THE

DRAINPIPE DIARY

by

TRESSA R. CATES, R.N.

VANTAGE PRESS   •   NEW YORK

WASHINGTON   •   HOLLYWOOD   •   TORONTO

AN UNCOMMON VALOR REPRINT EDITION
Complete and Unabridged

Printed in the United States of America

ISBN: 979-8-8690-8723-2

To all prisoners of war, living and
dead, this book is humbly dedicated

Foreword

Today from our home in the Santa Barbara foothills, my eyes take in a scene of wondrous serenity. The velvet green of carefully tended lawns, complemented by low and rambling pastel-colored houses. Red and green roofs. High terraces with multicolored ivy geraniums in such magnificent profusion that one is reminded of the Garden of Eden.

On a clear day, as far as the eye can see, there is the ever changing blue of the Pacific.

In the back of our home are the purple-shadowed mountains that seem close enough to touch. Below these same magic mountains, the tall grass undulates slowly with the breeze and the wild mustard dots the hills with gay patches of sunshine.

Horses graze peacefully all day in the lush grass, and the quiet of the day is broken by their loud neighing and the gleeful voices of happy children playing.

Here there is freedom; also happiness, peace, love, and security, just as there is everywhere in this happy land of ours. But complacency, smugness, and unpreparedness are here too, just as back in 1941.

My diary lies open before me, and its pages hold a lifetime of memories.

Bombings! Panic! Invasion and fear of the enemy, and the seemingly endless years of internment, out of which grew suspicion, prejudice, greed, hate, love, pity, self-sacrifice, sickness, and death!

This I have seen and known! This is my story of yesterday, and it could be your story today!

T.R.C.

January 5, 1942

January, the 5th! We could never forget that date, for it would have been our wedding day! Instead of a wedding, the large iron gates of our prison slammed shut on Catesy, my fiancé, and me with a finality that chilled our hearts.

What a nightmare we had lived in since Pearl Harbor! Yet there was always that one small hope that help and reinforcements would arrive before the enemy reached us.

But we waited in vain.

Bombings! Fires! Death and Destruction! Nursing the wounded! Panic and Invasion. This had been our life for the last month. Now imprisonment!

Strangely enough, Catesy and I had never given up hope that help would arrive — not until two weeks ago. That was the time we realized that escape had been cut off by land and sea.

We had driven to the piers to take a last look at our bombed ships which lay like useless driftwood in Manila Bay. The enemy had done a thorough job, as most of the ships were half-submerged, and their masts were leaning tipsily, parallel to the water.

As we gazed, sadly, at all this destruction, we recognized one of the destroyed vessels. Once it had been a sleek and beautiful freighter, and the accommodations for twelve passengers had been luxurious. Now it was a useless piece of junk.

This was the freighter that would have taken us on our honeymoon trip to Europe! But what was the use of thinking about that?

Our immediate problem was to dislodge ourselves from the crowded passenger car which had conveyed us from our homes to the prison that loomed before us.

Prisoners of the Japs! Just to repeat the phrase made one shudder.

There were six of us in the tightly packed car, and we had bundles, suitcases, and bulging pillowcases around us, between us, and on our laps. Because the Japs had instructed us to bring food for three days, we were surrounded by small and large bundles of canned food and other edibles, and our suitcases contained clothing, additional food, and some bedding.

The bulging pillowcase filled with a ten-pound wedge of rat cheese, two huge boxes of crackers, and other food items, on my lap, was in danger of splitting.

I had to stretch my short neck to see above the mound on my lap. I turned and smiled at Catesy, and he squeezed my hand in a reassuring manner. Thank God, we were together!

Catesy was dark-haired and handsome, but of course I would be prejudiced. His most outstanding traits were congeniality and kindness, and like most people with an Irish and Welsh background he had a sly and droll wit. He had his faults, too, like anyone else. He had a hot temper which flared up as suddenly as summer thunder and disappeared just as quickly. After one of these temper flare-ups, he was as meek and contrite as a small boy who had been caught red-handed stealing apples.

For the past eight years he had been employed by one of the largest Manila wholesale-and-retail drug firms in the entire Orient.

Henry, a bachelor of forty, with sandy hair and baby-blue eyes, was the second man in our little group of six. His perpetual grin and good humor helped to lessen some of the tension of the last month. Slightly built and of medium height, he walked on his tiptoes with a bouncing gait.

For many years he had been stationed in one of the southern provinces as an employee of one of the major oil companies in the States. To him fell the job of setting fire to several million dollars' worth of oil prior to the Japanese entry into Manila.

As we had watched the huge conflagration caused by this oil destruction from my sixth-floor apartment only a week ago, we had listened to ear-shattering explosions all day. Giant flames and mountains of dense smoke had hung over the city for days.

"I dare the Nips to find a jiggerful of gas when they reach the city!" Henry's voice, though tense and nervous, had been filled with complete satisfaction. He had followed the army's orders.

Sophie, a slender girl of twenty-five with brown hair and unusually large gray eyes, was one of the four women in our group. She was the wife of a mining engineer and, like so many others, had come to Manila to do her Christmas shopping; but because of the rapidly approaching enemy she had been unable to join her husband in the provinces. Nor had she been able to communicate with him. To add to her depression and worries, a favorite young cousin of hers, a flyer, had been killed at Clark Field about ten days before.

The other two women were mother and grown daughter, Belle and Toinette. Both were attractive, dark-haired and extremely vivacious. They had lived in the same apartment house I had, and the mother, like me, had been employed as a civilian nurse at the Sternberg General Army Hospital in Manila.

Usually they bubbled over with gaiety, but now they sat quietly in the car, staring straight ahead.

I was short and on the plump side, with light-brown hair and dark-brown eyes, and my complexion was fair. I was born in Hungary, and my parents came to the United States when I was only five. But I might add that I was as American as pumpkin pie.

Seven months after I had finished my nurse's training, I had saved enough money on private duty to see five countries in Europe. The fact that I had exactly forty-five cents in my purse when I reached home base in Pittsburgh never bothered me. My wonderful trip to Europe had given me a stronger urge to see more of the world, especially the Orient.

I scrimped, saved, and dreamed about China, Japan, India, Siam, and the Philippines. Finally, a few years later, with money in my purse, I left for California, and then Hawaii, Japan, China, and eventually the Philippines. When my funds became alarmingly low, I nursed, while in between times I went sightseeing and shopping. I saw all the famous tourist spots in Japan, Peiping, Nanking, Tientsin, Hongkong, and Shanghai. I would have been content to stay in Shanghai for a year or more, as the private nursing was plentiful and each day brought new faces, sights, and adventures.

My rickshaw and taxi fares were paid by my patients, and my living quarters, all for the princely sum of twenty-five dollars a month, were luxurious. If I was tired after a twelve-hour stint at a hospital or at a patient's home, if I wished, I'd have late tea or dinner served to me in bed at my quarters without extra charge.

With the exchange in my favor, what a happy time I had buying souvenirs, curios and brocades in Shanghai's fabulous shops! For one gold dollar I received enough Shanghai Mex to stuff a knitting bag. There had been so much to do, see, and learn! Jai-alai! Horse racing! Dinner parties, tea and garden parties! Sightseeing and night clubbing and eating strange and exotic foods! And always there had been an abundance of escorts.

But like all good things which had a way of ending, my exciting and happy life in Shanghai terminated almost overnight.

It was in the late summer of 1937 that the Japanese shelled Shanghai, and it was only a question of a few days before they would be in command of the city.

American and British nationals were evacuated to Manila and Hongkong, and because I was single I was one of the last to leave on the luxurious President liner, the ill-fated *Hoover*.

That was the time I escaped the Japs, but now, four years later, they had caught up with me!

Quietly and dejectedly, we sat in the car that was parked in front of a large four-story gray stone building. This was the Big House, the largest of the buildings on the Santo Tomas University campus.

The Santo Tomas University was considered the oldest university under the American flag, having been founded in 1587 by the Dominican Order, or Order of Preachers, as a secondary school. Later in 1611, the first university in the Orient was started by the Spaniards in the walled City of Manila.

If this was to be our home, I was grateful that the present site and structure were modern.

To the right of the Big House was a rambling, one-story administration building. To the right of the latter was another large building, used for classes and for housing nuns.

To the left of the Big House, separated by a wire fence and the Father's garden, was another large gray stone structure. It was the Seminary building, quarters for the Spanish priests who formerly taught at the university. The building also contained the Santo Tomas chapel.

About two city blocks beyond the Seminary building was a large gym. The spacious grounds in front of it and the Seminary building had been used for collegiate sports of all types.

Everywhere I looked I saw Allied nationals strolling about the grounds, and I recognized many familiar faces. Some appeared utterly bewildered and depressed, while others strolled about as though they didn't have a care in the world.

Several men recognized Catesy, and as they waved to him cheerfully I decided that things weren't so bad after all.

I was quickly jerked back to reality when Japanese soldiers surrounded our car and made guttural sounds and rapid motions with their hands.

"Everybody out of the car!" shouted an American who seemed to act as interpreter.

Grabbing our bundles and bags, we squeezed ourselves out of the car and walked toward the Big House. The hot sun felt good on my head and back. It was a beautiful day, and everything should have been peaceful and in order.

We walked into the large lobby and were met with bedlam.

Japanese officers, soldiers, and civilians, with the customary waving of hands and arms, were all shouting in Japanese, while men, women, and children of Allied countries were pushing forward to get near the officers in charge. All of them were asking for beds for their women and children, while many others were trying to get releases because of illness.

With difficulty, we inched our way through the tightly packed crowd in the direction of the wide staircase which led to the upper floors.

At the first landing, which branched off in two stairways, we were met by an American who instructed us that the men were to take the right staircase, while the women were to go left.

"Sheep to the right, and goats to the left!" I said flippantly.

"Well, don't forget, we are in Japanese custody, and in their opinion women are this low." With black eyes flashing, Belle demonstrated by placing her shapely hands a few inches apart.

We four women climbed the few short stairs and found ourselves in a long corridor.

To the left of us we passed many classrooms that were already jammed with women and children, benches, chairs, school desks, and mountains of luggage.

To the right of us we saw an old acquaintance of ours sitting on a window ledge that faced the west patio. We spoke to him, and though his staring eyes looked straight at us we received no acknowledgment. We passed on, worried and wondering. What was the matter with him?

Having turned the corner, we found ourselves in another long corridor with more classrooms filled with women and children with their belongings. Here, too, there were long windows on the opposite side, and when we looked down we saw the same patio. The building was U-shaped around the patio. On the other side of the building there was another U built around a second patio.

After walking past a dozen or more rooms, we came to an empty corner room. It was completely bare. It was a large room with tall windows on both sides and two doors leading to small balconies.

We dropped our bundles and bags, and for a long time we stood in the doorway. We picked up our luggage and walked over to the far side of the room and noticed that the room boasted a sink.

"And the bathroom is right next door!" remarked Sophie practically.

Since all the windows and balcony doors were closed, the air was stifling and the stench of urine was overpowering.

While Sophie and I opened all the large windows, Belle and Toinette went in search of brooms and dust rags. They returned in a short time with two brooms and several dust rags.

For more than an hour we kicked the dust around. We dusted, swept, and chose the far side of the room for our own. To insure squatters' rights, we spread out our belongings so that later arrivals would not jump our claim.

"But what about beds, tables, and chairs?" asked Toinette.

It was a good question.

"Let's go on a reconnaissance tour of the buildings! Surely, in a huge university like this, there must be furniture. Let's go, girls!" My voice sounded more confident than I felt.

In a room three doors from ours we found a bench and a chair, which we immediately dragged to our room.

Halfway down the corridor to the left of our room, we opened large double doors and found ourselves in a museum. The three sides of the enormous room were lined with glass cases filled with reptiles, birds, and animals, large and small, native to the Philippines and the Orient.

"Just what we're looking for! Stuffed and repulsive-looking iguanas and a friendly looking python!" exclaimed Toinette facetiously.

Just then my eyes spied an old Victorian marble-top table and I shrieked with delight. Like vultures, we pounced on it, and despite its weight we swiftly carried it to our new home.

Our search for beds took us much longer. We searched all of the rooms on the second and third floors of the Big House. We went outside and looked in the administration building, but there were no beds.

In the rear of the Big House there was a large, rambling frame dwelling. We combed every inch of this building, but we found nothing but large and heavy machinery. Apparently, the building had been a classroom for engineers.

Directly across from this building was another long frame dwelling, to the left of the Big House. Here we saw stoves, refrigerators, tables, chairs, and an abundance of cooking utensils. But there were no beds!

Next to one of the refrigerators was an extremely narrow door. I looked inside, and when my eyes alighted on the three native beds I yelled like a cheer leader.

"Look what I've found!"

The girls crowded around me to admire the beds, that were narrow and probably infested with bedbugs.

What a windfall! Though we had comfortable innerspring mattresses at home, yet now we went into ecstasies over narrow bejuca (native straw) beds which had probably belonged to servants.

While Belle and Toinette stayed to guard our prizes, Sophie and I went in search of the boys to help carry the beds. We found them on the third floor in a room directly above ours, and they were overjoyed to hear that we had found three beds.

After the men carried the beds to our room, they set them up. We found that between the four of us we had three sheets and three mosquito bars.

How would four white women squeeze into three single native beds that were less than thirty inches wide? It would take a Solomon to figure that one out.

While the boys went in search of beds for themselves, we hustled around to make our new home habitable. We removed the dirty mosquito nettings from the beds and attached our own clean ones to the crossbars. Since we had no mattresses, pads, or extra sheets to place over the straw matting, we placed half of a sheet over each bed, while the other half we planned to use as a covering.

A short time later the boys returned with the sad news that there were no more beds to be found. For days to come, they slept on the hard cement floor.

For supper that night I had only to thrust my arm into my fat pillowslip to produce cheese, crackers, and tea. From the well-supplied kitchen in which we had found our beds, the boys made tea in a saucepan they had pinched.

The marble-topped table gave our simple meal a certain elegance, and though we tried to be gay we did not succeed too well.

However, the hot tea and sugar revived us, and we felt that the future looked less dark and hopeless than a few hours before.

By nightfall it seemed that every cubic inch of space had been taken in our room, but people continued to pour in. All the women and children, ages ranging from eleven months to seventy-nine years, were tired and nervous, and I, who had been a want-to-be-alone Garbo from the time I could toddle, was in the midst of all this confusion and noise!

It was past bedtime, and the problem of accommodating four women in three single beds still remained unsolved. Finally, Belle suggested that she and Toinette would double up in one bed, and Sophie and I readily agreed. For once in my life I was grateful for my generous adipose surplus as my body hit the hard and resisting bejuca matting.

January 6, 1942

I will long remember my first night in Santo Tomas. Throughout the night, Japanese soldiers flashed lights on us as they barked restrictions and orders through an interpreter to late arrivals. Though we were already crowded, more people continued to join us. Frightened children screamed and cried in their sleep, and the eleven-month-old baby near my corner wailed most of the night.

On top of the noise, confusion, and glaring lights, we were chewed by bedbugs and mosquitoes.

At the first sign of dawn, just as my sixty or more roommates were beginning to settle down to sleep, I sat up in my torture bed, wide-awake and wild-eyed. I was wretchedly uncomfortable, and my body was peppered with mosquito and bedbug bites.

Since I couldn't sleep, I thought I would record the events of the previous day's happenings in my notebook. I had started to keep a diary a few hours after Pearl Harbor. It had given me something to do and think about, and if and when Catesy and I were free again, it would be something to read and remember—not that we would want to remember everything.

For over an hour I wrote, undisturbed by any noises or interruptions. The wailing baby had finally fallen asleep and so had our Nipponese friends. At any rate, they had probably run out of ideas on ways of disturbing us.

Like a stealthy savage bent on ambush, I quickly lifted my mosquito net and crawled out of the creaking bejuca bed. Carefully, I eased my way out of the room so as not to disturb my sleeping roommates. It was still very early, and I felt sure that there would be no long line at the bathroom.

I was never more wrong in my life! About fifty or sixty other women had had the same idea, and so I joined the end of the long line that stretched out to the corridor.

There were three washbowls, one shower, and three toilets for more than five hundred women and children on this end of the building. As I waited in the long line, my thoughts were anything but gay and cheerful.

A little old lady, frail and thin as a worn-out linen sheet, shuffled up to the long line in her shenalis (grass slippers). She was wrapped in an old-fashioned cotton kimono. In the harsh morning light, the hastily applied pancake make-up appeared ludicrous, and it emphasized the network of tiny wrinkles in her face. She paused when she saw the long line, and a puzzled look came over her face. "I guess I'll come back next week," she said to no one in particular.

I burst into uncontrollable laughter, and the women near me joined in. The women further up the line, who had missed the little episode, stared at us as though we had lost our minds.

When I finally returned to my room, the baby had started to cry again, and several of the older children were whimpering. One of them kept repeating, "Mom, when are we going home? I don't like this place!"

After dressing quickly, I walked down the long corridor to the front of the building and down the wide staircase. When I passed the Japanese guards in the main lobby, I looked straight ahead until I reached the outside.

Catesy had been waiting for me for over an hour. How good it was to see him and to be in the open, away from the appalling congestion of my room!

He too had spent a sleepless night on the hard cement floor, but at least he had been free of bedbugs.

When the other four joined us, it was time to think of breakfast.

Our first breakfast was prepared by Catesy and me. We went to the kitchen where we had found our beds to prepare our coffee. With a little further reconnaissance, we found another saucepan, which was ideal for cooking the Cream of Wheat which I had thrown in my suitcase as an afterthought.

By the time we had prepared our simple breakfast, the kitchen was crammed with nervous people trying to get near the stoves. Talk about the Russian community kitchens! This was far worse. Surely, there wouldn't be this congestion at every meal! How could four thousand people prepare meals in such a tiny place without losing their minds or developing bleeding ulcers?

It was a relief to get outside and join our party in front of the Big House, where we ate our breakfast, picnic fashion, on the ground.

We felt much better after the hot cereal and coffee. When Henry and the girls left to wash the dishes, Catesy and I were left alone.

"Well, honey, at least we are together. That's something, isn't it?" he asked as he squeezed my hands affectionately.

"I couldn't stand this madhouse without you," I answered firmly and a bit heatedly. Another comforting squeeze of his hand cooled me down, and I began to wonder what to give my gang for lunch.

Everyone we talked to had one thing in common — all were plainly bewildered by the noise, the confusion, and the lack of privacy.

To the can of oxtail soup contributed by Belle I added two cans of vegetable soup. This gave us a good lunch of soup and crackers. For supper we again had cheese, tea, and crackers.

The loveliest part of the day, sunset, was yet to come, and as long as we sat outside, away from the gloom and congestion of the buildings, we felt cheerful.

Suddenly we heard a shrill police whistle, and Japanese guards poured out of the buildings to shoo us into our quarters.

The most beautiful part of the day had to be spent in the boiler factory!

My room seemed noiser than ever, and no wonder! While we had

been outside, more women and children had been squeezed into
the room, and all of them seemed to be talking and crying at the
same time. When one child began to cry, the rest of the children
joined him.

January 7, 1942

My second night in Room 25, Japanese number, and Room 221,
American number, was just as restless and disturbing as the first.
Bedbugs and mosquitoes were busier than ever, and so were the
Japs. With their raucous voices barking orders to more late arrivals
and with their childish love of flashing lights in our faces, they
succeeded in keeping everyone awake.

The baby wailed so much that finally, in desperation, I slipped
on a housecoat and went over to the mother's mat. When I lifted
her mosquito net, she became frightened, and for a moment she
struggled.

"It's all right!" I whispered. "I'm one of your roommates. I want
to take the baby for a while."

Without any further argument, she handed me the crying child.
I carried it into the hall and wandered through the long corridors
until I must have walked several miles. Though the baby finally
fell asleep, I still kept on walking. Though tired and bleary-eyed
from lack of rest, I felt considerably relaxed.

When I slipped the sleeping baby under the net, the young
mother never moved.

Before coming into the darkened room, I had looked at my watch
and discovered it was only a few minutes after eleven.

I crawled under my net and lay awake for a long time, thinking
about that last wonderful night Catesy and I had had at Jai-alai.
It seemed more like years instead of exactly one month ago. So
much had happened since then!

That carefree, happy night at Jai-alai we made final plans for
our wedding, which was to take place in less than a month.

The Latin-American music, the dinner, and the wine were perfect, and I had on my favorite evening dress of red and white
splashy flowers. The neck was cut square and low, and the dazzling
white native shells I wore around my neck set off my deep tan.

Catesy, in his white sharkskin suit and healthy tan acquired from
daily golfing, looked more handsome than any man in the dining
room.

We left Jai-alai shortly after midnight, as I had to be on duty
by 7 A.M. at the army hospital.

How vividly I remembered my happiness that morning in the
taxi en route to the hospital! I thought of my four happy years in
the Philippines. They had all been good years. I had liked the

climate, my work, my comfortable apartment, and my many fine friends.

After having done twelve-hour duty as a private nurse in Pittsburgh and New York, which more often stretched into fourteen hours a day, counting commuting time, my six hours of duty at the army hospital were easy. No standing in rain, sleet, or snow to catch a bus, subway, or street car! No long hours of commuting time! I rode by taxi to work and Catesy brought me home. After duty I was still fresh enough to go swimming, sailing, riding, picnicking, or dancing.

When I reached my apartment after work, my faithful little servant, Adoracion, and my Skye terrier always met me at the door.

I had only to step out of my uniform and Adoracion was there to remove the buttons and place them in a freshly laundered uniform for the next day. The table was always set, the supper ready, and my clothes were laid out for the evening's activity.

What a glorious life! Especially for a working girl. Swimming and sun-bathing daily. Picnics. Sailing on Manila Bay. Cruising through the lovely southern islands. Fascinating trips to the colorful land of the Igorots. Shopping trips to Hongkong and Shanghai. Dinners and dancing every night under a tropical moon at the Army and Navy Club, Manila Hotel, and Polo Club if one had the inclination and the constitution, and I had plenty of both.

I attended stately and social functions at Malacanan Palace, and the Filipinas and mestizas in their beautiful costumes and diamonds dazzled eyes far more sophisticated than mine.

High-born Siamese, Burmese, Chinese, Japanese, and Indian ladies attended these balls, and their gorgeous costumes added to the brilliance of the occasion. The Indian ladies in their exquisitely woven saris with diamonds worn in the flare of one nostril were the most colorful and beautiful of all the charming ladies at these functions. The well-groomed American and European women, though less colorful, looked lovely in their summery evening clothes.

There was so much about Manila to charm an Occidental; The hoarse cry of the cocky street vendor! The hauntingly beautiful chimes of St. Paul Cathedral in the Walled City! The cheerful tinkle of the sleigh bells that were attached to all calesas and carramotas (two-and four-wheeled carts drawn by small Mongolian ponies.

Yes, my four years in Manila had been happy years, and that morning of the eighth of December I had a special reason to be happy. In less than a month I would be married to the man I loved!

But when I reached the surgical ward at the Sternberg General Army Hospital where I worked, I learned that Pearl Harbor had been bombed!

January 8, 1942

Again I awakened early, but since I had slept a little, I felt and looked less like a shadowy zombie.

My roommates, old and young, were quieter last night, and the Nips awakened us only twice with their flashlights, grunts, groans, and orders that no one understood.

The bedbugs, however, had multiplied and were on the march, but by now I was less disturbed at the thought of sharing my bed with them.

It was too early to go outside, as the large double doors in the front and rear of the Big House were still barricaded.

Lying on my bed fully dressed, I listened to the symphony of snoring, coughing, and crying, which was occasionally relieved by the characteristic creak of the bejuca beds.

A few of my roommates were preparing to get up, and the little boy near me was back on his old refrain, "Mom, I don't like this place. Let's go home!"

I reached for my diary and read what I had written a month ago, and the memory of those clouded and disturbed hours came back to haunt me.

1 9 4 1

STERNBERG GENERAL ARMY HOSPITAL

MANILA

December 8, 1941

When I heard about Pearl Harbor, I knew that my happy little world had crumbled about me. All of us were as certain as night follows day that we would be next. As we went about our work in stunned silence, we wondered gloomily how soon the Japs would strike in the Philippines.

In a few short hours we knew. It was nine hours after Pearl Harbor that the enemy bombed and destroyed nearly all of our planes on the ground at Clark Field. But why were our planes on the ground? Why? *Why?* We asked each other in bewilderment. Wasn't the Pearl Harbor treachery sufficient warning?

December 9, 1941

Today was like a ghastly dream! Beds that were empty yesterday were now occupied by mangled and horribly burned patients.

In a few short hours, the simple routine of our lives was completely changed. We worked twelve and fourteen hours at a time and felt no exhaustion—only numbness. We couldn't quite believe what had happened!

Heavy bombings daily, sometimes several times a day! Blackouts! Evacuation plans! Servants leaving for the provinces! Food prices skyrocketing!

Fort Stotsenberg and Clark Field had been bombed repeatedly, and our wounded and dying continued to fill the beds.

December 10, 1941

Today we heard that the Japanese had made a landing in northern Luzon! It can't be true!

DON'T BE DEFEATIST signs were posted throughout the hospital grounds, and in a small way they lulled our fear and suspicion that the enemy had made a landing.

Early in the morning our hospital was thrown into the wildest confusion when word was passed that the enemy was using gas. We rushed for our gas masks only to discover that there weren't enough to go around. Those without masks were given a cup of soda bicarbonate solution with a small piece of gauze. Useless, no doubt, but one had to do something for those wounded and helpless men. Fortunately, the rumor proved to be false.

This afternoon sixty-six Japanese bombers flew over our heads in perfect formation, and our entire hospital staff rushed out to see them. They looked like giant silver birds. Beautiful and harmless!

Then, suddenly, they started to unload their bombs! Over Cavite Navy Yard, Nichols Field, and Manila Harbor!

"This is another case of Crete! Those G... D... bastards in Washington have betrayed us!"

The army captain who had spoken those words stood beside me watching the bombs fall, and for a moment I felt a nausea and pain at the pit of my stomach.

In a short time the wounded began to arrive, and soon our wards, receiving rooms, operating rooms, as well as the large hospital yard, were filled with the wounded and the dying.

American and Filipino men, both civilian and military, were lying everywhere on the well-kept lawn. Many of them were charred and burned beyond recognition. Blood as crimson as the hibiscus flowers which bloomed in profusion in the yard was scattered everywhere.

Black-robed priests and army chaplains knelt by the dying to comfort and give last rites.

Doctors, nurses and corpsmen worked around the clock.

December 11, 1941

It was true! The enemy had landed at Lingayen!

Nichols Field and Fort Stotsenberg had been bombed again!

Those who had the time stayed near their radios for news from Washington, and while we braced ourselves for the next blow, we kept asking each other, "Will reinforcements come in time?"

We nursed and eased the pain of the wounded and dying, and when word was passed that Fifth Columnists had poisoned our city water supply, I was too tired to care. It proved to be another rumor.

When Catesy met me at the hospital to drive me home, his attempt to appear cheerful and normal was a complete fizzle. We talked nervously about the weather and inconsequentials, but we never mentioned the rapidly approaching enemy.

At the door of my apartment I met Jinnie, another civilian nurse and resident of the building. Tearfully but proudly, she told me that her husband had joined the army that morning.

December 12, 1941

There were ghastly sights in all the wards at the hospital. Young American boys with legs and arms torn off and with bad burns. Our large army hospital was already filled, but more wounded were expected this afternoon.

The wounded and what was left of our air force at the Iba Air strip had arrived. They filled an entire ward. Their planes had never left the ground, and subsequently they were all destroyed by the enemy. The men who took to the ditches for cover were ruthlessly machine-gunned from the air.

The wounded survivors were stunned, bitter, and bewildered. Who was to blame for this fiasco? When some of the boys told us that General MacArthur had never given the order for the planes to leave the ground, we were more stunned than ever.

December 13, 1941

Nichols and Murphy Field had been bombed again!

All hospital personnel had been instructed to sleep fully clothed.

During the night I was repeatedly awakened by heavy bombings, anti-aircraft, and machine-gun and rifle firing.

Sixty Japanese bombers dropped their bombs over the city shortly after our patients had completed lunch. More wounded and dying!

After a long and exhausting day at the hospital, it was good to come home to a well-cooked meal and an orderly apartment. How fortunate I was to have Adoracion, as many servants had already left for the provinces. Selfishly, I was beginning to think that her pregnancy, a major disaster a week ago, since she was single and only eighteen, had proved to be a blessing in disguise. Because she was a loyal girl and so young, I promised to take care of her. When I asked her to stay in the apartment at night, she was happy about it.

"This building is safer, mum, than my nipa shack!" she explained.

December 14, 1941

The Japanese seemed to have the freedom of the skies. They raided the city several times a day, and there never was any opposition from our bombers. After each air attack there were more wounded and dying. We did what we could for them, and we went about our work in a daze.

There was no reassuring news by radio and there was nothing in the local papers. We had no idea what was happening. But we all knew that we needed help and plenty of it, before it was too late.

December 15, 1941

The Japanese again bombed the city just as our patients were having lunch. Fort Stotsenberg continued to take heavy punishment many times a day.

People continued to ask, "Where are our planes?" Hospital personnel had only to look at the grim faces of our wounded pilots to know the answer. But we still didn't want to believe what was whispered everywhere—that our planes were all destroyed in those first surprise attacks.

But why were they surprise attacks? Wasn't the nine-hour interval between Pearl Harbor and the first attack on the Philippines sufficient time to put our bombers in the air?

Morale among the patients and hospital personnel was high.

We've had only a few of the dreaded gas-bacillus cases; and thanks to sulfathiazole and gentian violet, our wounded and badly burned were recovering.

December 16, 1941

Fort Stotsenberg had five air attacks yesterday, and Joyce, the army nurse who worked with me, lost her sweetheart during one of the raids. She went about her work silently with red and swollen eyes.

My family at the apartment now numbered four, counting my little pet.

Sophie, the wife of a mining engineer, came yesterday. She had come to the city to do her Christmas shopping ten days ago and she had never been able to rejoin her husband in the provinces. The gold mine where he had worked was already occupied by the Japs, and all communication had been cut off.

When I reached my apartment today, she was standing by the window, weeping quietly. She had just heard that her twenty-three-year-old cousin, a flyer at Stotsenberg, had been killed. When I tried to console her, she wept all the more. "I think my husband is lost, too!" she cried.

From my living-room window on the sixth floor, I saw dense smoke rising from Nichols Field. I gazed hopefully toward Manila Bay for a sight of one of our navy ships, but the bay that once used to be filled with the ships of the Asiatic fleet was completely deserted. The fleet was elsewhere, I thought sadly.

Many local civilian nurses and missionary nurses from India, Japan and China had volunteered their services at the hospital. The entire city worked together, building air-raid shelters, helping the Red Cross, and starting vegetable gardens.

There was no more dressing for dinner, dancing, and the movies. The long walks on Dewey Boulevard with my little pet at sunset time were over. There was no time for anything but sleep and work, for which we were grateful.

Another tragedy struck Manila! The *S. S. Corregidor*, en route to the southern islands with a passenger list of fifteen hundred or more evacuees, struck a mine and sank in about six minutes. Several hundred were rescued from the shark-infested water by patrol boats from Corregidor, but the remainder perished.

Tokyo called the sinking of the ship "another stupid American blunder."

The enemy dropped incendiary bombs close to our hospital.

A few minutes later, the wounded began arriving but, unfortunately, many of them died en route to the operating rooms and wards.

For the last few days, soldiers, officers, and corpsmen had been digging trenches in the hospital yard for ambulatory and litter patients and hospital personnel.

Our commanding officer had seriously considered moving the patients from this hospital, as all the buildings which covered several city blocks were of flimsy frame construction.

When a raid started, the hospital was quickly emptied. Only those in cumbersome Balkan frames were left in the wards.

As the bombings increased, we discontinued the moving of litter patients so as to decrease fresh bleeding as well as agonizing pain.

Today, our ambulatory and litter patients spent more time under their beds than on them.

The last raid caught me at the nurses' home, where I had my lunch. There was nothing to do but cower under a bed, table, or bench. As I dived under the nearest bed, I heard a British voice which sounded familiar, calling to me from under the other bed. "Who's there?"

It certainly sounded like Brinny, an English nurse, whom I hadn't seen since 1937 in Shanghai under similar circumstances. When there was a lull in the fireworks, I saw emerging from under the bed a middle-aged woman, with matted and fiery red wig framing a pair of flashing brown eyes. It was Brinny all right, and she was snorting with rage. "Those blasted Japs!" she exclaimed venomously.

Then, recognizing me, she added in a milder tone, "What the blazes are you doing here?"

December 20, 1941

It was wonderful to see the high spirits displayed by both American and Filipino soldiers. Young men with an arm or leg gone actually considered themselves fortunate. Those with shrapnel wounds, who in another month or so would be recovered, were making plans to fight the Japs.

Dramatic developments almost every day. Fort Stotsenberg had been evacuated. Ambulatory patients had been moved to the Estado Mayor, which formerly housed the 31st Infantry. Some of our army nurses and doctors had already left for Bataan and Corregidor. Grocery stores were jammed with frantic customers who bought staple and canned goods. Bombings increased in frequency and intensity.

The broadcasts were alarming: Eighty Enemy Transports Landed in Lingayen, only 175 Miles from Manila; Tank Combat on the Lingayen Shores.

Fifth Columnists were at work, illuminating strategic areas for the Japs with lighted flares. Enemy planes visiting us three and four times a day (and we never saw an American plane). Manila declared an open city, though the enemy continued with their bombings. Civilians fleeing from mountains to lowlands, and from one province to another, only to find the enemy there already. Jap bombs dropping while we trimmed our Christmas tree. Dewey Boulevard packed with traffic, Army vehicles of every description racing out of town. The Army was leaving! Four mammoth fires, with the giant flames licking the sky. It wasn't a very Merry Christmas that was being ushered in.

December 25, 1941

The Filipinos have named this day well. Black Christmas!

The blackness of despair and resignation was everywhere. Only the Axis nationals and the Fifth Columnists were happy.

Catesy met one of the released Nazis today and he said he was tempted to wipe the smirk off his face. There was a special smirk reserved these days for the Americans. The handwriting was on the wall, and all of us knew that soon we would be the enemy nationals—behind bars.

Apparently the Japanese were not guided by international law and ethics. Open city meant nothing to them. They raided the city six times today and four times yesterday!

The patients in my ward ate their Christmas dinner under their beds when the bombs started to drop all around us.

"A Day of Hope," said our local radio commentator. President

Roosevelt had promised us "adequate help." We continued to pray that it would come soon. A few more days, and it would be too late for those hopelessly outnumbered and ill-equipped men in Bataan.

Catesy tried to join the army the other day and the officer in charge told him to go back home. He had added bitterly, "We wouldn't even have a gun to give you!"

As the bombings increased in frequency and intensity, I considered myself fortunate to be living in an eight-story apartment house constructed of steel and concrete. Catesy, who had lived in a frame dwelling moved in a few days ago and we were happy to have a man with us. There were many others living in frame houses, who hinted openly about moving in but already we were crowded. My former house boy, Catalino also was made welcome and there was plenty of work for him now that my family had increased.

Patients and hospital personnel had the jitters. Continuous bombing and lack of sleep had worn nerves to near hysteria. In a few days the hospital would be evacuated.

At my apartment there was an atmosphere of normalcy that was most reassuring. The morning paper was folded neatly by my coffee cup and the telephone and doorbell still rang. I tried to kid myself into believing that everything was as it should be. But the moment I unfolded my paper and looked at the headline, I was jarred back to reality. "Baguio and Davao Are Occupied!"

Was it only a few months ago when we read newspaper and magazine articles concerning the menace of twenty thousand or more Japanese civilians firmly established and controlling all the big business in Davao? What an excellent opportunity for Fifth Column work, predicted the writer of the article, who had come from the States to investigate this situation. No one heeded him, but now, thanks to the cooperation of the Japanese civilians, Davao had been taken without any effort on the part of the invaders.

The Japanese were getting closer to the city, and they boasted that they would be in Manila by New Year's Day.

Despair, anxiety, fear, and resignation gripped us. My wedding day, so close, was almost forgotten.

December 27, 1941

A suspected Nazi civilian doctor in my ward was shunned like a mad dog by patients and staff alike. Several times I tore up his orders and prescriptions in his presence and, instead of marching me to the C.O., he looked at me with astonishment in his watery blue eyes. "Why did you do that?" he asked me in a wheedling voice.

He could no longer harm us, for the hospital was being evacuated to the Sta. Scholastica, the Philippine Women's College, and the La Salle College.

Though the fall of Manila was expected soon, we behaved like children who believed in fairy tales. We hoped desperately that a miracle at the last moment would stop the enemy.

How pathetically we listened to our radios for news of some great victory, but the news was always about Germany and Russia.

The Chinese grocery stores were packed with panicky customers who kept buying more staples and other food supplies.

Just as I returned to my apartment from work today, Jinny, the nurse whose husband was fighting in Bataan, came to see me. She was breathless and excited.

She asked me to leave with her for Bataan. Her husband had sent a soldier with a car to fetch her and myself. In his note he had written that we were to leave immediately and to bring food, bedding, and cooking utensils, as a nipa shack had been provided for us.

I had only half an hour to decide and pack. I looked at Catesy, who stood by the window with his back to us. I went to him, and when I saw his depression and sadness, I knew that I could not leave.

When he said, "I can't make the decision for you," I had already made up my mind.

"I'm staying, Jinny. Give Dick my regards and thanks for asking me."

Catesy kissed me tenderly and asked me, "Are you sure?" There was a doubtful note in his voice.

I knew definitely that my place was with him, but how could anyone tell which was the frying-pan and which was the fire?

Sophie embraced me, and when I heard Adoracion and Catalino giggling nervously in the kitchen, I knew that they too were pleased. Even Rags seemed to know that something out of the ordinary had occurred, for she kept scratching my shoes for attention.

We all went down to Jinny's apartment to help her pack. In less than half an hour the car was piled high with bedding, cooking utensils, food, and clothing. When we lingered over good-byes, the soldier fidgeted nervously and finally advised her to start.

We watched the car disappearing rapidly around the corner on Mabini, headed for Bataan.

December 28, 1941

The heavy bombing began overhead just as patients in cumbersome Balkan frames were lifted into the large army trucks, which were to convey them to convents and colleges. Those helpless patients were an open target for the bombers above.

In the midst of all this fear, confusion, and deafening noise, Major Greene sidled up to me and shouted into my ear, "Are you doing anything tonight?" He was watching me and leering like a wicked satyr.

What a guy! I thought.

"Aren't you nervous?" I asked.

He touched his generous paunch tenderly and answered, "I never did like butterflies."

When we wheeled our poor doomed Lizzie out of the ward, he wept like a child and we wept with him. I gave him a stiff opiate and promised to visit him, but I never saw him again.

The less wounded were not apprehensive. Happy Harris, as usual, joked about the fun he would have living in a convent for the first time in his twenty-one years.

December 29, 1941

The army nurses had left for Corregidor and Bataan, and only a few of the medical officers of the administrative staff were left. The civilian nurses, like myself, stayed on to complete the evacuation and packing of equipment.

One of the city's former American civilian doctors, now in the army reserve, came to my ward to bid me good-bye.

I had met him three years before on my first private duty case in Manila, and what a time I had had with a rambunctious patient who insisted on having six doctors, each of them countermanding the other's order. When I confided my troubles to the doctor who stood before me, he had said, "Just ignore the other orders. I'm the one in charge!"

He was still giving orders, for when he saw the civilian Nazi doctor in the ward, he took a menacing step toward him and in a voice filled with hate, demanded, "What are you doing here, you S..O..B...of a Nazi?"

The Nazi ran like a whipped dog, and he was out of the door before anyone could say another word. The next time I saw him, a day later, he was standing at the paymaster's window in front of me.

I wanted to make a scene, to shout and tell the paymaster not to give him his money. Instead, I did nothing. What was the use? The U. S. Army had left, and soon the Japs would occupy the city.

Before Jinny left to join her husband in Bataan, she had asked me to look after a friend and co-worker of her husband. Both men had been employed by the same Stateside Oil Company: I readily agreed and now my family had increased again.

Henry came today. He was a bachelor, shy and quiet, but his

friendly manner and homespun sallies helped to ease many tense moments. It was difficult to believe that this quiet man had set fire to huge installations of gas and oil in carrying out the U. S. Army's scorched-earth policy. He had done a good job, and it was doubtful that the enemy found any gas when they entered the city.

December 30, 1941

The evacuation of the hospital was almost completed. There was confusion, tension, anxiety, sadness, and mad rushing about as last-minute instructions were shouted throughout the hospital grounds. Army trucks filled with men and equipment moved rapidly out of the grounds. Most of the men in the trucks looked like young high school boys. I wondered what their fate would be. And ours! We civilian men, women, and children—left behind.

A voice whispered into my ear. "It's your last chance to date me!"

It was Major Greene again with his libertine grin and nonsense. As we shook hands, he slipped a small object into my hand. With eyes misty with tears, I waved to him as the truck moved out, and that was the last time I saw him.

I looked at the small vial in my hand. It was filled with one and a half grains of sodium luminal. This time the tears blinded my eyes because of his regard for my safety. I prayed for him and for myself—that I would never have to use the drug.

December 31, 1941

The demilitarization of Manila had been completed now that General Francisco, chief of the Philippine Constabulary, had left with his staff.

On the front, General MacArthur narrowly escaped being struck by a bomb.

The scorched-earth policy was carried out by our retreating army, and American demolition squads had been working for days, blowing up bridges, barges, and burning oil. They mined strategic areas in the north and south to delay the advancing enemy. Henry had been out all day to help set fire to several million dollars' worth of oil.

There had been ear-shattering explosions since six o'clock tonight, and as we watched the heavy black smoke to the north and south, we knew that the Japs wouldn't find any oil. Henry, though extremely jumpy, wore a satisfied grin on his face. We watched the awe-inspiring conflagration. Mountainous pillars of hungry flames licked the sky, and thick black smoke spread over the entire city.

We spent New Year's Eve sitting around the attractive second-floor terrace of Belle's apartment. Though drinks were passed and toasts were made, no one tried to be gay.

Someone a little bolder than the rest suddenly asked, "How soon do the Japs reach the city?"

We were relieved that at last the terror had been brought into the open.

1 9 4 2

January 1, 1942

The radio was dead!

We continued to hear deafening explosions, immediately followed by clouds of thick black smoke and pillars of dancing orange flames.

As far as the eye could see there were dense curtains of black smoke and flames.

A blood-red haze hung over the city, blotting out the sun. I thought of Doomsday and Dante's Inferno.

People stood in the streets and on their rooftops to watch the fires and destruction that surrounded them.

On the City Hall building there were huge signs painted on cloth bearing this message: OPEN CITY. BE CALM. STAY AT HOME. NO SHOOTING.

We stayed in our homes and waited. But how does one remain calm?

January 2, 1942

The enemy dropped thousands of leaflets over the city. Uncle Sam was depicted as a Death's Head in repulsive caricature. Underneath the picture in large letters there was one word: "Destiny."

My neatly folded morning paper was reassuring until I unfolded it and read the headline: "City Awaits Occupation. Avoid Hostilities When Foe Arrives." The fires at Pier Seven and Port Area were beyond control, and millions of dollars' worth of merchandise went up in smoke while bonded merchandise continued to be looted by hundreds of people.

The U. S. quartermaster stores were the first to be opened to the poor, followed by commercial stores in the Port Area.

Traffic was tied up for miles with an endless procession of push-carts, bull carts, bicycles, carromatas, carretelas, and automobiles filled with radios, typewriters, expensive rugs, adding machines, barber chairs and other equipment from bonded warehouses.

29

Many people set up shop on the sidewalks and bridges to sell these articles at ridiculously low prices.

Tonight it was Catesy's turn to guard the large wholesale-and-retail drug firm where he worked from looters. I pleaded with him not to go, since the enemy was on the outskirts of the city. But nothing would change him.

"You're guarding the store from looters! What a laugh! So that the Japs can have everything neat and intact!"

I stormed and raved. But it was no use! All the other American employees had taken their turn in guarding the store nightly, and it was his hard luck to have his turn fall that night.

With Catesy downtown, the suspense of waiting was more fearful. Sophie, Henry and I wandered from room to room with Rags whimpering at my heels. Adoracion and Catalino talked in whispers as they squatted in the corner next to the kitchen door.

Then, just as the sun set, the Japanese entered the city!

The victory parade on our street, which was Mabini, seemed unreal. It was as ridiculous as an old 1911 film. Yet they were our conquerors, and our beloved Stars and Stripes were replaced by their Rising Sun flag.

It was a shabby and poorly equipped army that passed down our street. They rolled by in four trucks and a half dozen or more bicycles led by a lieutenant. The soldiers who followed wore badly tailored uniforms, and their boots were dusty and oversized.

We weren't impressed. We could only marvel that these badly equipped men were a part of the mighty Imperial Japanese Forces.

There were very few people on the streets. Most of them, like us, watched the victory parade from behind shuttered windows. But the Spanish mestizos across the street from us stood on the sidewalk, and as the soldiers passed they shouted, "Banzai!" while the soldiers enthusiastically returned the salute.

We heard a tumultuous cheer, like the roaring of thousands of lions, coming from the direction of nearby Rizal Stadium, where apparently a more impressive parade had been staged. At the sound of the loud ovation, a cold fear stabbed our hearts. Had the Filipinos already abandoned us?

Now that the enemy was here, some of our tension lessened.

But where was Catesy? I tried to reach him by phone, but the line was dead, and I knew that the Japs were in the downtown section.

January 3, 1942

Though I couldn't reach Catesy by phone, my phone rang continually. Friends and neighbors called to see if we were still in our home or to inform us that other friends had already been taken by the Japs.

When I phoned the Oriente Hotel in Walled City where Zenia, the missionary nurse from India, stayed, the Filipino operator said in a frightened voice, "Do not call again, mum! The Japanese are already here and all the Americans have been taken away!"

The hours dragged by and there was still no word from Catesy. Finally at 1 P.M., he returned, tired and footsore, without his car.

"But where's your shiny new car?" we chorused.

"The runty little bastards took it!" Catesy grinned sheepishly.

Anticipating that this would happen, he had prepared a receipt before he left the store. Just as he got behind the wheel of his car, two Japanese officers stopped him and politely asked him to get out. When Catesy asked them to sign his prepared receipt, they willingly obliged.

How like the Japanese to be always polite! My mind leaped to Ogden Nash's "The Japanese":*

> How courteous is the Japanese!
> He always says "Excluse me, please"
> And climbs into his neighbor's garden
> And smiles and says, "I beg your pardon."
> He bows and grins a friendly grin,
> And calls his hungry family in:
> He grins and bows a friendly bow:
> "So sorry, this is my garden now."

With Catesy safely returned, much of our tension and worries of the last eighteen hours lifted. Henry, ever alert for an auspicious moment to do a bit of celebrating, ordered our favorite drinks, which Catalino prepared and served expertly.

People stayed in their homes. Few dared to go out.

A few hours later an American living nearby came to our door and cautioned us to stay in the apartment and to destroy our liquor. While Catesy and Henry sadly emptied Scotch, bourbon, rye, gin and brandies at the sink, I hurriedly hid a bottle of brandy and one of Scotch under my bed. I thought that the time would soon come when we would need a little morale boosting.

Later in the afternoon, we heard that many who had destroyed all their liquor were now making hurried trips to town in an effort to buy a bottle to ease the tension of the next few days.

All the liquor at the Army and Navy Club, the Elks Club, the

---

*Ogden Nash, "The Japanese."
By permission of Little, Brown and Company, Boston, Mass.

Polo Club, and other American controlled bars was destroyed. Those who helped with the wholesale destruction sampled and guzzled freely until they became roaring drunk.

January 4, 1942

We had abandoned all wishful thinking and hopes that a miracle at the eleventh hour would occur to prevent the Japs from taking us into custody.

At last we were convinced that it was only a question of time, perhaps a few hours, before they reached my home. My home suddenly became very dear to me, and the thought of leaving my newly furnished apartment filled me with sadness.

We packed, unpacked, and repacked a dozen times a day. Each time we took something out of our luggage, only to return it a few hours later. We had no idea what to pack. We had no precedent to follow, and if we had, our minds were too confused to follow anything through.

The morning paper was still delivered at my door, and this semblance of normalcy was reassuring. I was still kidding myself.

MARTIAL LAW AND A NEW PHILIPPINES FOR THE FILIPINOS! It didn't take a seer to figure out the headline. Already the Nips controlled the newspapers.

The telephone rang constantly, and from our friends we learned that Americans in the Ermita section had already been rounded up. We were next. We were in the Malate section.

The British nationals who had congregated at the Manila Club, as far as we knew, were still there.

Catesy hovered around me like a worried mother hen. When he scolded me for using lipstick and powder, I was astonished. Then it dawned on me! I realized the torture and concern that he was going through. The same torture that all men were experiencing at this time over their women. He smoked one cigarette after another as he nervously paced the living-room floor. Suddenly, he asked me sharply. "Haven't you something less becoming to wear?"

Meekly, I went into the bedroom. Sophie followed me. We removed all make-up and changed into shapeless and baggy slacks.

We ate lunch, and everything tasted like sawdust.

When the doorbell rang loudly and imperiously, Catesy went to the door, while Sophie, Henry and I stood behind him. When Catesy opened the door, Rags jumped out of my arms and scooted to her sanctuary under my bed, where she began to whimper loudly.

Two Japs and our own Filipino landlord, the latter anxious and worried, stood before us.

One Japanese was a civilian, the other a noncommissioned officer.

He was less than five feet tall and had the most delicately tinted pink cheeks and the longest and most straggly Fu-Manchu mustache I have ever seen, on or off a stage.

Our midget conqueror stood before us, talking loudly and rapidly, while the questions were relayed to us by the civilian Japanese in English. Were we Americans? Were we one family? How long had we lived in the Philippines?

We answered mechanically as we stared at his ridiculous mustache. Despite his midget size, the mustache and the long sword that dangled at his side gave him a sinister and Sax Rohmerish air.

While he shouted and gesticulated extravagantly, he strutted back and forth in the living room, while his long sword made a clanking and somewhat childish noise on the cork floor.

We watched him as in a trance. Everything about him seemed absurd and ridiculous, like a character in *The Mikado.*

He lifted cushions off the sofa and chairs and threw them on the floor. He looked behind some of my books on the shelf, and he dashed into the kitchen to peer inside the kitchen cupboards.

Catesy and I had often discussed the possibility of Japanese invasion, but we had never believed it could happen. As long as the American flag flew over this country, we had felt safe. After all, hadn't our own leader, General MacArthur, assured us and the rest of the world that the Philippines could be defended?

Suddenly, I was jarred back to the present as the Mikado rushed into the living room. He hopped around, looking at one bric-a-brac after another, until his attention was riveted on the Chinese horses that I loved. With one sweep of his sword, he knocked them off the shelf. No one moved or dared to pick up the pieces.

The questioning continued. Did we have cameras, flashlights, and telescopes?

When he dashed into the bedroom to look under my bed, Rags growled uncertainly. A few hours before, I had removed the Scotch and bourbon, for which I was thankful now. In a moment he returned to the living room, triumphantly displaying an army coverall which I had worn in the last few weeks at the hospital. What a yakamashi he made over that one innocent coverall!

Our kindly landlord came to the rescue by explaining that I was a civilian nurse who had worn those coveralls during the heavy bombings.

The Mikado sucked in his breath, nodded, and motioned us to stand in a group outside the front door of my apartment, while he and his party hurried to my next-door neighbor.

Since their door was partly ajar, we heard the mother of the new baby crying hysterically. This made the Mikado shout louder.

The husband was told to leave without his wife and infant, and when he joined us in the hall, his wife, red-eyed and distraught, clung to him in a last embrace. There was more shouting, and the Mikado became noticeably impatient.

"We'd better go!" cautioned the landlord nervously.

We picked up our bags and bundles and meekly followed the Japanese down the six flights of stairs, while our heavy suitcases bumped into our legs with each step we took.

The downstairs lobby was jammed with Americans and other Allied nationals. Men, women, and children were milling around, talking to neighbors or sitting quietly on their bags. They tried to appear nonchalant, but they failed miserably.

Two Japs, one in uniform, the other a civilian, conducted a disorganized and half-hearted inspection. They pawed through the bags, looking for money, flashlights, guns, cameras, scissors, knives, and other sharp objects.

Nervously, I glanced toward my bag which contained a large butcher knife, scissors, and a flashlight. There was nothing to do but hope for the best.

We wrote our names, nationalities, and apartment numbers on slips of papers; then we sat on our bags while the men chain-smoked nervously. We talked in whispers and furtively shot quick glances in the direction of the miniature men.

We waited. Finally, a few hours later, we were told that because there weren't enough cars to take us to our destination, we could spend another night in our homes. Best of all, our bags hadn't been searched. We were also instructed to be in the lobby at six in the morning and to bring food for three days.

We decided to repack. Somehow, that last command to bring food for three days struck a false note.

This time we discarded many items, such as clothing and shoes, from our bags, in order to have more room for food.

Into a pillowslip went ten pounds of rat cheese, two big boxes of crackers, coffee, tea, canned milk, and cocoa. Sophie and the men added another large assortment of canned meats, soup, and milk to their bags and bundles.

When it became dark, we hid a hundred-pound sack of rice, several huge hams, and several five-pound slabs of bacon on the wide ledge outside my dressing room window.

We tied money in oilskins and hid them in flower pots in the hanging airplants outside the living-room windows and in the tank of the water closet.

I gave the stub of my traveler's checks to Catalino, and I divided the checks into equal parts and placed each in my shoes. The psychological lift of these unusual arch supporters was most comforting.

During dinner we discussed other possibilities of safeguarding our food supplies, and we decided to store the rest of our hams and bacon with a Swiss family in the building and with a Free French family living nearby.

We lingered over the fine dinner and relished every bite. Though none of us voiced our thoughts, I am sure that we all wondered when we would eat another meal in the apartment.

January 5, 1942

By 5:30 we had breakfast, and fifteen minutes later we were in the lobby of the apartment, surrounded by our bags and bundles.

After an hour, when we saw no movement of any kind, we marched back to our apartment, and our luggage seemed to increase in weight with every step.

At 10:30 the doorbell rang; two sloppily dressed soldiers, a Japanese civilian, and our landlord stood at the door. The apartment was again searched, but this time with less bluster and drama, and the same routine questions were asked. Again we were told to wait outside while they went next door.

While we waited, we heard the young mother crying bitterly and pleading with the Japanese to allow her husband to stay. Her baby screamed lustily, but its cries did not drown out the shouting Japanese. In a quiet voice the landlord cautioned the wife to cease her pleadings, and he urged the husband to get his bags.

Single file, we descended the stairs for the last time. Out in the warm sunshine we quietly climbed into the large truck that stood outside the apartment house. When all the other tenants had been rounded up, the truck moved off in the direction of Rizal Stadium.

Feeling like Marie Antoinette on the way to the guillotine, I glanced back to take a last look at my home. From the first to the eighth floor, servants, tenants of neutral countries, and the landlord's family were leaning out of windows, doorways, balconies to wave to us. The Filipinos who stood on either side of the streets gazed at us sorrowfully.

In a few short blocks we were at Rizal Stadium, where we had watched baseball, softball, and other sports during happier days.

We jumped out of the trucks and placed our belongings in a neat mound before we joined a long line of other Allied nationals who were waiting to show their passports or residence taxes to a group of Japanese officers and civilians.

Sophie, of course, with her home in the provinces, had neither, but after considerable palaver with the Japanese military she was permitted to pass on.

35

I was next. When the Japanese officer saw my passport, which showed that I was born in Hungary and a naturalized American, he broke into excited Japanese and went into a conversational huddle with the Japanese civilian sitting beside him.

What was up? I waited anxiously while Catesy fidgeted nervously.

Then, in perfect English, the uniformed Japanese said, "You are not American! You can stay out!"

Terrified, I edged closer to Catesy and my friends, and I declared most firmly that I was an American. If I had dared, I would have told him that I was safer with my fellow Americans.

His annoyed expression showed that he thought me a fool and not worth bothering about, and to my great relief he waved me aside impatiently.

As the stadium became more crowded with people, several Japanese civilians divided us into groups of five.

Since Belle and Toinette had joined us, and there were six in our party, we persuaded the Jap to allow us all to go in one car. Including the Japanese driver, who drove like a maniac, there were seven in the car. We were wedged in so tightly with our bags, bundles and bulging pillowcases that we supported each other on the dangerous curves.

"That guy must have been a cab driver in Tokyo!" remarked Catesy as we narrowly missed the curb.

My front view was completely obscured by bundles on my lap, but occasionally I would get a quick glimpse from the side.

The Rising Sun flag was everywhere—on public buildings, trucks, and the tanks which lumbered past us.

We passed the Estado Mayor, former home of the 31st Infantry, and later the Hospital Annex, but it was gone. It had been leveled to the ground.

Tired and unarmed Filipino soldiers marched dejectedly between Japanese soldiers.

No one spoke, not even when our lives were threatened on the dangerous and crowded corners.

In a short time we saw the high tower of a large and gloomy-looking gray stone building, and we saw other large buildings nearby. It was the Santo Tomas University! Was this to be our destination?

On either side of the wide gates leading to the university, Filipino men, women, and children watched us solemnly. Their expressions were sad, and one could see that they were deeply moved.

When Japanese sentries opened the wide iron gates, we passed through. We were inside our prison!

January 8, 1942

I closed my notebook with a sigh. At least in here we would find less tension and anxiety in our daily existence than we had experienced in the last month.

After straightening my bed, I reached under it to get my pots and dishes for our breakfast.

As usual, Catesy was waiting for me outside the Big House with a smile and a kiss.

Suddenly, we heard a commotion beside us. It was loud and excited talking in Japanese. We turned around and looked into the eyes of two Japanese soldiers who were talking rapidly and moving their hands back and forth in a negative gesture.

We shook our heads, shrugged our shoulders, and eased out of the picture.

"What do you suppose they were so excited about?" I asked Catesy.

"I guess the little runts don't approve of kissing," he answered glumly.

With everyone in our party taking turns at the kitchen that now had all the earmarks of a medieval madhouse, we were spared from ulcers. Again we had Cream of Wheat and coffee for breakfast, crackers and cheese for lunch, and cheese, crackers and tea for supper.

When would the Japanese start feeding us?

Perhaps never, for a notice appeared on the large doors of the Big House with these two ominous lines. INTERNEES IN THIS CAMP SHALL BE RESPONSIBLE FOR FEEDING THEMSELVES.

People stopped to read the notice in a dazed manner. Who then would feed them if not the Japs? Were we not in their protective custody?

The enemy had concentrated over three thousand men, women, and children in this camp, and more were coming in daily, and yet they had made no provisions for feeding them.

Furthermore, there were no beds, extra toilets, showers, sinks, cooking stoves, or hospital facilities to care for the sick.

The university had been a day school, and there were no facilities of any kind to house men, women and children.

Fortunately, the weather was in our favor, and we were able to stay outside in the sunshine.

As more people from the city joined us, the camp had all the appearance of a busy ant hill or an Iowa picnic at Long Beach.

People sat in groups on the lawn, eating the provisions they had brought into the camp. The more ambitious and enterprising ones scurried around, trying to build a makeshift fire to heat food and to prepare tea and coffee.

Something would have to be done soon about our cooking, for the small kitchen where we had been preparing our simple meals was becoming more impossible and crowded. And what about our supply of food? When my ten-pound wedge of cheese was gone, what would we eat?

Several days ago a camp hospital was started in the frame building to the left and in the rear of the Big House with makeshift equipment and drugs.

To acquire more equipment and supplies, our doctors had to use patience, tact and flattery. These were important when dealing with the Nips, since the hospital couldn't get a roll of bandages or a bottle of aspirin without requisitioning it through the Commandant's office.

I volunteered my services at the hospital today. After I completed my four-hour shift, I went into the kitchen and hinted rather delicately to the woman in charge about doing a little cooking for breakfast.

January 9, 1942

The people who had homes, servants, friends, and business associates on the outside were fortunate indeed!

We were able to contact Catalino, and he brought us cooking utensils, charcoal, native stove, food, and other essentials. But there were many people in this prison camp who had nothing. They had been picked up by the Japanese on the street with no warning about bringing food and other necessities.

There were many others who were transients and seamen from various parts of the world. The ships which would have carried them to their destinations were bombed and destroyed in Manila Harbor, and passengers and crew escaped with only the clothes on their backs.

These people had no outside contacts from whom to obtain food and clothing, they had little or no money and those with traveler's checks were reluctant to cash them for a shakedown discount.

I tried to cash a traveler's check today and learned that I would lose exactly thirty percent. Already a few of our fellow internees— the opportunists, Shylocks, and leeches—were in operation!

Interned Red Cross officials were working on the Japanese to get food, utensils, and kitchen equipment. These interned Red Cross officials, with the co-operation of outside people, stepped in to help these destitute people with food, clothing, and bedding. They also tried to bring in field kitchens, but our benevolent jailers refused.

We already had a Central Committee, a self-governing body of Americans and Englishmen elected by us and approved by the Japanese.

These conscientious and hard-working men had daily contacts with the Nips. It was through their efforts, farsightedness, and courage that the camp was able to obtain food, hospital supplies, and equipment. It was through their patience, tact, and constant nagging that our handy men were able to install additional toilets, showers, sinks and stoves.

Other committees, such as discipline, work, morality, education, and recreation, were formed.

Buildings and grounds were thoroughly policed, and small particles of paper and refuse were picked up from the grass. Not so much as a tiny piece of paper was permitted to remain, for the Commandant, a strict disciplinarian, ordered that if so much as a cigarette butt was found on the grounds or in the buildings, our privileges would be taken away from us. If trash was thrown out of the windows, the windows would be sealed. The mere thought of closed windows in this intense heat had us leaning backwards to keep everything spotless. If anyone threw a scrap of paper on the grass, there were half a dozen self-appointed guards to pounce on the offender.

A monitor was appointed for each room. His job was to see that the room was kept clean and to appoint occupants of the room for various duties, such as guarding the room and keeping the toilets clean.

Our room monitor was Rainbow, a charming southern woman with an abundance of tact and an even disposition. She would need it for the rough days ahead, for with over fifty women and children of various ages, nationalities, races, and backgrounds and temperaments, jammed together in one room, it spelled dynamite.

Catesy and Henry were assigned to garbage detail. They went about their work in high humor, as though they enjoyed their task thoroughly.

Their detail started at eight every morning. The large wooden cart holding the garbage resembled a sedan chair, minus the gilt, and the liveried sedan bearers. There was no lovely lady peeping coyly through silken curtains. Only mountains of garbage and two grinning and perspiring men who went from floor to floor to collect the refuse.

I watched for them every morning, and the moment they saw me they broke into the characteristic dog-trot of a rickshaw coolie as they whined in a high and discordant sing-song.

The hospital already had forty patients, and we gave cholera,

typhoid, and dysentery shots to over thirty-seven hundred people
in the clinic.

Today, a young American girl with typhoid was hustled out
of camp to an outside hospital. Her case was passed on to a German doctor appointed by the Nips. When he approved her case,
she was immediately sent outside.

We had doctors from the Rockefeller Medical Center in Peiping
and missionary doctors from China and remote provinces of the
Philippines. We had our own local civilian doctors and Red Cross
Filipino doctors from the outside. The nursing staff consisted of
American, British, Burmese and Filipino nurses.

Zenia, the nurse from India, and my old friend Brinny, the
British nurse, worked on the same shift with me.

The Burmese and Filipino nurses came in daily from the outside,
and their cheerful presence helped us forget our worries. How
faithfully they tried to keep us posted on news from the outside
world!

Before passing on any information, they'd ask in a conspiratorial
manner, "Where can we talk?"

Their news was always good, and we wondered sometimes why
we were in the clink when our forces were so victorious.

The Red Cross set up a kitchen for mothers and children where
coffee, milk, fruit juice, and cereal were served. A second kitchen
was completed to serve old men and women and those who were
destitute or with no local contacts.

With close to five hundred children running around more or less
wild and unsupervised, it was imperative to start schools functioning from kindergarten through high school.

Classes were in daily session in empty rooms and on the fourth
floor of the Big House, and, of course, all the teachers were internees.

Today, as I left the hospital, I saw a dancing class in session.
What next? With jaws slack, I stood gawking at the young terp-
sichorean hopefuls trying to imitate the graceful movements of
their teacher.

A dwarfed figure, complete with rifle and sloppy uniform,
stepped up beside me.

This was my exit cue!

January 10, 1942

Each morning I rushed like the Mad Hatter to the hospital
kitchen to cook the cereal and coffee for our breakfast. Each morning I expected to be thrown out, but so far the woman in charge
refrained from any violence. But her grumbling and disapproving

glances were hard to take so early in the morning.

Belle and Toinette left our mess, but there were still four of us to be fed, and we knew that soon we'd have to make other cooking arrangements.

Our patients at this time had influenza, dengue, and gastro-enteritis. In all my years of nursing, I had thought that gastro-enteritis was a fancy name, put into textbooks to confuse the young nurse.

My mind was quickly changed when I saw how ill and prostrate these patients were. When I succumbed to the disease, not once, but many times, I had a healthy respect for cholera sufferers. Always there was nausea, vomiting, high temperature, and acute diarrhea, which left the patient extremely weak and near collapse.

There was a large tent to the right of the hospital in which fifteen seamen were being treated for venereal disease. As I passed out the sulfa pills, I had many interesting chats with these men about their home states and the countries they had visited.

Mr. Smith, an old-timer from the Philippines and well known throughout the Orient for his fine carnivals, was given permission by the Japanese to set up three of his large carnival tents. One was for the venereals, one for the TB's and the third for nurses and women who worked in the hospital and kitchen.

When the nurses kept urging me to move into the tent, since there was less congestion than in the buildings, I went to investigate.

As I walked into the tent, the hot breath of air almost knocked me down. It was like standing in front of an open-hearth furnace in one of the steel mills in Pittsburgh. I viewed the thick dust on all the cots, chairs, benches, and tables, and I speculated about living in a tent during the typhoon season.

No, thank you! The Big House was a boiler factory and a mad-house with its congestion, but the walls were thick. Rain and typhoon couldn't touch me—only bedbugs, lice, scorpions, and disgustingly repulsive flying cockroaches as big as fifty-cent pieces.

January 11, 1942

There was a steady trek of people trying to get near the Commandant's office in order to be pronounced unfit for concentration life, and fortunately many of the frail, the sick, the aged, the pregnant, and mothers with young children were granted permission to live outside.

Before applying for permission, they were cautioned by our ever-alert Central Committee that they must have homes intact—that is, not looted or commandeered by the Japs—and they must have plenty of money to meet the sky-high living costs. Furthermore, they had to have good outside contacts among neutrals, Spaniards, and Filipinos.

The empty spaces in the rooms caused by the exodus of these adults and children were most gratifying to those remaining. Though our room monitors repeatedly warned us that more internees were expected from all parts of the islands, we continued to spread out.

Surreptitiously, we spread inch by inch until we had gained a foot or more in our castle.

Many children, especially those with only one parent in camp, were sent to outside orphanages, convents, and homes of friendly neutrals. Mothers with more than one child or with extremely young children were moved from rooms that were occupied by adults.

Most of the mothers and children were housed in the Annex, the long frame building to the rear and left of the Big House.

Just to pass the Annex on the outside was a nerve-racking experience. Such bedlam and confusion I had never heard or seen. No wonder the poor mothers were tired, wild-eyed, and irritable.

Children, accustomed to the constant attention and attendance of Chinese amahs and Filipina ayahs since infancy, ran wild, and the inexperienced mothers seemed to have little or no control over them.

Children who once had been well-behaved and controlled were now wild, restless, and buoyed with excitement because of the many playmates and unusual surroundings. They galloped through the long corridors and the grounds outside, screaming like savages, and Lord help those who got in their way!

Those children with both parents in camp were naturally better behaved and supervised, but the mothers who had the responsibility of looking after two, three, or more children while their husbands were fighting in Bataan, Corregidor, or elsewhere, were having a tough time.

The morality committee had its own peculiar problems.

We had been asleep in our room for several hours when we were brutally awakened by loud talking. The ceiling light had been turned on, and someone was flashing a light in our eyes. Fifty-five of my roommates sat up dazedly to stare at a Japanese soldier and one of our American men, standing in the middle of the room.

The American cleared his throat and read from a piece of paper in his hand, "The Japanese Commandant issued a proclaimation that there will be no display of affection between married or unmarried couples before any of his junior officers. Not so much as a kiss or a hand squeeze, or the morality squad men will swoop down on the offenders."

When the intruders left, lights were turned off, and when the buzzing of my roommates had ceased, I lay back on my bed and pondered for a long time about these Japanese.

What strange people according to our standards! Many of their public baths and toilets were for both sexes. Their Yoshiwara or red-light districts were models of decorum and cleanliness, and they were sanctioned by the government. In front of each establishment there was a brilliantly lighted marquee, like in our own movie houses back home. Adorning the walls and billboards were pictures of fancy girls, so that the prospective customer could choose his lady before entering.

In the big-city drugstores in Japan, for all the world to see, were strange-looking aphrodisiacs and still stranger-looking contraceptives openly displayed in the windows with their hair tonics and aspirin. But to kiss or hold hands in public was strictly forbidden!

January 12, 1942

The long wide road from the Big House to the front gate led to the outside world. Tall and shady acacia trees lined each side of this road, and here we stayed all day after our camp and personal chores were over. Here we ate our meals, napped, played cards, read, or swapped rumors. It was good to be in the open, away from the congestion and depression of the gloomy rooms and corridors. But our happiness was short-lived, for the Commandant no longer allowed us to clutter up that part of the grounds.

It was a blow to us, for the trees farther away from the road were small and scraggly with little or no shade. But we were thankful for the blessed sunshine and the dry season.

We continued to remain outdoors, usually until we were near the sunstroke stage. Then we'd gather our belongings and square our shoulders as though bracing ourselves for added courage and strength. It took courage and strength to stand the pandemonium found in the buildings.

The one bright spot in our lives at present was the enormous crowd of people who came to the outside gates to see us. They came daily, two hours in the morning and two hours in the afternoon, and they brought us food, clothing, clean laundry, bedding, cooking utensils, and messages of cheer.

Knowing that our servants, friends, and business associates hadn't forgotten us gave us a tremendous lift. Knowing their loyalty, interest, and faith that the Americans would some day return gave us added faith. It made us feel that we weren't isolated and alone in an enemy world.

With hundreds of faces pressed against the outside fence, it was clear why many of the Filipino houseboys carried long bamboo poles with the name of master and friend printed in huge block letters.

When a Filipino boy finally spotted his master in camp, it was touching to see his face light up as though he had seen God. No wonder eyes grew moist on either side of the fence at this mass display of loyalty, faith, and affection! Undoubtedly, it was a great demonstration of Filipino loyalty and faith in the American people, and of course our jailers were considerably perturbed by it. They could not understand why we hadn't lost face with the Filipinos now that we were prisoners.

The congestion on our side of the fence was just as great. Since we were not permitted to get close to the fence, we motioned our friends and servants to move down to the lower end of the fence where we thought congestion was less. But others had the same idea, and soon there were hundreds of others beside us. All were screaming different messages back and forth across the fence. No wonder we rarely understood.

After one of these fence sessions, most of us were emotionally and physically exhausted from the heat, from the sight of a faithful and familiar face, and from complete frustration.

I tried to understand what Catalino was screaming about, but I finally gave up. Every other day Catalino sent us cooked food and clean laundry.

Inside the gate there was a long table presided over by several Japanese soldiers and civilians. Six internee men helped carry the bundles and other articles to the Japs, who inspected the baskets of food and other packages.

After the article had been inspected, another internee, chosen, no doubt, for his hog-calling talents, bellowed the name on the package, and the happy recipient stepped up to claim his prize.

By eight in the evening I was ready for bed. Four hours of hospital work, preparing meals, and washing dishes under conditions existing in the days of the Pilgrims had worn me out completely.

Five-thirty A.M. came around quickly the next morning, but I was never early enough to beat the line at the toilets, despite the fact that additional facilities had been installed.

One of the first things our new Commandant did was to order the long front fence covered with swali, a native woven grass, and now we were no longer able to see and talk to our friends from the outside world.

Catalino brought us twenty-five pounds of dried navy beans, sugar, several cases of canned goods, and enough cooked food to last for two days.

In his note, cleverly concealed in the hem of my freshly laundered slacks, he had written that the Japs had been snooping in my apartment on several occasions and that Rags was sick.

So far they hadn't taken anything, for which I was grateful. Other internees were less fortunate. The Japs looted their homes, and many of them returned to help themselves to whatever appealed to their fancy.

In the hem of my other slacks which I sent out to be laundered, I had a note instructing Catalino to take what was left of my belongings to Adoracion's home and to contact Mr. Nagy, an old Hungarian friend, to look after my dog. Mr. Nagy, though impractical, temperamental, and argumentative, was a loyal friend, and I felt sure he would take Rags.

I first met Mr. Nagy at his Hungarian restaurant in Shanghai in the spring of 1937. He had just finished playing a sobbing Hungarian tune on his violin when I entered the restaurant. It was an old tear-jerking folk song that I had often heard played as a child by gypsy musicians.

The excellent food, the wine, and the delightful atmosphere of the restaurant made me happy and very much at home. I wanted to hear more gypsy music. So I wrote him a note in Hungarian and asked him to play several of my favorites. He played all of my requests with a great deal of feeling, and this time the violin sobbed tremulously. When he came to our table and stayed the rest of the evening, the long, thin nose of my nice but rather stuffy Scotch escort quivered dangerously.

I learned that Mr. Nagy was a political exile from Hungary and that he was of noble birth. He spoke five languages fluently, and wrote light verse and prose in a faintly Dostoevski vein. He painted, sculptured, played the violin, and wrote political articles for the Shanghai daily papers. With his broad knowledge of Europe and the Orient and with his flair for interpreting news behind the news, his articles were interesting and often tinged with prophecy. Had I believed in his political predictions in 1937 and later in 1940, I wouldn't be in a prison camp now.

After the first meeting, he would call me by phone and send me flowers and notes, begging for a date. But I was too busy with my nursing, shopping, dancing, and visiting interesting spots in and out of Shanghai.

The truth was that I considered him too old, pedantic, and continental. He affected a ridiculous monocle. This wasn't too hard to take, but when he bent over my hand and kissed it with each meeting and departure and said, *"Keset cshokolom, Terushka"* (I kiss your hand, Tressa), it was hard to keep from going into wild laughter. Yet I had seen my newly arrived relatives from Europe doing the same thing when I was a child.

Because I spoke Hungarian with no trace of accent, to him, I was someone dear and familiar from his home country. Because I liked wine with my meals and loved Hungarian music, I was a true countrywoman of his.

Dear Mr. Nagy! So kind and impractical. Had he been younger and less romantic, he would have sensed that I was as American as hot dogs and hamburger.

Eventually, he stopped asking me for dates, but the few times I saw him at his restaurant he remained as charming and cordial as at our first meeting.

In August of 1937, when Americans in Shanghai were evacuated to Manila because of the rapidly approaching Japs, I stopped to say good-bye to him. His monocle was suspiciously cloudy when he bade me farewell, and after kissing my hand he added with a gallant sigh that he would always look upon me as his daughter.

A year and a half later, he too came to Manila, and when the Axis nationals were first interned a few days after Pearl Harbor, Mr. Nagy packed his bags in expectation of being interned by the Americans. At army headquarters he was told that he was too old for prison life and that he could come and go as he pleased. So instead of our handing him comfort kits and packages over the fence, he was handing them to us.

In his notes to me he always wrote that he prayed for us daily and hoped we would be as well treated as he had been during four years of internment in Siberia under the Czarist regime in the first world war. Four years of internment! How could he bear it?

We hadn't completed a month, but already the confinement, the noise, the lack of privacy, the bedbugs, the hundreds of people always around us, the primitive conditions under which we lived, and the uncertainty and anxiety with which we viewed our future made us edgy and irritable.

Women were already losing weight and having menstrual disturbances, while many others were afflicted with unsightly boils.

One woman was removed to a mental institution today, and the man who failed to recognize us on the day of our arrival in camp committed suicide in a psycho ward outside.

The Red Cross was already serving two meals a day to about fifteen hundred internees, and the Red Cross officials urged all of us to eat in the line in order to conserve our canned goods. Perhaps pride and cloudy thinking kept many of us from joining the line. As long as we had a reserve food supply, a little money, and outside contacts, we planned to feed ourselves as long as possible.

The Japanese ignored letters of protestation regarding the internment of Red Cross officials and the confiscation of Red Cross property as a violation of international conventions. In addition, the Red Cross was unable to communicate with the outside world by letter, cable, or wireless, and it was dependent entirely on the money and supplies it could raise locally.

Fortunately, interned Red Cross officials were able to organize an outside surveying and purchasing squad while inside, the officials had charge of receiving, storing, and disposing of food and supplies.

On paper this sounded simple. But in reality it took a great deal of effort, time, disappointments, and endless and pointless arguments and conferences in order to get Japanese permission for more supplies and food.

From notes in our packages and from buyers who went out daily to make purchases, we learned that business on the outside was more or less at a standstill. The large business houses were closed, for most of the executives were with us. Other business houses were naturally reluctant to sell their merchandise in exchange for the Mickey Mouse currency, the nickname for occupational money.

It was clearly evident that the Nips were certain of victory, for the Japanese government had brought shiploads of the currency with the first invading forces. The moment they landed on Philippine soil, the country was flooded with Mickey Mouse money.

So was Santo Tomas! The paper notes resembling tobacco coupons and stage money bore this short and sweet legend: "The Japanese Government," and also the denomination of the note in pesos.

Our room monitors constantly reminded us that no one should make a direct appeal to the Commandant for passes or for permission to live outside. All appeals were to be made to internee men who had been appointed by our Central Committee to handle all such affairs.

But the hardheads, the thoughtless, and the fools were here as elsewhere in the world. One internee wishing a pass went directly to the Commandment with the tale that his wife had been bitten by a mad dog. The story proved to be a lie. He went on a drunken toot and didn't show up in camp for several days. Naturally, the Commandant was furious, and as a result he banned the passes for many days.

January 15, 1942

The bedbugs in our native beds continued to fatten and multiply, and our nights became more sleepless and uncomfortable.

As soon as the insecticide squad was organized, we appealed to them. They went into immediate action with boiling water and chlorine solution. After that treatment, we slept alone in our beds.

47

In addition to the insecticide squad, we had suggestion, sanitation, recreation, supply, building, plumbing, electricity, vice, education, room direction, hospital, kitchen, and discipline committees. Our self-government was functioning smoothly. In fact, the present Commandant remarked that he was "amazed to see a group of Americans and other Allied nationals governing themselves so well."

The Commandant had cause to admire our smoothly run camp when one considered that we were indeed a mixed group. Bankers, business executives, millionaires, doctors, lawyers, engineers, teachers, nurses, scientists, explorers, newspapermen, photographers, dancers, sword swallowers, clowns, contortionists, musicians, priests, preachers, and artists rubbed elbows with confidence men, gamblers, pickpockets, thieves, prostitutes, and pimps. There was even a murderer in our midst, according to the report given by one of our fellow members, who had spotted one of his roommates as the man "Wanted for Murder" in *True Detective Magazine*.

In addition to our varied professions, we had many nationalities and races represented — Americans, Britons, Poles, Czechs, Dutch, Germans, Russians, Hungarians, Arabs, Syrians, Assyrians, Egyptians, Chinese, Hindus, Hawaiians, Chamorians, Negroes, and mestizos (half-castes of various races and nationalities).

Though we were not exactly happy, we were one big family, with everyone doing his best to keep the oil in the machinery of the camp humming. Above all, we leaned backwards to stay out of the Nips' path, as we carried out their orders to the letter.

In a camp of this size there were many interesting personalities. One of them was Don Juan. He was short, dark, and handsome in a matador fashion, and he loved blondes. When his bold and roving eyes cast their fluoroscopic rays on a girl, he didn't miss a trick.

Before the war he had been a successful businessman and had many friends, especially among the fair sex. Here in camp, with his good humor, Rabelaisian wit, and easy spending, he was surrounded by friends of both sexes. And here in camp, where money truly talks, he had no trouble in finding a good-looking blonde — er-r-r . . . I mean *blondes*.

I met him today in front of the Big House. Two eye-filling blonde beauties were on either side of him, clinging to his arm in a proprietary fashion. Either blonde would have caused a second look on Hollywood and Vine.

"How are you, D. J.?" I asked rather superfluously.

"Never better!" he answered with a wicked wink.

From all appearances, his little world hadn't been too greatly disturbed. In fact, it had improved. Now he could pursue blondes as a full-time occupation.

It was siesta hour, and most of my roommates were in their cubicles, a space large enough to hold a bed or mattress and various boxes and suitcases filled with clothes, food, pots, pans, and other cooking utensils. The women who had cots and beds stored their possessions under them. A few like us, who had arrived first on the scene, had a treasured table, school bench, or chair.

The enormously high ceiling and walls were unbelievably dirty, and so were the six huge pillars which supported the ceiling.

The old-fashioned sink in our room was our pride and joy. It made our room something special, and we were the envy of all the other rooms on the floor.

At this sink, only teeth, face, and hands could be washed, and the rules were most rigid. However, when we thought the coast was clear, most of us sneaked to the sink to wash a pair of panties or to rinse a cup or dish. To the right of the sink there was a large blackboard where notices were posted. On the first day of the month, a new calendar was drawn by one of the girls in the room.

Underneath the blackboard was a raised platform, the home of three attractive women of Spanish and Dutch ancestry. They were mother and two grown daughters. The daughters had flashing black eyes, creamy complexions, jet black hair, and large and beautifully proportioned hands, which they used in a graceful and expressive manner.

The mother, a pleasant and quiet woman, was always even-tempered, despite the fact that her husband was temperamental and extremely cantankerous. He usually sat outside our room, glaring at every woman that came out of Room 25, while he waited impatiently for his family to emerge.

To the right of my bed was the Smith family, consisting of a widowed mother and her two grown single daughters. Her third daughter, a divorcee with a young son, had moved to the Annex. Mrs. Smith was frail and ailing, and she worried a great deal about her son at the front and a daughter-in-law who lived on the outside because of her sickly child.

Beyond them toward the wall were two women and a child — a spritely little grandmother of seventy, her equally spritely and attractive married daughter, Daphne, and her eight-year-old grandson. Grandma had another married daughter in camp and many grown grandchildren. Daphne was slender, extremely nervous, and she believed most of the fantastic rumors that were spread in camp. And, brother, some of them were whoppers!

We loved to see her come around with her written radio transcripts which she read to us in a precise and clipped British accent. While she read, we watched her pretty black eyes shine with excitement and optimism. Our American forces were always just outside the gates of our prison as far as she was concerned. Her optimism and faith were contagious, and often we found ourselves wondering if we weren't a bit too cynical and pessimistic.

Perhaps it was true that a thousand of our flying fortresses had reached Corregidor!

To the left of my bed was Sophie's, and beyond her were Belle and Toinette. These three had already quarreled, and I had a difficult time remaining neutral. Perhaps Sophie had carelessly bumped Belle's bed, or perhaps she had hung a dripping washcloth near it. It didn't take much to start a fight in a packed room like ours.

Last night Sophie shouted at Toinette to stop making so much noise with her cream jars, and when Toinette told her to mind her own business, all of them lashed at each other with their tongues.

It was hard to tell which side had the most grievances. When Belle and Toinette switched to Spanish and French, Sophie was stumped. It was just as well, for what they said about her was hardly complimentary.

With this type of feminine warfare going on in my corner, I felt like I was sitting on the edge of a Vesuvius that would erupt at any moment.

Finally, Rainbow, our tactful and diplomatic monitor, solved everything. She switched Sophie's and my bed, so that I was next to Belle and Sophie was to my right. Now only my bed stood between War and Peace.

Sometimes, when feeling cussedly mean and bored with the monotony of this life, I would have welcomed a good knockdown fight — providing I was only a spectator.

The three corner cots in front of our beds were occupied by the wives of three mining engineers who had joined our forces at Bataan shortly after Pearl Harbor.

Leslie, the eldest of the trio, had short brown hair and wore glasses. She was quiet, reserved, and even-tempered. Though constantly boosting the morale of the other two younger women, one could see that she was greatly concerned over her husband in Bataan and her two grown sons who were somewhere in the war theatre.

Margo was a strawberry blonde, young, pretty, and affectionate, with a pleasing personality. She often talked about her handsome husband, and she prayed nightly that reinforcements would arrive in Bataan.

Kay had dark hair and eyes with high cheek-bones. Her slim waist and hips and her shapely feet and legs were the envy of all the women not so favorably endowed. Usually, she was quiet and even-tempered. Occasionally, her black eyes would flash with anger and bitterness, and it was usually when she berated those "fatheads in Washington for not sending reinforcements to Bataan."

Siesta hour should have been the hour of peace and quiet, but the women had difficulty relaxing. Those who weren't whispering were talking out loud, while half a dozen or more were fussing with pots and pans under their beds. Though I had cotton in my ears, I heard everything — the creak of the beds, the whispering, the coughing and the sneezing.

I tried to read. I tried to sleep. But there was just too much activity around me.

Kay and Margo chattered as Kay helped her to wash her lovely reddish-blonde hair. They were both squatting on the cement floor with three pails of water before them.

Suddenly the canvas curtain that hung over our door to give us privacy from the teeming multitude in the corridor was thrust aside, and we saw a face, complete with goggles, buck teeth, and peaked cap. He explained to someone behind him, "Radies, all radies!"

When they left, the radies all laughed, for we were becoming accustomed to goggled eyes peeking at us. It was just another guided tour of Japanese officers who had come to gape and leer at us.

The women continued with their gossiping, reading, knitting, napping, and swatting flies.

January 17, 1942

I rushed to the hospital kitchen at six every morning. If by some magic I could have obliterated myself into a tiny grease spot while I cooked our coffee and cereal, I would have done so. I knew that my welcome was being stretched dangerously thin in the crowded kitchen, and I expected to be thrown out without any formal notice.

Catalino had already sent us a native stove, plus my old iron skillets, pots, pans, and other kitchen utensils, and we'd have to put them in use just as soon as we found a place outside to set up housekeeping.

January 19, 1942

Four or five hundred of our fellow members jammed into the west patio of the Big House after curfew, for a community sing. The walls of this old Spanish university resounded to the lovely strains of "Old Kentucky Home," "Swanee River," "When Irish Eyes Are Smiling," and other favorites.

Songs of a patriotic nature were not permitted by order of the Commandant.

January 20, 1942

Most of our barbed-wire buddies were optimistic, and many firmly believed that we'd be out in a few weeks. They reasoned that in a few weeks our reinforcements would arrive. However, one brash young man at the hospital today said that he thought we would be imprisoned for a whole year, and for a moment it looked like the young man was going to be mobbed by his angry fellow internees.

January 21, 1942

It was interesting to watch the expression of an American when a Japanese soldier with untidy uniform and oversized boots shuffled past. Disgust and amusement could not be disguised, and more often a string of unprintable words were muttered after the retreating back.

January 22, 1942

With so many rumors going around, we were in a continual state of nervous anxiety. One day we heard that the men and women would be separated. A few hours later we heard that the women would all be released.

Most of us were afraid to live outside. We felt safer in the camp.

Occasionally someone less optimistic told us that though our men at Corregidor and Bataan were fighting like demons, it was only a question of time before they were defeated. A cold fear chilled our hearts. If Corregidor and Bataan fell, our chances of early release vanished.

The Internews, a camp newspaper, was started, and of course only camp news was printed in this tiny ten-to-fifteen page pamphlet. Since softball and football teams had been formed, one section of the paper was devoted to sports.

January 23, 1942

Nothing caused more exasperation and hate than seeing the Nips driving our cars. There were more unprintable words uttered when internees recognized their cars being driven into the camp by cocky Japanese! Catesy gritted his teeth every time he saw his car entering the camp. The indignity of being politely pushed out of his new car was bad enough. But it was far worse to watch a grinning Japanese soldier driving his car like a demented cowboy, while several high Japanese dignitaries on a rubberneck tour of Santo Tomas sat in the back seat.

We had a few dipsomaniacs, nymphomaniacs, and women who followed the oldest profession in the world.

The most colorful and notorious prostitute was Tientsin Mary! Her brassy voice, coarse laugh, and dancing hips were a familiar sight to everyone in camp. Her activities were discussed with avid interest, and it was whispered that in addition to an already full schedule, she shared her favors with the Japanese soldiers.

January 26, 1942

A ripple of tremulous excitement went through the camp when we heard many planes high in the clouds. There followed heavy anti-aircraft firing, and we heard the loud detonation of bombs.

A Japanese guard with bayonet bared came to our room to turn off our lights, while excited men, women, and children in corridors were hustled into their rooms by additional guards.

A ripple of nervous and excited giggles swept our room, and many felt that we'd soon be liberated.

It was a beautiful night. Clear and moonlit. Through the mosquito bars I saw Belle and Toinette praying on their knees.

January 27, 1942

By order of the Commandant, each room was given a copy of the Japanese-controlled daily *Tribune*, which we had nicknamed the *Nishi-Nishi*.

The morning headline made us positively gay. NIGHT RAIDERS MET BY A HEAVY BARRAGE OF ANTI-AIRCRAFT.

It won't be long now, we gloated!

January 28, 1942

The Japanese paper, the *Nishi-Nishi*, had us in a tizzy of merriment. How crude and fantastic could their propaganda be? The paper carried this astonishing bit of news: "The Santo Tomas Internment Camp has been ruthlessly bombed by Americans, and the Japanese condemn the bombing of Manila by Americans, especially the bombing of Santo Tomas, which clearly exposes the inhumanity of the Americans."

In anticipation of another raid by our bombers, many of us stayed in the west patio until 9 P.M. By the light of the full moon we scanned the heavens above us in hope of seeing our planes.

We waited in vain.

January 29, 1942

A Filipino ice-cream vendor was permitted to enter the camp with his push cart, and we flocked to him like eager kids.

On the third day, when he disposed of his wares, the Japanese guards took him to the Commandant's office. After beating him up, they took away his earnings. When he left the camp, one side of his face was a bloody mess.

I glanced back at the notes I had made a month ago. At that time I had been in a state of mind bordering on fearful anxiety, panic, and resignation. The U. S. Army had left the city, and we were expecting the enemy. Kind and thoughtful Major Greene had given me a vial of luminal. Yes, I had been fortunate. I had had no need of it.

But there were other women. Had they known the shame, degradation, mutilation and madness that awaited them, they would have sought blessed oblivion in some fashion on the day the enemy reached the Philippines.

January 30, 1942

We were sick at heart and depressed today. We heard that Churchill had said that "Singapore will fall." This news came as a bombshell after all the optimistic rumors we had been hearing.

People who had lived in the Orient for years had almost a fanatical belief in the impregnability of the Singapore Fortress. Now that illusion had vanished. They wondered about Corregidor. If Singapore fell, would Corregidor go next?

January 31, 1942

For four weeks we have been eating in the open, picnic fashion, while we fought ants and huge blowflies.

February 1, 1942

The front and rear double doors of the Big House were closed and barred every night at 6:30. This meant that two thousand or more people could no longer escape the heat, noise, and confusion of the rooms and corridors — unless they were young and fleet-footed.

Fortunately, Catesy and I were young, and nimble on our feet. the moment roll call was over, we literally flew down to the west patio to find a vacant spot.

But about five hundred people had the same idea. All of them carried petates, native grass mats, which were woven with such fancy inscriptions as "Happy Thought," "God Bless Us," and "Felicitations."

The patio was about the size of an extremely large swimming pool, and when we got there, puffing like a couple of steam-engines, it was jammed with men and women. Hurriedly, we leaped over arms, legs, and bodies until we found a spot large enough for our petate. We spread it on the ground and settled down with a sigh of relief.

"Happy, honey?" whispered Catesy as he squeezed my hand.

"Alone at last!" I sighed blissfully, though anyone hearing my remark might have taken me for a madwoman.

Every cubic inch of space was packed as tightly as in Coney

Island on a torrid Sunday in July. Instead of the sea and sand, we had hard ground and four stories of gray concrete walls on four sides of us. But how blessedly fortunate we were to see a small square patch of the sky and stars above!

Here men and women dreamed and planned their future, and for an hour or two they found peace. Catesy and I talked about some of the wonderful times we had spent together, and for a short time we almost succeeded in forgetting our sordid environment.

"We'd be honeymooning in Europe if —"

My voice choked in my throat, and Catesy took me in his arms.

"Just wait and see. The Americans will be back in a few weeks, and instead of a European trip, we'll go around the world. Would you like that, honey?"

My eyes were wet with tears and, as we kissed and embraced, for a moment we were far from Santo Tomas.

A flashlight glared in our faces. It was one of our morality squad men who patrolled the east and west patios.

He went into his speech, though his heart wasn't in it. "No demonstration of affection is allowed by order of the Japanese Commandant." He had repeated this phrase so often that his voice sounded like a tipstaff droning a jumble of meaningless words in a hot country courtroom.

We left shortly afterward.

February 2, 1942

Life in the Constipation Camp — nicknamed by our camp wits — went on!

We were all in our room this afternoon when Daphne, the eternal optimist, perked us out of our lethargy." Our boys are sending messages from the sky!" she shouted, as she saw tiny bits of paper dropping near our windows. Eagerly, we rushed to the windows in hopes of grabbing one of the precious papers.

Alas, there were no inspiring messages or instructions, but only charred scraps of worthless paper carried by the wind.

Disappointed, and feeling somewhat foolish, we went back to our beds, and our hopes for an early deliverance were somewhat dampened.

February 3, 1942

Apparently the bedbugs had nine lives. They were on the march again, and I spent another sleepless night.

The insecticide men again sprayed the bed with chlorine solution, and this time they assured me that they had liquidated even the great, great-grandpappies.

For several days there have been whispers that a few of our fellow members have escaped over the wall. This was quite possible, as at the present time the guard system was a colossal joke because of the few Japanese guards patrolling these extensive walls.

Escape over the wall was simple. The difficulty arose outside. A white face in a sea of dark ones wouldn't get very far without a pass.

Tonight we went to the east patio after roll call and sat beside a group of Hawaiians and Chamorians. They sang their plaintively beautiful melodies to the accompaniment of uke and guitar. Their music brought back nostalgic memories of Waikiki Beach to both Catesy and me.

Catesy voiced my thoughts when he said, "I wish you had been in Hawaii with me!"

When we compared notes, we discovered that we had been there in the same year. "I wish I had known you then!" I remarked.

Because our entertainment committee had prepared a program of music and dancing in the west patio, we left our musical friends a short time later.

Harvey Jones was a gifted professional dancer, comedian, mimic, singer, and entertainer. He was the perfect emcee for our camp. He made us laugh and forget our surroundings, and he lifted our morale tremendously. He was over six feet tall, with wispy and mousy-colored hair worn in a Skeezix bang which nearly hid a pair of the friendliest and kindest baby-blue eyes I had ever seen. With his unusual height, his bean-pole skinniness was accentuated. When he danced, his loose-jointed body seemed to move without effort, giving one the impression that he was made of rubber and completely devoid of any bones.

We were fortunate to have him as well as the other professional dancers, singers, actors, and musicians who were from the States, Shanghai, Australia, and India.

The Commandant and his henchmen apparently thought them good, for throughout the entertainment they bared their teeth as they laughed in appreciation of the excellent performance.

People were more relaxed after the good show. Rumors and the war were pushed back in our minds, and for a short while the future seemed less dark.

The *Internews*, our camp paper, had a cartoon of an American enjoying his whiskey soda in the pre-war days. On the opposite page, he was wheeling huge cans of garbage.

Millionaires, bank presidents, executives, and beachcombers took their turns at garbage detail. They cleaned toilets, mopped floors, and dug ditches to bury tons of tin and garbage.

There was a special detail nicknamed "Issue Tissue" which entailed bathroom duty and doling three squares of toilet paper to a customer. Only three! No more and no less! Small wonder that robust jokes had made the rounds of the camp regarding this detail.

An epidemic of pediculi broke out in one of the women's rooms, and it was Zenia's sad task to examine fifty-nine indignant heads. The fact that some of the heads belonged to the cream of Manila's society didn't help the situation. When Zenia, the missionary nurse, completed her grisly search and extermination, she was lousy, too.

We heard the heavy and muffled rumble of big guns today. It sounded a long way off. We prayed that they were our own guns.

Heads instinctly turned heavenward when planes flew over us. There was always the faint hope that they would bear the insignia of the star. But it was only the Flying Eagles decorated with the bright orange sun.

February 6, 1942

The boys surprised us with an exceptionally good lunch. To plain boiled rice, given us by neighbors on the other side of the abandoned truck where we had been eating for the last few days, they added tomato juice, fried bacon, and several cans of corned beef. It was good enough food for anyone, and we all agreed that ice-cold beer wouldn't have been out of order.

But it was not for us! No alcoholic drinks of any type were permitted in camp. It was just as well, as the camp had a few alcoholics. These former bottle-per-day men would have a grand opportunity to go on the wagon. Under the circumstances, it wouldn't be hard to imagine what would happen to a swaggering Jap who strutted past an American who had been drinking.

Again we heard heavy detonations coming from a distance. How desperately we wanted to know what was happening at the front!

My daily routine remained unchanged. After hospital duty, I showered with sixteen other women and then tidied my boudoir by pulling out the boxes, baskets, crates, pots, and pans under my bed prior to mopping.

February 8, 1942

Today was Sunday! The rotogravure section of the *Nishi-Nishi* was filled with idyllic scenes. The Japanese soldier was shown worshiping with the Filipinos in local Manila churches. Another picture depicted an old Spanish church in all of its seventeenth-century grandeur. Not a stone had been nicked, but all around there were half-destroyed buildings. Underneath the picture were these hypocritical words: "The Japanese respect the Filipinos and their religion." There was a dig at Uncle Sam and his people. "A nation that indulges in pretty dresses, nice food, physical enjoyment and expensive fashions can never succeed in establishing a strong nation."

The money that we sent to Catalino was made to stretch as far as possible. We ate well twice a week.

Today being Sunday, he sent us baked ham, vegetable salad, ubi (a sweet potato substitute with a bright purple shade), and apple pie with cheese.

I had looked forward to the Sunday meal, but a censored note from Mr. Nagy informed me that my dog was very sick. When Catesy found me, I was leaning against the abandoned truck and crying like a baby. Before putting his arms around me, he glanced quickly around to see if it was safe.

"It isn't only Rags," I wailed. "It's the flies, the bedbugs, the bedlam, and the lack of privacy!"

February 9, 1942

We've had intense heat the last few days, and the leaves of the fine acacia trees are beginning to turn brown and fall on the ground. In another month the trees will be naked and the grass withered and scorched.

The hot season in Manila was trying under normal conditions, which included lovely gardens, verandas, servants, iced drinks, fans, and air-conditioned rooms. But under these circumstances — that was something else again!

"Take each day as it comes and don't look too far into the crystal ball!" cautioned Catesy when I wondered about the hot season and whether we'd find a shady spot to cook and eat our meals.

While writing this, I happened to glance toward the door, and I was startled to see a Japanese guard holding up the canvas curtain to get a better look. Immediately, I stopped writing and looked around the room with the most innocent expression I could manage. Not daring to meet his glance, I slipped off my bed and eased my diary under the bed. Then I started to fuss with my pots and pans until I was certain he had left.

The women who had kept diaries in my room had long since destroyed them. One of them buried her diary with her silverware and jewelry in her garden at home, and now she was wondering if the rains would wash them up.

Seven hundred new books were added to some of the books given the camp by the university. The former head of the YMCA was able to have these books sent in from the outside.

How dearly we'd love to see the latest issue of *Time* or *Life.* Many of our people refused to read the local *Nishi-Nishi* because of its propaganda. It infuriated and depressed them.

Our little Filipina Red Cross nurse, Pura, who came from the outside daily, said, "One should invert the news in the *Nishi-Nishi* to get the real information."

This we often did, especially when the Nips were crowing about a particular victory. Our losses, of course, were always three times higher than theirs.

The *Nishi-Nishi* had a nasty habit of referring to all Americans as "those degenerate Americans."

February 10, 1942

Crotchety and old Mr. and Mrs. Greenshoes' dispositions didn't improve, living and sleeping as they did in the crowded corridor of the second floor. They've had several verbal tussles with our Internee Committee and the Japs, but so far they have won every round.

When informed by our committee that husbands and wives were to be separated, the old lady indignantly declared, "I've slept with my husband for forty-five years, and no G—— D—— Japs are going to separate us now!" And no one did!

Screens were placed around their bed at night, and these old people tried to rest with hundreds of people milling and prowling around the corridors until late at night. On several occasions, when the traffic and noise had become too much for them, Mrs. Greenshoes had appeared from behind the screen in her night-dress. Wild-eyed and furiously angry, she had lashed everyone with her sharp tongue. During the day she stomped about the corridors, and traffic had a way of parting for her.

I learned that the easiest way to divert the old lady from her scoldings, protestations, and colorful profanity was to ask questions about Buddhism. She was a devout Buddhist. When she launched into her favorite subject, the glint in her fiery old eyes changed to a seraphic gentleness, and her strident voice shifted to a soft purr.

February 11, 1942

This was a big day for the Nips! The Foundation Day of the Great Japanese Empire, which was started 2602 years ago! The morning *Nishi-Nishi* was filled with crowing over Japanese successes. They had done well! These little men that we never took quite seriously.

Today the Rising Sun flag waved over the High Commissioner's Office, Fort Santiago, Malacanan, and other public buildings. This was just one city! How many more cities and countries would their flag wave over before they were stopped?

Mr. Nagy sent me a box of chocolates with a note cleverly concealed in one of the wrappers. After Catesy and I read the last part of his note, we had our first good laugh in days. In his careful English he had written, "I visited your apartment yesterday, and I noticed that your girl, Adoracion, had conceived, and that it was plainly visible. So I asked her, 'Adoracion, are you married?'" And she had answered with bowed head, "No sir, but I am disgraced!"

February 12, 1942

SINGAPORE FALLS! This was the headline that greeted us in the morning rag. The camp was stunned. People went about their work sadly and dejectedly.

Would Bataan and Corregidor go next? We couldn't bear to think about it!

Christmas, New Year, and now Lincoln's Birthday — all of them spent in the shadow of the Rising Sun!

Tonight we heard of another tragedy. The whispers we had heard of an escape were true. Three Australians who had escaped over the wall had been captured and cruelly beaten. Fellow internees heard their cries of agony. After their wounds had been dressed by our camp doctors, they were taken outside for further punishment.

February 13, 1942

Another man escaped! This time it was an American, and those who knew him well thought he had a better chance of eluding the Nips, for he was married to a native woman and was familiar with the country.

We were sorry to hear about this escape though, as it meant more rigid rules and hardships.

February 14, 1942

After work at the hospital was over, nurses and patients made Valentines for their favorite doctors, patients, and attendants.

The most amusing and original one was made for our natty-looking Englishman who cleaned the toilets and bedpans. Despite his menial work, he managed to remain as immaculate as a floorwalker at Wanamaker's. From morning until night he remained at his post, always courteous and always smiling.

Laura, who was the poetess from my room and also at present a patient at the hospital, had written the following poem, which we ceremoniously presented to the Englishman in a spotlessly clean cellophane-wrapped bedpan.

The Only One

'Twas a quaint little room with quans on the wall
A wash bowl or two and a faucet not new.

In this quaint little room where we answered the call
Was a natty young man most polite to us all.

With a swab in his hand and a flourish gallant
He never did say, "Well, what do you want?"

But always was cheery and would say with a smile,
"Won't you sit on this box for a while?"

"There's a gentleman ahead of you, but he shouldn't take long."
So down you sit, tho you know 'twas all wrong.

To sit there and wait for a gent to emerge
From where we all go when we have the urge.

But oh, the tearing of paper, I'm sure he's most through,
But he's only preparing, and the joke is on you.

So you wait and you wait till the damn thing flushes,
Then finally out the occupant rushes,

Stumbling over your feet as he goes,
But where is your urge? Ah, nobody knows.

At last, up you get, and start for the can,
But into the door goes the gallant young man.

And finally when you sit down on the seat,
You feel that at least the darn thing is neat.

Forgotten the urge, and the impatient waiting,
Such gallantry lingers without deflating.

The three Australians who tried to escape were shot at the North Cemetery today; several of our leading fellow internees were asked to be present at the execution by the Japanese, and our men reported that the three men met their death bravely.

An air of uneasiness and gloom had settled over the camp. Passes and other privileges were canceled for the time being. There was no news about the escaped American.

February 16, 1942

To increase the gloom and depression that had settled over us, a mammoth balloon hovered over the camp. Printed in large fire-red print across its huge surface were these words: SINGAPORE HAS SURRENDERED.

Just in the event we had missed the above cheering news, we were further plagued by leaflets dropped from the sky bearing the same glad tidings. A giant victory parade, complete with marching and singing soldiers, tanks, trucks, and other vehicles passed our camp. Thank God, we could not see it! It was bad enough to hear!

The camp hospital was filled with gastro-enteritis, bacillary and amoebic dysentery cases. A health campaign was started by our doctors to improve the sanitary conditions in the camp.

Since we were almost eaten up by loathsome flies, anti-fly campaigns were accelerated, and all sorts of home-made booby traps for flies were invented.

Adult education classes were started in astronomy, Spanish, Tagalog (the dialect spoken in Manila), Russian, Japanese, English, mathematics, and many other subjects.

A bridge tournament was in session, and the second-floor corridor of the Big House was filled with serious players night after night.

A requiem mass was said yesterday for the three executed men at Santo Tomas chapel. After today, internees will no longer be permitted to worship at the chapel.

A large truckload of Filipino workmen came in today, and as they passed us they grinned sympathetically and held up two fingers à la Churchill fashion.

The workmen immediately proceeded to put up barbed-wire fences between us and the Seminary building which contained the chapel and housing quarters for the Spanish priests. The barbed-wire fence also cut off the ball diamond. Bit by bit, more ground was taken away from us. More rules were enforced.

From reading between the lines of the *Nishi-Nishi,* and from stories we heard from our people who had been out on passes, we learned that the Axis nationals weren't too happy either. They were beginning to awaken to the fact that the great "Co-prosperity Sphere in Asia" did not include them. "Asia for the Asiatics" was another mumbo-jumbo term with no true meaning. It was Asia for the Nipponese, and no one else!

February 19, 1942

Camp morale moved back and forth like a pendulum. We

heard that Germany was about to collapse and that Russia planned to declare war on Japan. But the best news of all was that our fleet had won many victories in the Pacific.

No matter how fantastic the rumors were, we wanted to believe them. But oh, the terrific letdown when we learned that we had been fooled again!

The Catholics were told at roll call tonight that mass would be said by a Japanese priest.

After roll call Catesy and I dashed down to the west patio to find a vacant spot to spread our petate. We stretched out on the petate and tried not to think of the four stories of concrete walls surrounding us.

The morality-quad man stalked back and forth between the two patios.

Since it took the inspector ten minutes to make the rounds in one patio, couples learned to time their embraces when the snooper was in the other patio. These stealthy and torrid little love scenes should have tickled my funny-bone. Instead, it made me infinitely sad.

February 20, 1942

It was still dark this morning when I hurried to the hospital. Suddenly, I bumped into someone with such force that I nearly lost my balance. The grunts and groans which followed made me realize that I had collided with a Japanese guard.

"Good morning!" I sang out cheerily.

"Ohio!" answered the Jap, followed by a string of unintelligible words that sounded friendly and neighborly.

"*Si! Si!*" I answered in confusion and made my escape.

February 21, 1942

One hundred thirteen British men, women and children arrived yesterday from Sulphur Springs, a small internee camp outside of Manila. These people had been the passengers and crew of the *S. S. Anhui* which reached Manila shortly after Pearl Harbor.

February 22, 1942

Washington's Birthday was not forgotten! The men in the room next to ours made an American flag from a white piece of cloth dipped into gentian violet and Scott's solution, and during roll call the improvised flag was displayed.

The Nips had a change of heart, and the Catholics were permitted to worship at the Santo Tomas chapel. While notices on the bulletin boards announced that a Protestant Japanese preacher would lead the services in the Father's garden, I saw no sign of a Nipponese.

From my window I had an excellent view of the Father's garden and I could hear all of the service, and I was happy to see that we still had an American minister as before.

When the organist at the wheezy old portable organ struck the first chords of the lovely hymn, "Faith of Our Fathers," I joined the congregation in the singing. Kay and Margo joined me, and for the rest of the service the three of us sat on my bed.

My little old corner I had chosen so long ago had its advantages. I could attend church just by sitting at my window.

February 23, 1942

F.D.R. States That American Shores Cannot Be Defended. Every headline in the *Nishi-Nishi* was meant to terrorize and demoralize.

I finally persuaded Catesy to shave off his beard, which he had planned to keep for the duration. Though the beard made him appear more handsome, it had a depressing effect on me. But Catesy was proud of his beard, and he was most reluctant to shave it off.

Finally, in protest, I wore my baggiest and most faded slacks, and I wore my hair in a homely Sis Hopkins style. For three days I looked sloppy and "Tobacco Roadish," but that was all I needed. The next day the beard was off! To show my appreciation for his sacrifice, I put on a dress, lipstick, and arranged my hair becomingly. After having worn slacks, I felt indecently exposed, but the interested look my man gave me more than rewarded me for the trouble I had gone to.

The men with beards looked unkempt and fierce. While the women kept themselves neat and clean, some of the men became careless about their appearance. The American beauty operator from the Army and Navy Club set up a shop, and those with money were getting manicures and finger waves. However, there were few women who could afford this kind of extravagance often.

February 24, 1942

Japan Is Prepared to Wage War for A Hundred Years. This was hardly the type of headline that would cheer us.

Daphne, our British roommate, could always be depended upon to cheer us when we needed it most. With Kay, Margo, and me on my bed, Daphne read us some of her absurdities. "Roosevelt has given the Japs forty-eight hours to clear out of Manila; otherwise he will lambaste them with a fireside chat."

Daphne produced laughs, and how we needed laughs in these dark days!

February 25, 1942

California Shore Shelled. This was our morning headline. Can it be true?

64

The Santo Tomas trots or acute gastro-enteritis caught up with me, and I had to leave my work at the hospital.

By afternoon I managed to stand in the food line for my plate of stew, which was pretty rough fare for me. In the evening I spent an hour on my weekly detail of "Miss Issue-Tissue." I was grateful that I could sit in a chair as I doled out three squares to a customer.

Laura, our poetic roommate, was still at the hospital, sick with bacillary, and when I went off duty today, she gave me the following poem:

February 26, 1942

> Remember when?
> For bedpans we all had a yen —
> Some claimed eight, and others ten,
> And even twelve or fifteen when
> We weren't as we should have been.
>
> Remember when?
> Among visitors we had men
> Which never stopped us when
> We needed bedpans brought again
> And by heck, we used them then.
> Remember when?
>
> Remember when?
> We swatted flies, and slept, and then
> We swore that if and where and when
> We ever got back home again
> We'd never have another yen.

February 26, 1942

Zenia, my nurse friend from India, went outside on a pass, and she spent the night at my apartment.

How happy we were to see her the next day, for she had brought us the money we had stored in the water tank and in the hanging air-plants.

I was too weak to nurse, but not too weak to spend most of the morning chasing bedbugs and cleaning my boudoir.

It was whispered that every room had an ear. A few minutes ago Margo pointed out a middle-aged American woman of German descent in my room. The woman had supposedly been on the G2 list of the U. S. Army before the war. As I looked at the woman's kindly and pleasant features, I thought, just as in a whodunit, that she would have been the last one I would have suspected.

February 27, 1942

F.D.R. Says: "It Is Hopeless to Send Reinforcements to P.I."

Each day, after reading the propaganda headline, I vowed that I'd never again look at the *Nishi-Nishi* — until I saw the lying rag the next day.

Daphne contributed some more of the latest news "right out of the horse's mouth."

"If the Japanese fail to get out of Manila in seventy-two hours, Roosevelt will send Eleanor to clear them out."

February 28, 1942

The Red Cross Filipina, Burmese, and Siamese nurses will soon leave us to care for wounded Japanese soldiers.

How we hated to see these fine girls leave! They never failed to cheer us with their optimism and news, and with their daily contact with the outside we were kept posted on what was happening in the city.

March 1, 1942

The Voice of Freedom, transmitting from Corregidor, had promised that soon the skies would be "darkened by American planes" and that General MacArthur was "preparing for the big push."

The Red Cross nurses gave us this news, and later in the day the same words were found in many smuggled notes, hidden in food and laundry bundles.

The Japanese granted the Red Cross permission to release part of their frozen funds to purchase food and other relief supplies for us.

March 2, 1942

"Bring food for three days!" Every time I met an elderly American on the campus, he greeted me with those five words. Then he added rather bitterly the time we had already spent. "We start our third month today!" he exclaimed unhappily.

March 3, 1942

Last night an Englishman was found wandering near the front gates and behaving suspiciously. With hands tied behind his back and escorted by two Japanese guards, he was taken to his room monitor. Our room monitors warned us repeatedly that the penalty for escape was death and that the same punishment would be dealt to the room monitor.

Fortunately, in the Englishman's case, our doctors were able to convince the Commandant that the man was suffering from a mental disorder brought on by worrying about his wife and child in China.

He was taken to the camp hospital, where no one could persuade him to eat. "We must conserve food. We must conserve food." Those four words were seared into his brain. Finally, he was removed to a psychiatric hospital outside.

This afternoon we were in our room when we heard the roar of many planes over us. We rushed to the windows in hopes that they were our own planes, but all of them bore the hated orange circle. We counted sixty-five bombers, and all of them were headed in the direction of Bataan.

Margo, Kay, and Leslie were noticeably nervous and depressed. What has been happening in Bataan? Were their husbands still alive?

March 4, 1942

I was taking my constitutional in front of the Big House when I saw an old man hobbling toward me with the aid of two heavy sticks. There was something familiar about the man. I thought that he resembled Nash, an old Sunshiner, army and local term for the Spanish-American war veterans who had remained in the country and married native women. I had last seen Nash about six months before at the army hospital when he had come for a checkup. But the man hobbling toward me seemed too thin and too feeble to be Nash. "Don't you know me, nurse?" he inquired.

It was Nash all right. When he told me how he had become crippled, I began to believe the atrocity stories that were seeping into the camp.

The Japs had imprisoned him in Fort Santiago for twenty-seven days. They had starved and beaten him. Periodically, they had tied his arms and legs and strung him up with head hanging down in an effort to make him reveal where U. S. Army guns and supplies were hidden. All this torture for an old, retired veteran who probably knew nothing.

He said that the pain in his arms was excruciating and that he could no longer walk without support.

There was a choice item in the morning *Nishi-Nishi* which I copied and would have liked to mail to the U. S. Ordnance Department in Washington. It was interesting to see what the Nips were offering in the way of reward to Filipinos who turned in highly expensive American guns and ammunition.

For Information		Turned in
Pistol	.30 pesos	1.00 pesos
Rifle	.30 pesos	1.00 pesos
Light machine gun	1.00 pesos	3.00 pesos
Heavy machine gun	1.00 pesos	5.00 pesos

100 bullets	.20 pesos	1.00 pesos
1 shell for above	.05 pesos	5.00 pesos
Trench mortar	1.00 pesos	3.00 pesos
Field gun	2.00 pesos	10.00 pesos
100 kegs of iron or other scrap metal	.05 pesos	.05 pesos

March 5, 1942

This morning a Filipina dashed through the wide front gates of Santo Tomas with the speed of a greyhound, while Japanese guards raced after her. As she ran, she dropped various pieces of wearing apparel on the ground. By the time she reached the entrance of the Big House, she was another Lady Godiva, minus a horse.

While one Japanese guard held her, the other one good-naturedly handed her a bra, panty, and dress. Then he gallantly helped her put them on. When she was fully dressed, they quietly escorted her out of the front gate.

"What do you suppose that was all about?" I asked Catesy.

"It may be a new kind of ambulating strip-tease!" answered Catesy with a grin.

The word "shanty" brought to one's mind a poverty-stricken picture of slum dwellers living across the tracks. Hobo towns, Grapes of Wrath, Tortilla Flats, and Tobacco Road!

It was not true in Santo Tomas. Shanties in our prison camp personified the epitome of comfort, convenience, shade from the scorching sun, and sanctuary and retreat from the mad bustle of the buildings and grounds.

Shanties cost money; therefore they were owned by the privileged and affluent. The shanty owner no longer had to lug heavy food boxes filled with groceries, cooked food, pots, pans, charcoal, and stove from the buildings to the grounds outside and then back to the buildings again at the end of the day. With a shanty, he could keep all his supplies and cooking gear under one roof, and he no longer had to stand in endless lines at the sink to wash his dishes. Shanties spelled Shangri-la and a certain degree of privacy and peaceful atmosphere. These shanties or nipa houses were made of bamboo and swali. They were assembled outside, and when completed the house was wheeled into the camp. Many of the shanties had commodious bungaras, wide ledges outside the push-out swali windows, and these bungaras held an earthenware water cooler, a charcoal stove, dishes, pots, pans, and other cooking utensils. Dishes were washed on these ledges and allowed to drip and drain through the bamboo slits in Spanish and Filipino style.

A "spit" — a form of showerbath — could be negotiated in the same fashion. By squatting on the bamboo floor and pouring water on oneself two birds were killed with one stone — bathing and cleaning the floor. There was only one catch to this type of bathing, the water had to be carried into the shack.

Families lived together in these shanties until nightfall. Then husbands and wives separated to different rooms or buildings. The daughters stayed with the mother and the older boys went to the father's room.

Just as quickly as the Commandant gave his consent, Shantytowns sprang up almost overnight, and they were given such names as Glamorville, Froggy Bottom, Jerkville, Over Yonder, Jungle Town, and Garden Court.

Internee contractors who took orders for these shacks were doing a landslide business. In fact, it was said that one of the young contractors was making more money than he had ever earned before the war.

As more shanties went up every day, those without funds eyed the comfortable nipa houses with envy and longing, I was one of them.

But there were many people who wouldn't invest in a shanty because of a childish superstition about owning anything as permanent as a nipa house. Why, a person would feel like he was preparing to stay a year in this damn place! As time went on, though, the resistance of many broke down, and they too ordered shacks.

The shanty tracts had their own mayors, patrols, and garden consultants, and everything was run as efficiently as a section in surburban Long Island. The streets in these shanty areas bore such names as Tiki-Tiki Road, Camote Avenue, and Telinum Lane, named after native foods and vegetables.

By 4:30 in the afternoon I was dressed and ready to join Sophie and the boys in a long queue that stretched four city blocks to get a plateful of mongo beans (small native beans resembling lentils and about as digestible as pebbles), a roll, a banana, and a cup of tea.

Joining hundreds of others, we took our supper to the large tent, in which long wooden tables and benches were already crowded with people. The buzzing of loathsome flies intermingled with the buzzing of hundreds of voices. But despite the heat, the smells, the filth, and the noise, we cleaned off our plates.

March 6, 1942

The Commandant cracked down on a peaceful and unsuspecting community — the shantytowners! He issued this brutal ruling:

Shacks may have only two sides covered, and the other two sides must be torn down immediately.

March 7, 1942

The Commandant commandeered our two large dining tents, but he promised to obtain sufficient lumber to enable our internee men to build a more permanent dining shed.

Any little joke, pun, poem, or rumor that would distract and amuse us was repeated and passed from room to room, from building to building.

The following poem, written by a man on the third floor of the Big House, described our life perfectly.

You can't do this, you can't do that —
You move around like an automat.

You can't go here, you can't go there —
You sit and think and think and stare.

You don't say yes, you don't say no,
You don't know where the hell to go;

You get your pass, there ain't no gas
You sit around and scratch your ———.

There is no light, mosquitoes bite,
And bedbugs work twelve hours a nite.

You can't stay out, you can't stay in,
To kiss your wife's an awful sin.

You cannot bathe, you cannot shave,
The water's off, you start to rave.

You can't do this, you can't do that —
You mope around and scratch your pratt.

Three sheets of tissue is the issue,
Oh, thunder-mug, how much we miss you!

You can't get inspiration from chronic constipation,
So come on, MacArthur, and relieve the situation.

March 8, 1942

How we looked forward to Sundays! The day when Catalino sent us a well-cooked meal. After a week of lean and poor food, it was something!

The *pièce de résistance* today was his caramel pie. This rich dessert made us smack our lips with appreciation.

Kay was finally given a pass to visit a sick sister and her two children on the outside. Her pass had to be signed by a witness and our room monitor.

After Leslie had signed as a witness, she said, "You'd better return, Kay, or I'll be shot if you don't."

"Oh, no," said Rainbow, our room monitor, quietly. "*I'll* be the one that will be shot!"

March 9, 1942

Twelve U. S. Navy nurses arrived from the Sta. Scholastica College where they had nursed our wounded men. The nurses were quiet and uncommunicative, but they told us that they had been well treated by the Nips.

How we missed our large dining tents! Especially when it rained. Carrying our plates of food and cups of tea, we scurried around like disturbed ants in search of cover.

Optimistic and fantastic rumors flooded the camp, and they became more fantastic with each repetition. When someone started to say, "I heard from reliable sources," I had a strong impulse to bash him over the head.

March 10, 1942

Many times a day I passed a handsome old gentleman and his wife, who sat in the first-floor corridor.

Because his wife was deaf, she used a large shell ear trumpet that was decorated with intricate designs. A bridge table was pushed against the wall, and there was always a spray of orchids in the center of the table. Two deck chairs completed their home. It was rumored that the old man was a multimillionaire.

They had come to the Orient in their own yacht to attend their son's wedding, but the war interfered. Their son, an ensign, had not been heard from, and they were extremely worried about him, for his ship had been in Philippine waters when the Nips invaded this country.

Coming from the chow line this afternoon, the old gentleman stumbled and dropped both his plate and his wife's, which had contained pechay, a leafy native vegetable, resembling swiss chard, and two desiccated and skinny-looking hot dogs.

He looked at the messy conglomeration on the ground sadly. "I won't miss the pechay, but I sure wanted those hot dogs!"

March 11, 1942

The hospital continued to be crowded with the same old ailments.

Food was fairly good and the beds were comfortable, so if there was any malingering among the patients, it was understandable. However, when I was ill and weak, which seemed to be often lately, I looked after myself.

I was ill again with a high fever and upset stomach.

What made me so ill? Was it the half-cooked cracked wheat that I had at breakfast? The overripe papaya, or the soggy buns peppered with cooked bugs? Or was it a combination of bad food, flies, and upset nerves caused by disquieting rumors?

Japanese planes roared over this building all day, and if one stood on the roof it would have been a cinch to spit on some of the showoffs who nearly brushed the roof.

We've heard nothing of Bataan or Corregidor. Despite the undercurrent of uneasiness surrounding us, optimistic rumors were a dime a dozen.

March 13, 1942

The morning *Nishi-Nishi* carried the inspiring headline: Crush Britain and U. S. Is Japan Aim — Tojo.

I existed on tea and crackers today and felt as a weak as a day-old infant, but I managed to clean my boudoir, as today was inspection day.

Rainbow, our room monitor, was doing an excellent job of soothing ruffled feathers. In a room of this size, with many nationalities and a wide gap in ages, one could expect friction. The grievances, real and imaginary, were endless, and it took infinite wisdom, patience, and tact to solve them; fortunately, Rainbow was blessed with all three.

All but three of the children in our room were moved to the Annex. The baby in our room, a lovable little fellow of five, was the darling of all the women.

The Red Cross was able to obtain five sewing machines, and our women volunteered to sew and mend garments of all descriptions.

In the far corner lobby of the Big House, machines hummed merrily all day, and one of the classic jokes that came from the sewing ladies should squelch all rumors that Englishmen had no sense of humor. An Englishman turned in a pair of shorts, or what appeared to be the foundation of a pair, as it had no crotch, no pockets, no belt — in fact, there was very little about the garment to identify it. But after the clever seamstress had finished with it, he was amazed to see the result. "By Jove," he said admiringly, "if you can do that, I wonder if you can make a shirt around a button I have!"

March 14, 1942

The cooks in the chow line had this sign on the blackboard: "Menu for today: Noodles au gratin, egg salad, tea, and fruit in season."

On the east corner of the Big House, next to the Commandant's office, several American Negro boys did a flourishing business shining shoes. Above their chairs they had printed this sign: "Lexington Avenue, 125th Street."

Harvey Jones, our gifted and versatile emcee, had an excellent show for us in the west patio. When the audience broke into loud and thunderous applause, it was heard by the Dominican priests in the seminary building nearby.

For an hour and a half we forgot time and place.

March 15, 1942

Another week went by, and today we ate Catalino's good Sunday meal.

After supper, we watched a softball game, and later on we listened to excellent recordings amplified through a P.A. system that our men had rigged up. Our recreation and music committees were doing a superb job of lifting our morale. The spacious grounds in front of the Big House were covered by hundreds of people, sitting in groups, chatting or listening to the music.

If it hadn't been for the Japanese guards shuffling around us, and the barbed wire, and the anxiety that filled our hearts, it would have seemed like any other Sunday night concert on the Luneta.

March 16, 1942

The days became hotter. Lucky shanty owners stayed in their shacks until nightfall, while the shantyless remained indoors and out of the blazing sun.

Mrs. Greenshoes, who could always be depended upon to be on some rampage about something, met her equal tonight in the person of a six-year-old boy. The mischievous little rascal kept racing back and forth in the corridor near the old people's quarters. Turning to her husband, Mrs. Greenshoes said in complete exasperation, "What's that damn kid doing here?"

Unfortunately for her, the little boy heard her remark, and it irked him. Placing both hands on his hips, he looked up at her fiercely and said, "How would you like to have me knock hell out of you?"

March 17, 1942

In the hem of my freshly laundered slacks there was a note from Catalino. He was worried because I had sent back the evening dresses, shoes, and other fripperies that he had brought me. I had as much use for them as for a sailboat on the Gobi Desert.

73

Because of the continued congestion of our living quarters, people over sixty were encouraged to live outside, providing they were self-supporting and had a guarantor among the neutrals, Filipinos, or Axis nationals. However, many internees in this group failed to take advantage of this offer, for food prices were naturally climbing higher, and the fear of incidents with the enemy was an ever-present threat.

It was whispered that permanent releases could be had for a price, and I had every reason to believe that this was true.

March 18, 1942

Today my work at the hospital suffered when Catesy was summoned to the Commandant's office for an hour of questioning regarding his photographing studio in the Walled City.

Immediately after Pearl Harbor, the U. S. Army had taken it over because of its close proximity to Fort Santiago. Apparently, the Army Signal Corps, in its haste to leave the city, had not destroyed all of its military pictures. When the Japanese entered the city, they found many of the prints, and they also discovered that Catesy had been the former owner of the studio.

After an hour of stupid questioning, he convinced the Commandant that he had had no connection with the studio since Pearl Harbor. When Catesy came out of the Nip's office smiling and unhurt, I could have shouted with joy.

March 19, 1942

The most objectionable aspects of our life were the bad food, flies, monotony, confusion, congestion, and din made by hundreds of people. That ever-present feeling of anxiety also contributed to our irritability, nervousness, and stomach upsets.

There were other annoyances, petty and trifling under normal conditions, but in here they became magnified. There was the characteristic cough of one woman, the high, nervous giggle of another one. There was the chattering type and the annoying way one woman dragged her feet. There was the lazy and irresponsible type who refused to help with the camp work. She primped and fussed with her hair and face and romanced with the camp wolves.

March 20, 1942

Japan's Aim to Save P. I. from American Exploitation. To-day's headline in the *Nishi-Nishi* was a hodgepodge of nonsense and hypocrisy.

An entire column was written about the flight of High Commissioner Sayre and General MacArthur.

"The Filipinos are left to suffer. The soldiers are being supplied one meal a day and their clothes are torn by thorns in the jungle. While the Filipinos were suffering hardships, General MacArthur

74

avoided the cannon shells deep in the tunnels of Corregidor and American soldiers with their families indulged in dances and delicious meals. Such is the so-called American democracy, boasting that they will always defend the Philippines and hoping for the happiness of the people, and yet trying to save themselves only. From these deeds, we come to understand what Americans are. We found out that their deeds are full of cowardice and falsehood. General MacArthur and Mr. Sayre's escape is nothing but an American comedy. The Filipino soldier in the meantime will come to understand with what aims the Japanese forces come to the Philippines. Our real aim is to save the Philippines from American exploitation."

Food prices were rising! A can of powdered milk sold for fifty pesos, and an ordinary can of evaporated milk that used to sell for sixteen centavos, or about eight cents, now sold for one peso and twenty centavos, or sixty cents.

Most of the canned goods that were sold to us at the front gates by Filipino vendors were looted stock from the warehouses. However, we were glad to pay their high prices as we were anxious to build up a reserve stock of food.

No more canned milk was to be served to adults, but fortunately the children and the patients still received a small supply.

Despite their limited funds and lack of supplies, the Red Cross was doing a superb job in trying to feed us. With most of the officials interned, they were constantly facing problems. The most difficult, of course, was dealing with our jailors.

People without money and outside contacts were in a sorry plight, for without additional food to supplement the meals served them they began to show deficiency disturbances. Boils, ugly-looking sores, red gums, aches and pains in the joints, and frequency of urination were common complaints. Doctors and nurses heard them every day at the clinic and the hospital.

March 22, 1942

MORALE IN CORRECIDOR REPORTED SINKING! This was our Sunday morning headline.

A letter, supposedly written by a Lieutenant Colonel Wilson to his wife in the States, and found among the contents of a mailbag seized by the Japs, was also printed in the morning's paper.

My dearest wife:

It is four months already since we parted. During that time, as you already know, Manila and Davao have fallen, and now we are leading the life of a mole in Corregidor fortress. It is a wonder that I am alive and able to write to you.

It seems as if the Japanese operations are being directed by

God himself. Attacks come like hurricanes. Food in Corregidor
is running out, and a water shortage is also looming. All of us
have come to fear and hate the war. As food daily decreases, we
are continually giving out hopeless sighs. Even the Filipino
soldiers are gradually beginning to disobey our orders, and daily
Filipino and American soldiers are fighting among themselves in
all places.

My dearest wife, in this melancholy atmosphere, the only light
I see is you and the children. I have thought of deserting, but
it is useless. I hope peace comes soon, so I can see your face again.
Please give my regards to Father in New York.

It didn't take an intellectual giant to figure out the author of
that letter.

Knowing that Adoracion's baby was expected soon, I had written
Catalino to get another lavandera, and his answer came back in
the hem of my slacks.

"With regards to the laundry," he wrote, "I am sorry to tell you
that I could not find out, so I offer myself to render the service,
though I could not do it quite well.

"So long, let us, however, extend our best wishes and love.
Catalino and Adoracion."

March 23, 1942

Rumors flew thick and fast today! The favorite and most repetitious of them all was that "we would be out in a week." Though
I knew that rumors, no matter how fantastic and stupid, served
a purpose, a sort of a shot in the arm, so to speak, there was a
limit to human endurance and credulity. I was ill again and extremely depressed.

March 24, 1942

Japanese Wild Eagles roared over our heads many times today,
and each time we'd rush to the windows in hopes of seeing a
miracle. But no matter how hard we prayed and searched for a
star, we saw only the familiar orange sun.

March 26, 1942

Corregidor Takes Heavy Punishment. The morning rag was
filled with threats and predictions that Corregidor would soon
be taken.

Selfishly, we knew that if Bataan and Corregidor surrendered,
our hopes for early liberation were doomed.

March 28, 1942

While my roommates attended a floor show in the patio tonight,

I stayed in my room to enjoy the beautiful solitude. But I was not alone! A huge rat, bloated and repulsive, spoiled my reverie by chewing on boxes and rattling pans in a most disturbing manner. I took a broom, and making ferocious sounds like a devil dancer, I chased it all over the room until I lost it.

March 29, 1942

Palm Sunday! Catesy and I went to church in the Father's garden. The minister prayed for peace, and an earnest congregation joined him. When the soloist sang "Palms," I recalled most vividly another Palm Sunday under different circumstances, when as a young girl of sixteen I had sung the same solo.

Catalino sent us a good meal, and we enjoyed every morsel. If only we could share our cooked food with those who were less fortunate! But already Catesy was worrying about our finances, and our budget was stretched to the breaking point by feeding our two friends.

March 30, 1942

CORREGIDOR HAS BEEN BOMBED EIGHT TIMES!

We visited our former neighbors who kept house on the other side of the abandoned truck. They now had an imposing looking lean-to made of swali and drapery material. While the boys played whist, the lady of the manor and I exchanged recipes, rumors, and gossip.

Suddenly we heard loud detonations, followed by many more. The boys threw down their cards and decided it was more fun to listen to the fireworks. The men were overjoyed. They were certain it was our bombs. More heavy detonations followed, and enemy bombers in great numbers flew over us.

A man from a nearby shack yelled, "I'll sell you my shack for three pesos! I won't need it after today!"

April 1, 1942

Pura, my little Red Cross Filipina nurse friend, lifted my mosquito net before I was up to tell me the great news that Toyko had been bombed by the Americans. By noontime, everyone in camp had heard the joyful news.

The morning *Nishi-Nishi* warned, "Filipinos, beware of misleading propaganda, and do not believe in American promises of aid ever coming to the Philippines, because the Japanese Army now has complete control of the whole southwest Pacific basin."

Catalino certainly had a stormy time looking after Adoracion! The note in my slacks from him gave the full story. "Adoracion gave birth to a boy at 6.30 A.M. She was struggling so hard from 2:00 A.M. sharp! She gave birth at the Malate Hospital. She has to stay there for three days, and if possible, I need money for expenses;

especially they called for a special doctor to assist. I tried my best to bring her to General Hospital, but sorry no available transportation. I even carried her to the said hospital myself. Thanks to God she is all right now. So long, best wishes. Catalino."

Sketched on the front page of the *Internews*, our camp paper, was an internee asleep on a deck chair, dreaming beautiful dreams. The vision of a banquet table with steaming turkey and other delicacies was realistically depicted. A waiter was opening a bottle of champagne, while luscious-looking native girls did the hula around him. Underneath the cartoon there were two brutal words— "April Fool!"

Thousands of bats hovered over our heads tonight as we sat outside. The flapping of their wings sounded like the distant hum of hundreds of motors tuning up. They swooped down, soared upward, and then swooped down again in a crazy and erratic fashion. Like all women, I covered my head with my hands to prevent one of these repulsive mammals from nesting there. Catesy laughed as he handed me his handkerchief to use for a headgear. Somehow, the presence of these bats added to the beauty and eeriness of the deepening twilight. I said: "Do you remember the time we went to watch the bats come out of the caves at Montalban several years ago?" (It used to be a tourist attraction before the war.)

"Uh huh."

Nothing more! He never mentioned the grand time we had had that day nor the wonderful picnic supper I had prepared.

I was worried about him. He was less talkative, less cheerful, and less optimistic, and he seemed to worry a great deal.

When the shrill police whistle pierced our ears, we picked up our camp chairs silently as Japanese guards herded us into the buildings. It was curfew time.

At the door of my room, Catesy said good night and I missed his usual smile and hand squeeze.

As I sadly crawled under my mosquito net, and a giant flying cockroach landed on my back, I brushed it aside indifferently.

Nothing mattered — except the wall that was coming between Catesy and me.

April 2, 1942

Just as Sophie and I carried the card table and eating utensils into the corridor outside our room in preparation for lunch, a group of Axis officers on a rubberneck tour bore down on us. It was too late to run and hide. There was nothing to do but sit down and try to cover my bare knees, as I had on shorts. I covered my nakedness the best I could with my hands and with the large cracker can I was holding.

There were twelve in the party. Six Japanese officers, and one of them was over six feet tall. As he passed me and saw my shorts, he raised one eyebrow in a characteristically American manner. The other six officers were German and Italian, and all of them would have been perfectly cast for movie roles of elegant and arrogant Axis officers. To complete the movie role, one of the Germans had a long saber cut on his cheek.

An explanatory note from Catalino bore this message. "The laundry will be brought here tomorrow, cause I was awfully busy. Every day, both morning and afternoon, I used to visit Adoracion, and I always brought her fruits. The child is well and the mother is all right."

I was beginning to worry about Catalino's attentions over Adoracion. It smacked of a dedicated devotion that seemed to go beyond the "call of duty."

Naturally I was worried, because I was extremely fond of his devoted wife Maria, who used to keep house for three of us American girls several years ago. Shortly after Pearl Harbor, Maria took their child of six to the provinces to be near her aged parents, while Catalino remained in Manila.

April 3, 1942

Exciting news swept the camp! The Commandant informed us that a neutral ship would leave for the States at the end of this month after negotiations for diplomatic exchanges were completed between Washington and Tokyo. Out of 3700 people, only about two hundred would go, so there was no need to get too excited.

Coming from the hospital today, I watched three young American matrons fraternizing with Japanese officers. Their deck chairs were placed directly in front of the Japanese office, and there they sat and waited until one of the Japs joined them.

The camp, of course, was scandalized and disgusted by their behavior, and if their names were bandied about in a light manner, they had only themselves to blame. As a result of their friendliness with our jailors, they went in and out of the camp as they pleased.

People were betting that these women would be on the much-sought-after exchange list to the States.

April 4, 1942

Easter was in the air! From my window I watched and listened to the women's choir practicing in the Father's garden.

Women and children were weaving tiny green baskets from palm leaves and filling them with chickens and bunnies made of cotton and yarn.

In the first-floor corridor of the Big House, several men dipped popcorn balls in sugar and chocolate, and the finished product looked like a large Easter egg from Schraft's, but it was more expensive. At the other end of the corridor a Polish woman ironed dresses with a large and clumsy-looking charcoal iron. It looked as though many of the women planned to wear their fineries tomorrow.

Another floor show in the west patio tonight gave me a whole hour of solitude in the room. It was heavenly!

April 5, 1942

We went to sunrise services and communion in the Father's garden, and it was like no other church I had attended on Easter Sunday.

The hibiscus bushes around us were in flaming bloom, and it was a gay contrast to the two gloomy buildings which flanked the Father's garden on either side. As we sang the familiar hymns, some of the Spanish priests from the seminary building watched us.

We prayed for our men in Bataan and Corregidor, and we prayed for peace.

After church, we watched and listened to the excited and delighted squeals of happy children as they scampered over the grounds hunting Easter eggs.

Catalino added a bouquet of flowers to the box of good food he sent us.

It was a hot and seemingly breathless day. After roll call we went to the patio to cool off, but the heat from the four stories of concrete walls made us feel as if we were in a huge oven.

April 6, 1942

A three-hundred-pound teen-age girl came to our room this morning with a pair of shoes that she wanted to raffle off at twenty centavos a chance.

As I looked at her misshapen body, I wondered if glands or food were the cause of her obesity. Time alone would tell.

We enjoyed the sacred concert given us by the mixed chorus in the Father's garden. Between Bach and Handel solos, Nipponese planes circled over our heads in an annoying fashion, while two frisky goats belonging to the priests stomped and gamboled about.

April 7, 1942

During the night we were awakened by the roaring sound of many planes speeding toward the west. How could we sleep after that? We knew that our hopelessly outnumbered and ill-equipped men were about to catch hell. How long could they hold out?

Yesterday Margo received a smuggled note from her husband in Bataan, and it made her deliriously happy. Throughout the day she sang the ditty her husband had written, "We are the fighting bastards of Bataan, we got no papa, no mama, and no Uncle Sam."

But today she was pitifully depressed. She had a premonition that Bataan would fall shortly.

We wondered what the Nips were up to when they asked us to fill out the following questions they had cooked up:

Which is more responsible for the outbreak of the present war among Japan, America, or Britain?

What is your forecast of the war situation?

Will this war be a protracted one?

Will this war end in a short time?

Will this war end in a decisive victory for one party?

Do you think this war will end in an armistice instead of a decisive victory for one party?

What is the big problem common to the countries concerned after the war?

Which treatment is more humane, the treatment the local Japanese here received from the American army or the one given to the Americans and Britishers?

April 8, 1942

An earthquake of considerable intensity awoke the camp, and the Big House shook like a shimmy dancer. Frightened and half-dressed, women rushed out of their rooms into the corridors to look for their husbands and children. The corridors were jammed with excited people and children, all screaming with terror.

Several women ducked under school benches, while one completely naked Negro boy rushed out of the building and hid in the hibiscus bushes. There he stayed until order was restored and all the lights had gone out in the building.

April 10, 1942

Though we refused to believe the *Nishi-Nishi* headline, TROOPS ON EASTERN FRONT OF BATAAN OFFER SURRENDER, we were unreasonably depressed. One could see small groups gravely discussing the headline throughout the campus.

But a note to Margo from Kay, who was still outside with her ailing sister, convinced me that it must be true. She wrote, "I hope you didn't hear the news until this morning. We have known for several days that it was coming. But I didn't know just how those three words would sound until the Voice of Freedom from Corregidor announced that 'Bataan has fallen.' Now I know. Sorry I don't feel like writing a cheerful note. I am damned mad and sick and tired of talking myself into believing things that aren't so."

When Margo and I finished reading the note, she burst into

bitter weeping, while Leslie, with a husband and two sons in the
war, remained tense and silent.

I thought of Kay and her delicate sister with her two small
children. The sisters were married to brothers, and both had fought
side by side in Bataan. What was in store for them now?

When I told Catesy about the morning headline and Kay's note,
he became unreasonably angry. "You girls must be working hand in
glove with the Japanese propaganda machine!"

Amazed and saddened by his reaction, I felt completely alone.
I felt that the news was true, and knowing it gave me a feeling of
desolation. If I could have talked about the surrender with Catesy,
it would have eased and lessened my anxiety. It was hard to understand that adults could behave so unrealistically. Yet there were
hundreds like Catesy in the camp. When the fall of Bataan was
mentioned, they became infuriated.

April 11, 1942

Seven civilians were brought in from Bataan today!

All their stories were the same. Hardships, malaria, dysentery,
inadequate equipment and food. While hungry and exhausted
men waited, fought, and prayed for reinforcements, the Japs ham-
mered at them from land, sea, and air.

People were slowly beginning to believe that Bataan had fallen.
Those with men at the front bore up wonderfully. The men in
camp, unlike the women, refused to talk about the surrender.

From radio transcripts smuggled into camp we learned that
President Roosevelt had said, "Bataan has served its purpose."
Just like that! "Bataan has served its purpose." One little sentence
that must have felt like a knife thrust in the breasts of the women
whose men had fought so bravely in Bataan.

Two of the Bataan women were assigned to my room, and I
learned from one of them that my nurse friend, Jinny, had malaria
and that her husband had been wounded. She also told me that all
the nurses had been evacuated to Corregidor.

April 12, 1942

The *Nishi-Nishi* had this cheerful information: "F.D.R. in his
press-conference speech admitted the impossibility of sending aid
to the Philippines to relieve the critical situation facing the
USAFFE." The paper also confirmed the news I heard last night
that "68 army nurses have been evacuated to Corregidor."

Not even the good food that Catalino sent us today could dispel
the sadness that weighed us down. We ate the excellent food in
silence. It seemed tasteless and flat.

April 14, 1942

On previous occasions we had witnessed Japanese flogging Filipinos whom they had brought into the camp. This afternoon several Japanese tied a young Filipino to a tree near the front gate and beat him unmercifully, while internees in stupefied shock stood and watched like wooden dummies. After stabbing him with their bayonets, they untied him and dragged him out of the camp.

Fellow internees, with rage in their hearts, dispersed silently and quietly. No one seemed to know who the victim was nor why he had been so brutally punished.

April 15, 1942

The morning headline filled us with dread. BOMBS DEMOLISH CORREGIDOR GUNS.

We felt the heat more than ever today as we dragged mattresses and other bedding into the sizzling sunshine to air. It was general house-cleaning day in Santo Tomas. Barbed-wire fences and clothes lines sagged with sheets, blankets, mosquito nets, and wearing apparel.

After hospital duty and house-cleaning chores were over, Catesy and I joined a couple who used to go sailing with us in the good old days. For the first time in many days, I was happy to see the interest in Catesy's voice and eyes as we planned a fishing trip to Borneo, if and when—with this same couple. They had made the trip in a yawl a few years before.

As they related their delightful experiences, we became more and more enthusiastic, and by curfew time we had the boat completely provisioned. Needless to say, the icebox was loaded with food, especially Italian salami and San Miguel beer.

April 16, 1942

A long line of elderly and ill-fed American men filled the front lobby of the Big House. They had come from the outside to register in accordance with the Japanese regulations.

A few of the Sunshiners had been old patients of mine at Sternberg Hospital, so I stopped to talk with them. Most of the men were old veterans of Dewey days, and they all planned to stay in camp rather than face the hardships caused by the rising living costs. The periodic search and looting of their homes by the Japanese and the confinement to their homes and gardens had begun to get on their nerves.

While these men were waiting to register, other internees, like myself, milled around the group to get news from the outside. While tongues wagged and ears were strained to catch every bit of rumor, Japanese guards jostled us around in an effort to break up the huddled groups.

The Commandant on more than one occasion had been most annoyed with all the news that came into camp. Several people had already been questioned by the Nips in an effort to track down a rumor or some news item. Our Nipponese friends ought to resign themselves to the fact that rumors were here to stay.

April 17, 1942

Corregidor Resistance Weak. A *Nishi-Nishi* correspondent at the Philippine front gave the following description of a fierce raid on Corregidor:

I had the thrill of seeing parts of the fortress being blown to bits when I accompanied a squadron on a raid over the island.

Unfolding in clear panorama under me as we started out on the raid could be seen the verdant ranges of Mount Natib, Mount Samat, and Mount Mariveles lying ominously silent. To the right could be seen the shipping surface of Manila Bay, while from everywhere could be seen black columns of smoke rising from the burning remnants of enemy pillboxes. Over the roads winding through the hills, long columns of trucks, horses, and troops could be seen advancing in the wake of the Rising Sun flags. In the harbor, the masts and broken hulls of sunken ships protruded above the water.

"That's the fortress!" the voice of the bomber commander boomed through the audiphone tube. We had at last arrived at Corregidor. Under me I could see the dark form of the island resembling a tadpole. As we circled over the fortress, the white puffs of exploding anti-aircraft shells surrounded our plane. It was as if balls of cotton were hurled at us.

"Our plane rocked heavily under the shock of the explosion. As I looked behind, I could see the remaining planes of the squadron continuing their flight in perfect formation. On the ground, the runways of the airfield and the military quarters and officers' residences appeared like the scene afforded by a sand garden. All the while the enemy's anti-aircraft batteries continued to pour an endless stream of shells at us.

The sound of the explosions caused my head to ache intensely. At this moment, the wing of the commander's plane rocked violently to the left and the right. This was the signal for the attack. Our planes began to dive madly. Bombs went sailing toward the ground.

An instant of suspense and prayer—and then I saw the enemy's anti-aircraft explode with a terrific concussion. Huge columns of smoke went curling up from the enemy's quarters and residences—my heart throbbed with excitement at what I had witnessed. I as well as the other members of the squadron returned safely to the base.

Every day the paper featured propaganda stories about the cruelty of Americans toward Filipino soldiers and of the antagonism between them.

"Even the captives' dress shows American tyranny. American captives wear khaki uniforms and steel helmets, every soldier is shaved, and they show themselves as Yankee-like dandies, while Filipino soldiers wear worn-out, drenched uniforms. Filipinos drink water from their flasks, dividing it among them, and smoke a piece of cigarette, handing it round from one to another, while some of the Americans kick them down from a truck in order to get their seats or keep a can of milk secretly in their pockets. They don't give it to those who happen to be sick or wounded. They are all selfish."

When I showed the article to Pura, my Filipina friend, she laughed and exclaimed: "My goodness, how stupid these Japanese are! No Filipino will ever believe that! They know how soft the Americans are! Why, they can't even bear to watch us beat our horses!"

Old-timers who had lived in the Philippines knew this to be true. Every time a cochero driver on the street started to beat his tiny Mongolian pony, an American would stop him and threaten him with police action.

April 19, 1942

The Japs had always been camera-crazy, but here in camp they had gone completely shutter-happy. Every day was a field day for them, as officers, soldiers, and civilians snapped our pictures at every opportunity. They took our pictures at the chow lines, at the gates while we waited for our packages, and in the corridors and grounds as we ate our meals. Apparently, they wanted to prove to the rest of the world what a cozy and comfortable group we were!

Compared to other prison camps, perhaps we were comfortable, and the food, such as it was, was not starvation fare. Many of us had beds, mattresses, cooking utensils, stoves, and a supply of canned goods, but it was our money that had furnished it. It was the Red Cross who fed us and helped to furnish the hospital and kitchens with equipment and supplies. It was money collected from internees that provided the additional plumbing facilities in camp, and it was internee labor that had installed all of it.

The Japanese dumped us into this university campus without food, supplies, or facilities to house close to four thousand men, women, and children.

As I looked at the faces of my roommates, I could see the changes caused by fifteen weeks of concentration-camp life. Many were thinner, and their faces were strained and anxious-looking. They talked more. Their voices seemed shriller, and their laughter verged on the hysterical.

Sophie had us all giggling like high school girls when she told us of the conversation she overheard between two precocious little boys near the Annex.

Said one little fellow mysteriously, "I know how to get out of here."

"I'll bet you don't know! How?" came from the second little fellow.

"Just get pregnant!" said the wise little man.

April 20, 1942

Pura, my little nurse friend, was still permitted to come in and out of the camp. If there ever was a harbinger of good cheer, she was the number one of them all! She delivered messages to friends on the outside, and she shopped for us.

But this morning when she lifted my net, I saw that her eyes were swollen and red. At first, she didn't want to tell me, but finally she broke down and told me what she had seen on M.H. Del Pilar Street.

A young Filipino with bayoneted chest and back had been tied to a telephone post since yesterday. He moaned piteously as flies swarmed around his wounds and the hot sun beat down on him unmercifully. Because two Japanese guards stood nearby, no one dared to go near him to dress his wounds or wet his lips.

April 21, 1942

U. S. Is No Match for Japan!

"Japan is about to secure full control of the Indian Ocean and consequently will be able to meet her Axis partners at the Suez Canal as a result of the fall of Singapore and Java."

How dearly the *Nishi-Nishi* loved to crow! This time they stretched out too far!

Tientsin Mary may be hard and coarse, but today I saw her bold black eyes change to a compassionate tenderness.

When the patient in the next bed to hers collapsed on the floor as she returned from the toilet, Tientsin Mary helped me put her back to bed. All morning after that I saw her looking toward her neighbor's bed in a most solicitous manner.

As I gave her a dose of paregoric and bismuth, she poured it down her throat with a quick and practiced gesture.

April 22, 1942

Faster-Than-Sound Planes Is Aim of the Japanese Scientists.
The morning rag certainly loved to startle and impress us.
Another one of my roommates was Jane, a civilian nurse who

used to work with me at the Sternberg Army Hospital. Four months ago she nursed, swam, rode horseback, played tennis, and danced. Now she was exhausted after taking a few short steps to the bathroom. Her wan face had an unhealthy color, and now she was despondent — as she had no word of her fiancé in Bataan. As I sat on her bed and painted her nails a brilliant red, we talked about the good times we used to have on double dates.

A short time later Daphne joined us to give the highlights of another fireside chat of Roosevelt's. In a portentously serious manner, she read, "The situation in the Far East is critical, and we should go back to Biblical days, like the Israelites who shouldered their picks, mounted their asses and camels, and set forth for the Promised Land. But you people in Santo Tomas should lay down your picks, sit on your asses, light a Camel, and wait for the Promised Land."

Maybe it was an old chestnut, but how we loved these absurdities and laughed over them!

April 23, 1942

Just as I gathered my frying-pan, dishes, and other utensils from under my bed in preparation for lunch, three American men entered the room, armed with a steel tape measure. As they measured the dimensions of the room and recorded them in a notebook, I became suspicious.

"How do we stock up for space with the other rooms?" I asked.

"Why, you girls have plenty of extra space!" one of the men answered.

My worst suspicions were confirmed, and I knew that soon more women would be squeezed into Room 25.

"My legs and thighs are black and blue now," said Margo in an undertone.

"Why, you couldn't swing a cockroach around here!" I replied indignantly.

We had become so accustomed to walking sideways to avoid hitting beds and other objects that it had become second nature to us. With an increase in our census, we'd probably have to hold our breaths and suck in our stomachs as we passed in the narrow aisles.

This week's camp paper described this congested situation beautifully.

Question "Do you feel that your present quarters insure you sufficient air space?"

Answer: "Show me the air, and I'll get the space!"

Question: "What would you do to improve the camp?"

Answer: "Open the gates."

April 24, 1942

The Commandant finally consented to a nine o'clock curfew. How happy and grateful we were to be able to stay in the front ground and plaza where the breeze was cool and the space was less congested than the high-walled patios!

When the shrill police whistle signaled us to start moving toward the buildings, we were ready. We felt less tense, and many expressed the hope that no one would violate any rules so we could continue to enjoy this privilege.

April 26, 1942

The lovely strains of "Rock of Ages" floated into my room as I watched the Protestant services in the Father's garden.

To the right of the Father's garden I watched the antics of an A. P. news correspondent with a wet sheet that he was trying to drape over the barbed wire fence. After several attempts he succeeded, and then he went through the same awkward motions with a faded blue shirt.

Half an hour later I looked out the window, and he was still there, hovering over his newly hung wash like a mother hen with her chicks.

From long and sad experience, we all learned it was best to stand guard over our wash until it was completely dry. It was no fun to stand in a long line to get near the tubs, and it was no picnic to wash with a microscopic bit of soap while mud and water splashed all around us. But to have clean clothes hijacked off the lines and barbed wire was downright demoralizing!

April 27, 1942

Our men were building large dining sheds made of wood, and soon they would be completed for the dreaded rainy season. There was an air of finality and permanence about those large dining sheds which made us uneasy.

There was something permanent about everything. One hundred and fifty more civilians were expected from Bataan, and the coming events, such as the Emperor's birthday, made us uneasy. Every day the glories and victories of the Land of the Rising Sun were splashed before our eyes in the local rag.

April 28, 1942

The *Nishi-Nishi* was most informative and educational. For the last few days it was filled with instructions on how to make the Rising Sun flag.

The people in the city were informed that the authorities would not interfere with the Nipponese soldier whose enthusiasm might be carried away by too much sake and beer, and that the common soldier would be given a free hand to celebrate.

88

We were not permitted to forget the Emperor's birthday! The pictorial section of the *Nishi-Nishi* showed victorious soldiers shouting as they dramatically planted the Rising Sun flag on a high ridge in Bataan. When we gazed at pictures of our captured USAFFE forces, the ache in our hearts was almost more than we could bear.

Our gallant men were so sorrowful and thin, while General Homma's picture, covering an entire page, grinned at us victoriously.

Many of the young belles of the camp wore hibiscus leis and flowers in their hair to celebrate May Day. My two Spanish and Dutch roommates, with their fresh, dark beauty, looked enchanting with the scarlet blooms in their black hair.

It was the last day of school for the camp kids. To show their glee, they tore through the corridors and grounds, screeching like painted savages.

Rainbow resigned as our room monitor, and Leslie was elected to take her place. With her quiet but firm way, we believe that she too will be able to handle a roomful of women of various ages, backgrounds, and temperaments.

No more bread was to be served in the line. This spelled hardship and hunger for those who had no money to buy the bread from the camp vendors.

Shocking and horrible stories were being repeated in the camp about the suffering of our captured forces. Forced marches without adequate food and water! Atrocities and brutality!

I saw several of the smuggled notes that had been written to wives by the captured men. Their stories were all the same. Hunger! Brutality! Death!

For quite some time the Japanese had been suspicious that we had a radio in camp, and no wonder! The other day American baseball scores were posted on the front bulletin board in the lobby of the Big House. The Japs were furious and puzzled. How did we get the results of the games so quickly? A thorough search and a crackdown of the entire camp was expected momentarily.

Meanwhile, life went on with the same deadly monotony, but fortunately there was plenty to do, for which we were grateful.

The drains at the sink were stopped up, and as we washed our dishes tonight, we struggled to keep our footing and balance in the foot-high muddy water.

May 4, 1942

Catesy was promoted from his garbage detail! He now helped at the front gate by handing out packages brought to internees from the outside.

For just a moment today he saw and talked to Catalino as he brought our package. Catalino remarked about Catesy's thinness, and he didn't think we were getting enough to eat. It was true. Catesy was thin, and he had been losing weight more rapidly than I, despite my frequent stomach upsets.

We could all stand more and better food, but the truth was, our budget wouldn't permit it. We were beginning to wonder how much longer we could pay for the good cooked food that Catalino sent us weekly, for the price of food continued to soar.

May 5, 1942

We listened to the happy and gay music of Gilbert and Sullivan recordings in the plaza. Usually, their music and rollicking lyrics cheered me, but tonight the music aggravated my depression and loneliness.

Yes, I was lonely, though Catesy sat beside me. Tonight he was far too low in spirits himself to cheer me with a comforting squeeze on my hand. We all felt low. The morale of the camp had touched the bottom of despair.

We were afraid to believe the dreadful news that the Japs were about to take Corregidor!

May 7 1942

No other topic interested us. Had Corregidor fallen?

On my way to get breakfast I stopped when I saw five men grouped around another man who was holding the morning paper. They stared in a dazed manner at the headline. I looked over their shoulders and saw what we had dreaded and feared the last few days.

JAPANESE LAND AT CORREGIDOR! Those four printed words ended our dreams and hopes for an early liberation.

We ate our wormy cracked wheat in silence, and for once Henry was silent, too. All his bounce and optimism were gone.

In my corner, of Room 25 Belle and Toinette were weeping quietly and staring out the window.

May 8, 1942

CORREGIDOR FALLS. Despite the morning headline, people still refused to believe. But when on the next page of the *Nishi-Nishi* they saw a picture of General Wainwright broadcasting from

KZRH studio and ordering the USAFFE forces to surrender in the Philippines—then they realized it was true.

Like robots, we went about our work.

The rich and nervous dowager in our room finally obtained a permanent release for herself and her husband. Those near her bed were happy to see her leave, for on more than one occasion they had been annoyed by her nagging and indignant fussing over trifles. As she left our room for the last time she frankly said, "It will be wonderful not to have to see anyone for a while!"

"Amen!" said Margo, sighing with relief and rolling her large eyes heavenward.

Mammoth victory balloons hovered in the sky to torment us. Attached to each balloon were long and tattered red, white, and blue streamers, dancing and swaying tipsily in the wind.

An endless procession of bombers made up the victory parade over our heads, while on the streets marching and singing soldiers paraded for hours. All over the city, effigies of a defeated Uncle Sam were being dragged by ropes through the filthy streets.

By the time I reached my room, I was ill again, and there were many like me tonight. We were too sick to care about anything.

May 10, 1942

We were saddened to hear the news that a woman whom many of us knew had committed suicide on the outside.

At the hospital we had a young woman who made her third attempt to take her life. She failed again.

The Japanese Navy was in! A large number of Japanese naval officers made a Cook's tour of the camp today.

May 11, 1942

The morning paper had this to say about Corregidor: LUXURIOUS BEYOND WORDS.

In the editorial section entitled "Corned Beef and Corregidor," the *Japan Times* commented on the American excuse that the fall of Corregidor undoubtedly was caused by lack of food.

The correspondent who explored the Rock after its capture described the underground stronghold in Malinta Hill as not only intact but "luxurious beyond imagination," with elaborate offices containing more than one hundred typewriters, air-conditioning plants, well-filled ammunition stores, a well-stocked dining room presided over by Chinese cooks, and a canteen with an abundance of coffee, tea, Camel cigarettes, and candy.

The Japanese troops were treated by the Chinese cooks to a sumptuous meal, including corned beef, which luxury the Japanese soldier could hardly imagine."

When Belle went out on a pass today, I asked her to inquire

about the hams and bacon I had stored with a Swiss and Free French family. When she returned late that afternoon, empty-handed, I knew that something had gone wrong.

"What did the French people say?" I asked excitedly.

"They said that the worms got into them!" replied Belle sadly.

"I'll bet they were Vichy worms!" remarked Catesy.

I felt like weeping when I thought of all that good bacon and ham. It was almost priceless in the present-day market. Many days passed before I had the courage to tell Catesy that the bacon I had stored with the Swiss family was also gone.

They told Belle that it had been stolen, but later we found out that instead of being Swiss, they were Germans, and ardent Nazis, at that.

May 12, 1942

One of our bird-brain internees was found stretched out in his shanty in a drunken stupor. From hoarded leftover cracked wheat saved from breakfast, he had made a highly potent brew. When aroused by internee guards, he became loud and abusive. After being subdued, he was led to his room, and the following day his shanty was torn down.

May 13, 1942

Mothers, wives, sweethearts, and friends eagerly scanned the five-page typewritten list of captured American and Filipino soldiers compiled by the Red Cross. The names were listed under exhaustion, dysentery, wounded, and heart attacks.

With Bataan and Corregidor gone, there was a lessening of the exhausting and emotional strain such as we had experienced in the last five months. Gone were the heated discussions and arguments regarding the arrival of reinforcements. Gone, too, were the wishful and childish rumors that our forces were outside the city.

Many of these once die-hard optimists now refused to believe anything, and they were particularly skeptical of the news from BBC and KGEI.

As for me, I was certain of one thing — that if I heard no news or rumor of any kind, I would become well again.

May 15, 1942

Stupid and disquieting rumors continued to plague us. Today it was rumored that we would be shipped to Portugal, and by evening our destination had shifted to Guam, Honolulu, Japan, Africa, and Australia.

When Pura came to my bed just before I crawled under the net, I asked her if she had heard anything in the city regarding our transfer.

"Nothing will be done! Not until Germany is smashed!"

For the last two months amateur gardeners have worked several hours a day, planting, weeding, and hoeing, and now these gardens were supplying the camp with greens. Shanty owners started their own little gardens around their shacks.

Grandma, Daphne's mother, was always furiously busy. She had been saving pineapple tops for the last few weeks, and today she planted them. When she came into our room tonight, she said seriously, "In two years they will bear fruit."

Her roommates laughed. Two years! The very idea! But I noticed that a few of my roommates remained grave and silent.

According to the paper, today was the hottest day in 57 years.

Because of the unbearable heat, I joined some of my roommates who sat on the school benches in the corridor. Like sad and neglected wall flowers at a dance, we sat stiff and straight on the benches lined against the wall.

"Here we sit — waiting. Not for a dancing partner, but for the war to end!" I said facetiously.

I don't know why, but we all laughed so hard that the benches creaked with our shaking bodies.

Smiling and victorious Japanese soldiers and generals leered at us from the pages of the pictorial section of the *Nishi-Nishi.*

As I gained strength and started to eat small portions of food, some of my depression disappeared.

I was starting to reread *The House of Seven Gables.*

Mr. Nagy sent me a box of peanut brittle, and I was cheered and amused by his note. In describing Rags, he wrote that she was "spoiled, lovable, companionable, and capricious as a beautiful woman."

After sharing my candy with my three companions, I saved a few pieces for myself. Perhaps in a few days I could eat it.

It was a night like many other nights when we sat in the plaza and on the grounds in front of the Big House and the Education Building, listening to recorded music. But tonight very few of us were aware of the gay Viennese music being amplified through the P.A. system, for our horrified eyes were riveted on a slightly built Filipino who had been tortured and tied to a post near the gate. Since early afternoon they had beaten him with their belts and rifle butts. When he had fainted, they had turned the hose on him and then started their sport all over again. It was almost dark, but we could still see his slender body, tied loosely to the post and swaying as though keeping time with the gay Strauss waltz. Like immovable statues at Toussaud's waxworks, we watched, horrified and numb.

Only a few brave and curious ones ventured closer. A Red Cross Filipino doctor tied a wet handkerchief around the victim's head and gave him a drink. After a while the swaying stopped, and the little men with the big guns carried their victim out of the camp.

May 21, 1942

Tonight the head of our executive committee, an American, a British woman, and a twelve-year-old American boy were permitted to broadcast a short message to the United States.

The broadcast, sponsored by the Japanese, lasted about ten minutes.

We sincerely hoped that many of our relatives were listening.

May 27, 1942

It was a big day for the Nips! Navy Day!

Many pages of the morning paper were splashed with pictures of the Imperial fleet's successes.

It was a big day for Margo! She heard from three different sources that her captured husband was well. She went about her work smiling and humming.

Passes and releases were canceled because of a drunken internee. The man had applied for a pass through our own committee, but he was turned down because of his alcoholic history. He appealed directly to the Commandant, who, of course, didn't know he was a bottle-a-day man. He was given a pass. When he returned a few hours later, he was drunk, violent, and fighting mad. After being subdued, he was taken to the hospital. The following day, for his protection as well as our own, he was sent outside to a psycho ward.

Now that bread had become more horrible-tasting and expensive, our noonday meal, which we furnished ourselves, was usually a masterpiece of ingenuity and culinary art.

To left-over boiled rice and duck egg from last night's supper we added left-over corn-meal mush, bacon fat, and onions, and we fried this conglomeration in my trusty iron skillet. With the fresh greens Catalino sent us, I made a vegetable salad.

May 29, 1942

The morning *Nishi-Nishi* contained an eye-witness account of the shelling of the Santa Barbara coastline in California.

Of course, we didn't believe it, but we read it just the same. The story was written by one of the Japanese lieutenants on board the raiding Japanese submarine.

The raid was timed at night, and when the U-Boat bobbed up off the coast line, there were no signs whatsoever of enemy patrol activity.

The illumination of Santa Barbara could be seen twinkling, while the beacon light of oil-storage tanks and derricks was clearly visible.

When the first shot was fired from the submarine, signs of consternation among the people near the shore were discerned immediately. Those on the U-Boat heard the distant shrieking of the sirens.

Everyone on board completely forgot the hardships they had encountered in making the crossing from Japan when the first shell shattered the stillness of the night, and when the second and third shots set the targets on fire, the entire crew danced with joy.

"I can still remember," said the lieutenant, "the painful bristles on the chin of one of the men who hugged my cheek."

May 30, 1942

Memorial Day! I would have forgotten it if someone hadn't reminded me.

It was just another day in here, but still I had to serve something a little extra for lunch. But what?

At breakfast I instructed my three companions to save part of their corn-meal mush. Then, swallowing what pride I had left, I went on a reconnaissance tour of my rich friends who kept house in comfortable shanties. As delicately as possible, I hinted for a handout. From one friend I received a can of tomato sauce, and from another a clove of garlic, a pepper, and a large onion.

Although the mush didn't harden for frying purposes, it didn't stop me. I fried it anyway, and the result looked like a thick and gooey wallpaper paste. The next problem was camouflage, to give it eye appeal. After drowning the mess with tomato sauce and the other handouts, we ate our Memorial Day lunch and enjoyed every bite.

The ban on singing patriotic songs apparently had been lifted, for when I reached my room after supper, I heard the voices of my fellow internees singing "God Bless America" and "My Country 'Tis of Thee" with great feeling in the Father's garden.

Memorial Day was remembered, after all!

May 31, 1942

My roommate Margo was in a special kind of seventh heaven today. She dashed into the room with blonde hair flying and eyes shining. Then, throwing her arms around me, she squeezed me until I yelled for help. Only a letter from her husband could have brought about such wild exuberance and joy.

"I just received the nicest and most wonderful letter from my husband!" Her voice sang with joy. She wept and I wept, and we both had a wonderful time!

June 1, 1942

When I think of the days I used to tear around in a seventy-five-bed ward at the army hospital and of my twelve-and twenty-four-hour private nursing days, I wondered how I managed and still had enough pep left to go dancing afterwards.

Those were the days! Now I was completely bushed after four hours of nursing.

Because of my frequent stomach upsets, I left my nursing job.

Every morning for three hours or more I sat with thirty other women in the dining sheds to de-bug mountainous piles of cracked wheat and other cereal. Picking webs, worms, and weevils out of cereal for three hours was a tiresome job, but compared to nursing it was a snap.

Today, while we picked and drowned the worms in tin cans filled with water, another Cook's tour of Nips came by to watch and snoop. For a long time they watched us as we removed worms, webs, and weevils from the huge mounds of cereal in the center of the long wooden tables. With the utmost gravity one of the officers placed several of the wrigglers in an envelope that he had taken from his coat pocket. All eyes watched him as he neatly folded the envelope and returned it to his pocket.

June 2, 1942

Although the smuggled note that Sophie received from her husband today had been written in January, she was relieved to know that at that time he had been well.

This afternoon I watched a pitiably emaciated father greeting two of his equally emaciated sons who had come to visit him at the front gate. His sons looked like pictures of starved children I had seen in my pediatrics textbook during my student days. Spindly legs, large abdomens, and thin necks supporting rachitic-looking heads. There was something inhuman and infinitely sad in the noises the father made as he embraced his sons. While tears streamed down his face, he made whimpering noises like a whipped dog.

I fled. I could not take any more.

June 3, 1942

The big military parade was on today to celebrate the fall of Bataan and Corregidor. Tanks, cars, trucks, and other vehicles rumbled through the streets, followed by thousands of marching and singing troops, while overhead the Wild Eagles roared back and forth in parade formation.

Across the street from the front gate, all the wide and large windows of the old Spanish-style houses were jammed with leering Japanese. They sat in the windows in their underwear, and their eyes never left us as we strolled about on the grounds.

June 4, 1942

"I wonder if the Japanese internees in the States had to clean and de-bug filthy cereal like this!" remarked one of the women as she emptied her tin can filled with drowned worms.

"Are you kidding?" said another women. "I'll bet their Wheaties come in cellophane-wrapped boxes!"

This morning I awoke with a feeling of thankfulness that I was safe in a prison camp.

I dreamed that Japanese parachute troops had made a landing, and just as one of them was creeping toward me, I awakened.

June 6, 1942

The hospital beds were always filled the day after chili con carne was served. Internee cooks were doing their best, but the half-cooked mongo and navy beans used for the chile made pretty rugged diet for most of us.

Harvey Jones, our happy and tireless emcee, gave us another excellent floor show. There was a condensed version of Ibsen's *Hedda Gabler* and a delightful skit entitled "Internees in Heaven." The novelty number, "The Doll Shop," included all professional entertainers and dancers, and they were excellent.

June 7, 1942

Another internee, a seaman, and a one-time Sing Sing inmate, was found drunk from home brew. He told members of our discipline committee that he was sick and tired of Santo Tomas where privileges were less than at Sing Sing.

We had a few drunk and disorderly characters in camp, just as one would find anywhere in a group of 3700 or more people.

For the safety of the law-abiding and respectable people, these incorrigibles had to be disciplined and punished, and it was our own internees who acted as jury and judge.

June 8, 1942

The present regime was starting to crack down on the people in the city. The morning headline stated: 44 LAW VIOLATORS PUT TO DEATH. Twenty-three of them were guilty of having counterfeit Japanese war notes, while the remainder were spies.

The Grand Central Station with all trains in the yard and the terminal filled with passengers going and arriving never had such chaos and noise as existed in our corridors in the Big House.

Screaming and running children. Babies crying in cribs and buggies. Parents rushing around trying to heat and prepare food.

The daily rain forced many families to abandon their shacks for the time being and subsequently the corridors were more impassable and impenetrable at meal time and curfew time than the jungles of the Uganda.

June 9, 1942

This has been an exhausting day, filled with minor mishaps, which under the circumstances seemed exaggerated to major catastrophes.

After waging another all-out war against bedbugs and ants in my bed, and de-bugging cereal for three hours, I was hardly fit for human society.

To add to my aggravation, I upset a large pot of precious bean soup, which I had momentarily placed on my bed, while I fiddled with pots and pans under the bed.

Thick, gooey bean soup ran all over my bedding and down on my worldly possessions under the bed.

After cleaning up this mess, I fervently hoped that it wouldn't start the voracious ants on another binge.

By evening, I was conditioned for any minor or major mishaps, and when it happened, I didn't bat an eye.

I bumped into my fancy marble-topped table that I had snitched from the museum, and my last bottle of toilet water went crashing to the cement floor.

June 10, 1942

Catesy was not well. His color was bad and he was quiet and more depressed than ever. As often as I dared, without irritating and worrying him too much, I urged him to see one of the camp doctors, but he always had an excuse.

June 11, 1942

Rumors of a naval battle at Midway have circulated in the camp for the last three days, and the morning headline verified them.

June 12, 1942

Japanese Navy Nears Absolute Sea Mastery. Panama Canal Now Exposed to Attacks.

This headline caused the most optimistic to have a moment of fear that the news might be true.

When I met the optimistic Mr. and Mrs. Mack at the dishwashing sinks, I asked them about the latest news, and for the third time today I heard the same news word for word.

"That half of the thirty Japanese ships engaged in the naval battle at Midway had been destroyed and that there was absolutely no truth in the headline that the Japs were occupying the western portion of the Aleutians."

June 13, 1942

A savage storm, with howling wind and lashing rains, kept most of the camp awake all night, and during the day the corridors were filled with people forced out of their shanties.

Tragic news came to one of my friends this morning. Her fiancé, a flyer, who had lost both legs in Bataan, had died a few weeks ago.

Whenever we saw a person with red and swollen eyes, or a mournful group in the corridors or rooms, we knew that they had just heard of the death of a loved one.

June 14, 1942

AMERICA ADMITS ALASKA LANDINGS. According to the paper, looting and killing had increased in the city.

Forty-eight internees, some of them former residents in Shanghai, were leaving for China tomorrow, and the entire camp seemed to be stirred up with excitement. Oh, delightful possibility! Perhaps we would be on the next exchange group.

One of the British girls on the exchange list, at the last moment, decided not to go, though her twin sister and mother were leaving tomorrow. She had a good reason. She found romance in camp, and yesterday her engagement was announced in the *Internews*.

June 15, 1942

ALEUTIAN LANDINGS SHOCK U. S. PUBLIC. There was no doubt that the *Nishi-Nishi* stirred us up and for that reason many stopped reading it. Each day I promised myself, never again! But when morning came, I almost broke my neck to rush to the desk at the front of the room to take a quick glance at the headline.

June 16, 1942

PACIFIC COAST TENSE. ALEUTIAN LANDINGS CAUSE FEAR.

I surprised my gang at lunchtime with fried croquettes, made from left-over rice, dipped in cornmeal and then fried in coconut oil.

Just as the sun set, a busload of tired and worn-out looking Americans arrived from the Baguio camp.

One of the most touching reunions was between a husband and wife and their young son. The mother had lost a leg during the first aerial attack on Baguio, and her young son had been badly wounded.

It was a joy to watch their happiness. They met for the first time since last December.

June 19, 1942

The deadening and demoralizing monotony of our existence went on day after day. Though life in a concentration camp was safe in comparison to a battleground, it was certainly an inglorious and useless way to sit out the war.

Did I say sit? What I really meant was stand. We stood in long lines at the toilets, the sinks, the food line, and the various stalls where anything from a two-way girdle to a vitamin pill could be bought.

Thank goodness, I was busy from dawn to dusk with de-worming, Issue Tissue detail, and housekeeping chores. Today I joined a bi-weekly Spanish and Shakespearean class sponsored by our Adult Education Committee.

It happened once in a neglected adult's life, that he was sur-rounded by scientists, musicians, writers, teachers and professors of every subject imaginable. Best of all, the subjects were taught free, and nearly all the classes were concentrated under one roof.

We learned today that the people who left for Shanghai the other day were still camped at the pier awaiting the freighter which was to take them to their destination. Fortunately for them, they had their bedding, food and cooking utensils.

June 21, 1942

My jaw dropped to my chin this afternoon in the corridor when I looked into a camera and a pair of slanted eyes. Click went the shutters, followed by a sucking of breath, the usual prelude to a "Sank you!"

The camera bugs had a Roman Holiday taking pictures of women lying in their beds, and of groups eating and sitting around on the campus.

The raw and angry-looking ulcer on my ankle, forerunner of diet deficiency, was improving, thanks to wet compresses and powdered sulfathiazole which I had brought to the camp with me. However, I was still hobbling.

June 23, 1942

It seemed that the Nips lacked a complete sense of the ridicu-lous. Today I received a staggering electric bill for P190.00 from Meralco, the local electric company, which was now Nipponese-controlled. Needless to say, I didn't rush out of my prison to pay it.

In the advertisement section of the local paper, there was an item that made our mouths water. It concerned the shipment of Baguio potatoes to Manila.

Baked or boiled potatoes. What we wouldn't give for either!

My roomies chuckled over another ad — a typically Oriental one: "Wanted — a masseur for prostate gland. Please state price per massage."

Night after night, men and women congregated in groups in the corridors, playing cards, reading, knitting, talking or just sitting and staring — waiting for the war to end.

Tonight, Catesy and three of my roommates sat outside our room. As we talked, we noticed that Mrs. Greenshoes, wearing an especially belligerent expression, was stomping back and forth in front of us.

Suddenly she stopped before us, and fixing her fierce old eyes on us, she went into a tirade on who had started the war. We listened politely and impatiently as she went on in this fashion: "This world is peopled by a lot of G... D... cantankerous fools, and until they get rid of the money system, and accept the teachings of Buddhism, there will always be wars. One of these days, I would like to have you join me in an hour of prayer."

On the last sentence, her fierce expression changed to a seraphic smile. Then swiftly she shifted to an angry mood.

"May those who started this war die the death of a thousand tapeworms."

After delivering this malediction in a harsh and bitter voice, she again changed to a sweeter vein.

"Now, in Buddhism —" But we weren't privileged to hear the rest, for just at this point her shiny and black silk skirt slithered to the floor at her feet, and she stood before us in a pair of men's long, white duck shorts, the type Englishmen wore in the tropics.

The sudden transition from black to white had a bewildering effect on our eyes. We wanted to scream with laughter. In fact we did.

June 25, 1942

Planes, bearing the insignia of the "fried egg" as we called them lately, were still zooming over us. We still rushed out to watch them. How desperately we wanted to see a plane with a star!

Tonight, while we watched a softball game, about a hundred Nips started to drill nearby and they broke up the game. Before one could say "Nuts," players and spectators had disappeared into the buildings.

June 26, 1942

The floor show that had been scheduled for tonight was canceled because of rain. Instead, a dance was held in the plaza and music was furnished by a three-piece internee orchestra. Only a few people danced, and most of them were teen-agers.

June 28, 1942

Attack on Japan Called Impossible — Occupation of Strategic Bases in China Removes Threat.

In the editorial section there was an appeal to small guerrilla bands still operating in provincial nooks to surrender by the end of the month if they wanted the protection given to war prisoners in accordance with International Law.

Flies, bedbugs, heat, rain, noise, confusion, poor food, lack of privacy, and fantastic rumors summed up our present life.

The army nurses from Corregidor arrived today, and we were in a tizzy of excitement!

As the nurses stepped off the buses to go into the Commandant's office, we crowded around to greet them, and many others pushed forward to inquire about relatives who had fought at Bataan and Corregidor.

There was very little opportunity to communicate with them as Nipponese guards quickly herded them into the Commandant's office. While we waited outside, the area around the Nip's office was roped off by internee guards.

By hook or crook, I was determined to speak to the nurses, and the quickest way was to waylay them in the bathroom. Sure enough, about ten minutes later, I talked to six of the girls.

Jinny, the nurse who had tried to persuade me to go to Bataan, appeared ill and she was naturally worried about her wounded and captured husband. Zest, another one of my friends, was thin and unusually nervous. How good it was to see them!

The chief nurse of Corregidor, another old friend, appeared, and she, too, was tired and just recovering from dengue. We talked nervously and excitedly for only a few minutes.

The nurses were taken to the Santa Catalino College, about three city blocks east from the Big House, and directly across the street from our camp.

July 2, 1942

The nurses were being held incommunicado, but we were hoping that soon they would join us. We saw their second-story quarters, and as we passed near the wall of the camp many of the girls waved at us.

July 4, 1942

We were de-bugging cereal this morning when a girl sitting next to me was told that her brother was one of four captured soldiers who had brought the army nurses' luggage into camp. Throwing her pan of cereal and can filled with worms into the air, she dashed excitedly to the front of the Big House, while some of us ran after her to watch the happy reunion.

Strangely enough, the Japs allowed them to converse for a few moments, but by the time the mother appeared breathless and deathly pale, the four soldiers had left the camp. The disappointment of that mother cannot be described.

We listened to a recording of "America" over the P. A. system, and we were grateful that Independence Day hadn't been entirely forgotten.

July 6, 1942

The morning *Nishi-Nishi* had this to say about our Independence Day:

> Is not this Fourth of July a golden opportunity for the peace-loving American people to think of the treasured heritage from the wise fathers of the Declaration of Independence —in its true and unadulterated form — equality of men, the rights of liberty and the pursuit of happiness, justice and humanity and, above all, non-intervention and non-entanglement which alone can insure America's security? It will at once become clear to them how wise the American fathers in their counsel for posterity and how priceless their legacies were.
>
> The founding fathers do not know that Oriental peoples have been shut out from the "Land of Freedom" by the mere reason of difference in color and that the latter's descendants are made the object of discrimination and ill-treatment for the only reason that they were born of Orientals. The founding fathers do not know that by no other reason than they happened to be the Japanese on the Pacific coast and forced without even a single hearing to leave their lands and their homes which have been built with long years of sweat and labor and are concentrated in the unbearable desert land of the interior. The founding fathers do not know that these American citizens of Japanese parentage who have pledged their loyalty to the American flag are about to be stripped of their constitutional rights of citizenship only because they were born of Japanese.

JAPAN WAGES EAST ASIA WAR TO SECURE LASTING PEACE.
Where have we heard this type of nonsense and hypocrisy before?

Again Catesy talked to Catalino for only a moment at the package line. He asked about my health, and he proudly told Catesy that Adoracion's baby weighed sixteen pounds.

July 8, 1942

After Catesy and I had hastily kissed in the dimly lighted second-floor landing, I asked him what to write in my diary. I expected to have something impressively profound for today's entry in my diary as, for a moment, he looked gravely serious. Then with a sly wink and a grin, he announced. "The Russians

are still fighting, the British are retreating, and the Americans are
still talking."

July 9, 1942

Because of the daily rains, strange costumes were seen on the
campus. The most colorful and bizarre were the short straw cape-
like native raincoats, which fanned out over the wearer like a
miniature hut.

Wooden bakias or clogs, half boots and hip boots, galoshes,
rubbers, Stateside raincoats, and umbrellas were worn by shanty
dwellers and those who had to go to the front gates for their
packages.

July 10, 1942

Six Japanese from the dreaded Military Police at Fort Santiago
searched the entire camp today. They searched the shanties and
all the rooms. When they came into our room, I was extremely
apprehensive, and when two of the brutal-looking M.P.'s walked
out to the balcony, I felt as though my heart had stopped beating,
for only a week before, I had wrapped my diary in oilskin and
a dirty old rag, and then I tied it to the drainpipe next to the mops
and brooms.

They stood on the balcony for only a minute but it seemed like
hours to me. One of the M.P.'s looked searchingly at me, and as I
droppped my gaze, I prayed fast and furiously.

When they walked toward the front door, my respiration became almost normal.

July 11, 1942

Juan de la Cruz was the Voice of Freedom, now that Corregidor
was gone. This courageous Filipino broadcast daily from his
renegade radio station somewhere in the city. We heard about
him from people who had been outside and from the daily
Nishi-Nishi.

Kay, who was still outside with her sister, had written to Margo
about Juan de la Cruz. He had started his broadcast: "Well,
General Homma, you almost got me that time, but now I have
a better hiding place."

We were afraid that this brave young Filipino, who defied the
enemy and put courage and hope into his people, would eventually be caught.

July 12, 1942

One of our friends received a smuggled note from her officer
husband today. He wrote that he was still free and from that she
assumed that he had joined a guerrilla band.

The morning rag continually alluded to misguided patriots who
had joined with guerrilla forces. They were assured complete

amnesty if they surrendered immediately. It gave us hope to know
definitely that guerrilla bands were forming throughout the
country.

Several hundred missionaries, with their families, came into the
camp for pass renewals.

They congregated in the Father's garden, and after considerable
powwow and yakamashi, they were given another extension on
their pass, providing they signed a pledge which read: "Released
because of promise to the Japanese authorities to cooperate with
them through religion."

Some of the people who had never sought for any privileges or
passes criticized the missionaries for staying outside.

July 13, 1942

On the front page of this morning's *Nishi-Nishi* there was a
picture of the Imperial Japanese Forces making their surprise
landings on Attu, Agattu, and Kiska Islands in the Aleutians.

We were eating our worm-infested cereal this morning, when
pandemonium broke loose in the dining sheds. We quickly jumped
on the bare tables in order to see what the commotion was about.
Two women were battling furiously.

"One of them is Tientsin Mary, your pal!" cried Catesy excitedly.

It was Tientsin Mary, all right! She clawed, scratched, kicked,
and spat at her opponent, a fiery-tempered Eurasion girl.

"My money is on Mary!" declared Henry admiringly as he
watched Mary's flying hands and feet. The other girl was smaller
and no match for Tientsin Mary's ferocity, though she hung on to
Mary's Medusa fringe with all her strength.

Just as the audience became larger and the battle more ferocious,
the Eurasian girl suddenly dropped her grip on Mary's bangs, and
she shouted threateningly, "You . . . of . . . stay away from him!"

Tientsin Mary laughed coarsely and boisterously as she pulled
herself together. Then, shrugging her shoulders nonchalantly, she
calmly sat down to finish her breakfast.

July 14, 1942

Margo and Leslie were radiantly happy women today! Each
had received a smuggled note from her husband in Cabanatuan.
All the notes from military prison camps were the same. The men
begged for money, food, medicine, and clothing.

The women sold their jewelry and other possessions to raise
money. Through the Number One men of the companies their husbands had formerly worked for, they were able to get a monthly
allowance, which they hoped to send to their men.

The Nips made another search of the shanties today but they
did not find the much-sought-after radio. Instead, they found a

few home-made stills and a dozen or more men under the influence of their home-brew.

Liquor was also being smuggled into camp by bird-brains in many ingenious ways. One of the most original containers was the dry coconut. The milk was removed, and gin, tuba, and other native drinks were substituted.

Our leaders immediately organized a liquor Control Squad, and it was their job to remedy this grave situation, which threatened the few privileges which we enjoyed and the possible security of the entire camp.

Daphne loved to tells puns on the British though she was British herself. After roll call, she stuck her head under my net and told me this one:

"England will fight to the last American dollar and Aussie!"

A good laugh at this time was better than a sedative or a vitamin tablet.

July 15, 1942

Anything that broke up the monotony of our daily existence was welcomed. Today it was another hair-pulling and exchange of profane words between Tientsin Mary and the Eurasian girl. Just as quickly as they started their battle, the man who was the cause of the fight faded out of the picture. Apparently, internee guards had been alerted, for they rushed to the scene and broke up the fight. But there was still plenty of battle left in Mary, as internee guards led her kicking and swearing to her room, where she was made to stay for several hours.

July 16, 1942

364 Allied Ships Sunk Since Pearl Harbor Tragedy.

I read the hateful *Nishi-Nishi* from cover to cover, in hopes of finding some good news, but there was nothing hopeful for our side.

July 17, 1942

Kay wrote that the inspiring and courageous broadcasts of Juan de la Cruz had ended. The Voice of Freedom had been silenced. We shuddered to think what punishment awaited him.

Still raining. Our clothes, our bedding, and the gear under our beds were damp and musty smelling, and we hadn't seen the sun for several days.

Few women in camp looked as bedraggled and awful as I did at this time. Everytime I looked into the mirror, I became more depressed. My light-brown hair was dull, stringy and straight as a ruler, giving me the look of a frustrated Vermont spinster. Something had to be done! I decided to get a permanent, and when I told Catesy of my plan, he readily agreed. Had I looked that bad? I wondered.

My traveler's checks in my shoes were becoming ragged and shopworn from constant friction by my arches, and I decided to cash one of them, even though the camp brigand charged me thirty percent.

I paid the thirty percent and rushed to the shack where the beauty operator was in business, and I made the appointment for the afternoon.

The permanent changed me completely! The frizzed hair made my face appear fuller but, best of all, it gave me a mental lift.

Now I could appreciate why beauty parlors in mental institutions were a part of the mental therapy.

We were not paranoids, manic-depressives, and schizophrenics, but we all had moments of darkest and deepest despondency.

The rains continued. Today, shortly after I had cleaned and mopped under my bed, a large and violent deluge of water rushed in from the balcony door. Hastily, I grabbed my cardboard boxes filled with food and clothing. But it was too late! Everything under my bed was drenched.

To complete a day of minor mishaps, I burned the last of our precious cocoa on the charcoal stove, and in the evening I dropped the heavy lid of the garbage can on my bare toes.

July 19, 1942

Today was Henry's birthday, and what a spread we had!

Once a week, Henry's boss, who was not interned because he was a neutral, sent him a box of cooked food. There was always enough for four.

Today he sent roast turkey, dressing, gravy, sweet potatoes, and a magnificent-looking birthday cake.

When I cut the cake an overpowering and unpleasant odor assailed our olfactory. It was over-ripe duck eggs and cassava flour!

"Holy mackerel!" said Henry, holding his nose.

"Never mind!" All this cake needs is some fresh air!" And with that, I cut the cake in four generous portions. After thoroughly airing the cake, the smell completely disappeared, and we ate every crumb.

Catesy, Henry, and Sophie were in excellent spirits after the fine meal and I tried to join in the cheerful conversation, but it became too much of an effort.

Waves of nausea and weakness spread over me like an unhealthy mist, and by the time I reached my room I was too ill to care what happened to me.

What was the matter with me? Six days a week I ate poorly

107

cooked and scanty food and I remained fairly well, but on the days we ate well I became sick.

July 21, 1942

As usual, I was completely absorbed in trying to balance my clean dishes on the narrow pipes above the sink when I heard a man ask me, "Are you trying to high-hat me?"

I looked at him. Blond, thin, and with prominent blue eyes. I was just about to say that he was a complete stranger when I suddenly recognized him.

"For goodness' sakes, Mr. Neal — no wonder I didn't know you! How many pounds have you lost?" I asked in surprise.

"Sixty!" he replied sadly. "And I've lost all my teeth, too, and two years' supply of vitamins, thanks to the Nips who kept me in solitary confinement at Fort Santiago for six months."

July 22, 1942

Military Police Arrest Many for Hostile Acts.

From the headline, we gathered that the Filipinos throughout the country were having a difficult time under the Co-Prosperity Scheme.

Kay returned to camp, but her delicate sister with her two little children were given another extension.

As we sat on Kay's bed today, we fired eager questions at her as we knew she had been near a radio.

"Is it true that the Americans landed in Mindanao?" I asked eagerly.

Kay looked at me sadly and shook her head. "I've had my ears glued to the radio, but I never heard that one!" she said.

"You can't believe a damn thing you hear around here!" said Margo disgustedly.

July 23, 1942

I spent another miserable night with the bedbugs, and just as soon as it was daylight I went to work picking them off my sheets and net.

This building was crawling with them. During supper, Catesy started to squirm and itch, and when Henry told him to examine his belt buckle, he lifted the metal and found it alive with bedbugs. For one awful moment, we thought we'd lose our supper.

July 25, 1942

Another American escaped! When last seen, he had been under the influence of alcohol.

For the protection of the camp, our internee guards notified the Commandant, who was decent enough not to refer the matter to the Military Police at Fort Santiago.

A member of our Central Committee, with several Japanese

108

guards, went in search of the man, and late in the evening they found him at the home of a native girl friend.

To save his skin, which most of us agreed wasn't worth saving, he was guarded day and night by internee guards at the camp hospital.

What his punishment will be depends on the doctor's verdict and the leniency of the Commandant.

Many of the British internees were upset over the news that they would be shipped to Africa. Grandma, Daphne's mother, was one of them. She broke down completely and sobbed when one of our roommates jokingly said, "Forty years in the Philippines and now on to Mozambique!"

Grandma wept bitterly and she said indignantly, "It's no joking matter! I don't want to leave the Philippines! This has been my home for forty-five years!"

Her sympathetic roommates understood her pain and sorrow.

One of our friends, a well-known Manila matron, had cancer. Yesterday, she and her husband obtained a permanent release to live outside. But her beautiful home, once a showplace, and scene of many happy parties, had been stripped of all its comforts and fine furnishings by the Japs. Here in this empty house, she will spend the few precious months remaining to her.

July 26, 1942

The Smith family, whose beds were near mine, were a sorrowful little group today. Mrs. Smith was notified by the Red Cross that her son had died in a military camp.

The bereaved group, consisting of mother, three grown daughters, and a grandson, sat on their cots weeping quietly. The widow of the dead son lived outside with an invalid child.

If only they had a little corner in which they could be alone in their grief. Nothing was private in here! Not even grief!

The entire camp sighed with welcome relief when the alcoholic who had tried to escape was pronounced a psycopath and shipped off to a mental institution outside.

When two more men were found in a drunken state in their shacks last night, the discipline committee went into action. The drunks were locked in a small room, and tonight, with their hands tied behind their backs, they were exhibited throughout the campus.

Shades of Hawthorne and pillory days! Instead of Puritan dress, the two shamefaced men wore regulation Santo Tomas garb — skimpy shorts, bare chests and wooden clogs. As they were paraded around the campus, the gay and rollicking tunes of Gilbert and Sullivan came loudly over the P. A. system.

When the music stopped, there was a short pause and a squawk,
like someone was clearing his throat. It was our official announcer,
an Englishman. He informed us that the next one who was caught
drunk would be placed in a pillory.

July 28, 1942

The *Nishi-Nishi* admitted that "due to the high cost of living
and prevailing hard times, the number of needy families had
increased."

Yoshiwara (red light) districts had sprung up throughout the
city, and many an internee was appalled to learn that his home
was now used as a house of prostitution.

July 29, 1942

The Commandant has requested that the following be circular-
ized among the internees:

"Your attention is directed to the recent order of the Imperial
Japanese Military Army prohibiting acts of hostility by civilians
toward the Imperial Japanese Forces, as expressed in the newspapers of July 21st and subsequent issues. These orders apply
equally to those interned and it is my order that they be strictly
obeyed.

"Specifically, internees must refrain from expressions of sympathy
to our enemies and hostility toward the Japanese, for example:

"1. Rumors and criticisms relative to the Imperial Japanese
Forces and their movements.
"2. Criticisms of Japan and the Japanese, etc.
"3. Rumors and criticisms relative to the government of the
Philippines.
"4. Criticism of living conditions of Filipino people.
"5. Rumors and criticisms relative to the life of Internment
camps.

"Such actions have been observed in the past and reported to
this office. We have made due allowance for certain principles
which Americans and British deem to be their right, but at the
same time all internees must recognize that they are in detention
and must govern themselves accordingly out of the ordinary
courtesy and desire to maintain the harmony which I hope will
continue to prevail in this camp."

Mr. and Mrs. Greenshoes had been moved into the College
museum.

For seven months, these old people had slept in the busy corridor opposite the museum doors. Internees had automatically
lowered their voices as they tiptoed past their screened beds.

Now, at last, they were alone. Only the repulsive-looking

110

stuffed specimens in the glass cases on three sides of the huge room shared their privacy.

Idly, I wondered what would happen if either of them were an alcoholic. For their unique Grand Terminal size bedroom, with its riotous display of nightmare-producing iguanas, lizards, pythons, birds and wild boar, would have thrown an alcoholic into delirium tremens.

August 1, 1942

ORDER LIQUIDATION OF HOSTILE BANKS.

The headline made me smile, and I thought of Mr. Neal's vitamin tablets stored in the bank vault. Would they be liquidated too? Next time I saw him I would ask, and maybe we'd have another good laugh.

Leslie, our room monitor, returned from a ten-day stay at an outside hospital. A gall-bladder upset had weakened her considerably, and of course, she was worrying about her husband at Cabanatuan.

About twenty-five men, women, and children came into the camp from the southern islands. Among the women were several army nurses who had worked with me at the Sternberg Hospital. They had been on the second plane that had left Corregidor bound for Australia, but due to engine trouble the plane had to make a forced landing in the southern islands.

August 3, 1942

Internees made a collection to buy an artificial leg for the American woman who lost her leg during the first bombing in Baguio.

An expert American prosthetic man had been delegated to make the artificial leg and just as soon as the Commandant gave him permission he was going outside to obtain the tools and supplies for this worthwhile undertaking.

August 4, 1942

SPIRITUAL REVOLUTION IS NECESSARY — GENERAL HOMMA.

As Grandma finished reading the headline in an impressive voice, Margo said scornfully, "Look who's talking? General Homma! The Butcher of Bataan!"

I always wanted to live in the Orient because I had heard that life was easy for a working girl. It had been easy and wonderful — before the Japs arrived.

Now it was a life of montony and drudgery. Cereal and rice debugging daily. Cooking on a charcoal stove, washing dishes and clothes under primitive conditions, fighting flies, mosquitoes, bedbugs, and standing in long lines. Bathroom detail, room-cleaning detail, and now I had another job. With thirty or forty other women,

I pared and cleaned enough vegetables in two and three hours for over three thousand people.

August 6, 1942

Religious Instruction in School Is Abolished.

The corridors and rooms were more congested than ever because of the rains. To escape them, I crawled under my net, and for an hour I lost myself in the fascinating pages of *The Sun Is My Undoing*. The title of the book intrigued me, for I, too, followed the sun, until it "done me wrong."

The air was charged with irritability, nervousness, and explosive tempers as the rain kept us cooped inside. It didn't take much to set off a fuse that would explode into a first-class fight.

One of my roommates just stumbled over her neighbor's suitcase, and out loud, she said, "Damn!" Her neighbor flew at her and, for a moment, I though I'd be the witness of a first-class brawl between two refined women.

August 10, 1942

We knew definitely that most of the news we received was from the secret radio in camp, but by the time the news had been repeated several thousand times, the original broadcast was completely unrecognizable, and no more reliable than the ridiculous dribble that we read in the *Nishi-Nishi*.

The sun came out this morning hot and bright, and we all chirped happily. Isn't it a glorious day?

Barbed wire and washlines groaned with bedding and clothing as people washed or aired their belongings in the blessed sunshine.

Everywhere women were seen washing and drying their hair, while near them were their moth-eaten suitcases, baskets, and paper boxes filled with their worldly goods.

In the afternoon, when the sun still favored us, I put on my best dress and the giddiest and prettiest shoes I owned and I took a walk on the plaza. How good it felt to wear a dress and high heels! But my legs felt indecently exposed after wearing slacks for so long.

I stopped at the bodega (warehouse) scales to get weighed and I was astonished to find that I had lost eighteen pounds. However, my roomies and friends told me that I never looked better. But, of course, by now, we all had learned to lie. It was our way of saying, "You look like a sea hag."

It was impossible to keep one's weight in here, for even when we had good food to eat, it seemed that something always happened to ruin appetites and digestions.

Today, just as we sat down to the good food that Catalino sent us once a week, an inspection party of eight Japanese naval officers came by. Immaculately dressed in white and gold braid, they stared at us and at the good food on the bridge table.

It upset me. I wanted to shout that the Imperial Japanese Army hadn't provided us with the food, that as far as they were concerned we could starve. I looked down at my plate. My appetite was gone, and I felt ill again.

August 13, 1942

Solomon Sea Battle Shows Japan's Might. American Fleet Surprised in Night Encounter.

From our secret radio reports, we heard that the Solomons were definitely in American hands.

Considerable betting went on today when word spread that Formosa had been bombed by the Americans.

Leslie, our room monitor, had another stricture, this time more serious than the others. For one moment, before adrenalin was administered, I thought her lungs and heart had failed entirely.

She was taken to the camp hospital and from there transferred to the Philippine General Hospital. We hoped and prayed that the hospital had a doctor with the necessary training and instruments to dilate the esophagus.

August 16, 1942

All the pleasure in seeing Adoracion, her baby, and Catalino this morning, was completely spoiled when Catalino denied that he had a wife.

Catesy had arranged the three-minute meeting for us at the front gate, and I had looked forward to seeing them.

After I had fussed over Adoracion's fat little rascal, who kept smiling at me as though I were an old friend, I noticed Catalino's proprietary interest in Adoracion and the baby.

"Catalino, do you ever hear from your wife, Maria?" I asked pointedly.

"I do not have a wife, mum!" There it was! A flat denial, and he looked me straight in the eye.

My blood pressure jumped.

"Don't you dare stand before me and tell me such a lie! You and your wife Maria worked for me for three years! And what about your little girl? Are you going to deny her, too?" I shook with anger.

"Easy, honey," whispered Catesy.

Just then the Japanese guards hustled them out of the gate and Catalino was spared from answering me.

As Adoracion turned to wave good-bye, I saw tears coursing down her cheeks, and some of my anger against Catalino disappeared. But it quickly returned when Catesy, a native Iowan, with a completely un-Iowan shrug of his shoulders, remarked, *"C'est la guerre!"*

"Don't you *'c'est la guerre'* me in that Latin fashion! There's such a thing as decency and loyalty though the world is at war!"

"Easy, honey! Just look around you in here and you'll see what the unnatural life and segregation has already done to couples. Some of them look forward to the end of the war because they want a divorce. They argue, nag, and hate the sight of each other. You see that middle-aged man over there? I never saw him look at another woman before the war, but with his wife in the States he was lost and lonely until he started to go with that woman he's with."

I looked at the couple in astonishment. They had been inseparable ever since the begining of internment, and I had naturally assumed that they were husband and wife.

"But suppose after the war, he didn't want to go back to his wife!"

"C'est la guerre!" repeated Catesy.

War was hell! It not only maimed and killed, but it did many other devastating things to heart and soul. People stopped thinking straight. Values were lost. Loyalty, faith and devotion to each other were smothered as people sought to forget their anxiety and dreary loneliness, in the companionship of others.

Catesy had changed, too. Though he never looked at another girl in camp, I worried about him for other reasons. He had frequent spells of despondency, and he was easily irritated. I missed his droll wit and the affectionate way he used to grin at me, and I missed our friendly and cheerful chats about our future. When I discussed our future or an exciting trip to some far-off place, he remained silent, or he quickly changed the subject.

After I crawled under my net, I remained troubled and wakeful.

Perhaps, I too had changed. My frequent stomach upsets had hardly improved my disposition. How else had I changed? I asked myself a hundred times as I tossed and turned on my bejuca bed.

August 18, 19̄42

10 Allied Vessels Lost in Australia. Offensive Against Japan Impossible.

If only I had enough will power to stop reading the morning paper with its upsetting news I believed that I would get well. Some of my roommates expressed the same thought.

The Commandant permitted the army nurses to mingle with us, and we were all very happy about it. Jinnie, Zest, and the former chief nurse from Corregidor joined us in the plaza, and for three hours we listened as they talked. We were anxious to catch up on all the news since we had last seen each other.

August 19, 1942

Zest, the army nurse, was dark-haired, with dark eyes and a creamy complexion. She was an attractive girl, even in her drab khaki uniform. When I introduced her to Henry, I was surprised and delighted to see the interest in his baby-blue eyes.

The following day, I was more surprised when like a flustered schoolboy at his first prom, he asked me whether Zest could join our mess. It was a big favor, for our fund and food supplies were hardly adequate for four, let alone five. After talking it over with Catesy, we decided to take Zest into our little circle.

Today was Catesy's birthday, and Catalino sent us a well-cooked meal. The excellent food did wonders for our morale and we talked happily about many things.

Henry, the confirmed bachelor, was most attentive to Zest, and my woman's instinct told me that Zest was equally attracted to him.

We were getting corn-meal as our morning cereal and it was certainly an improvement on the wormy cracked wheat. However, the corn-meal was hard on inflamed intestines.

To the corn-meal, we added coconut or carabo milk, which we bought from camp vendors. Those with no funds ate their corn-meal dry. Sugar, however, was still served at this time.

August 22, 1942

About eight Filipino vendors opened fruit and vegetable stalls in the area behind the Nip's office.

Every morning between the hours of eight and ten, we lined up with our baskets and bayongs to get near the counters to make our purchases. All transactions were in Mickey Mouse when the Japs were around, and if we made our purchases in dollars or Philippine pesos we had to be quick about it.

August 24, 1942

Brazil Declares War on Germany and Italy.

I was beginning to be less skeptical about the news that was circulated around here. Apparently, it wasn't all fiddle-faddle.

The army nurses moved from the Santa Catalina to the frame building that formerly housed the camp hospital, while the patients and hospital equipment were moved to Santa Catalina, the building the nurses vacated. It was like moving day in Pumpkin Center! Three hundred men and young boys had volunteered to help move patients and equipment. It was surprising how efficiently and quietly the transfer was made without trucks or other moving equipment.

One of our own local civilian doctors will be in charge of the hospital, now that the Rockefeller Foundation man has resigned, and the army nurses will take over the nursing.

I started to read *Berlin Diary* tonight, and I was struck by the

similarity of the steam-roller tactics of the Nazis in the low
countries to that of the Japs out here.

August 25, 1942

If a person were in the mood for laughs, this place was chock
full of crazy sights and incidents. At tonight's chow line, we saw
an indignant woman hit her husband with a cupful of pudding.
For a moment, we thought we were watching a Mack Sennett
comedy. The sticky mess was in his eyes and nose, and it trickled
down his chin.

Without a word, he calmly proceeded to wipe his face with a
towel that he always wore in his belt; then he quietly went into
the building.

"Now I know why he wears that towel in his belt!" remarked
Catesy.

While we sat in the plaza tonight, a Japanese guard, pleasantly
inebriated from sake, went around shaking hands with internees.
As he shook hands in a most neighborly manner, he smiled and
chuckled good-naturedly. Finally one of our own guards led him
toward the guard shed, but before one of his colleagues could
hold him he dashed into the street and jumped on a bus, where
he started to slap Filipinos in a most unneighborly manner.

Early to bed to read a 1938 issue of the *Reader's Digest*. It was
just old enough to be new.

August 26, 1942

Mr. Nagy sent me a box of candy and a note that perked me up
considerably. Apparently, he had become tremendously attached
to my little dog. He wrote that Rags was frisky and playful, and
that without her his life would be dull.

August 27, 1942

STALINGRAD IN FLAMES. GERMANY ONLY 30 MILES FROM BOMBED
CITY. After finishing *Berlin Diary*, I planned to re-read Lin Yutang's
Importance of Living.

August 28, 1942

A frail and elderly couple whom Catesy and I both knew
before the war were granted a three-months release. Because
their home in Cavite had been bombed, I told them to go to my
apartment. When they left today, their happiness was touching
to witness.

August 29, 1942

U. S. TROOPS RAISE MORAL QUESTION.

At first, I thought Margo and Kay, who took turns reading the
following article, were making it all up, until I saw for myself.

The increasing number of American soldiers in Britain is

threatening to alienate the hearts of thousands of British women from their "Tommies" according to information received here. It was reported that the British war office issued a note to the wives of sweethearts of two million British Army men suggesting that when writing to their men about visiting places or doing things to write, "I should have enjoyed it so much more with you." The note warned the women against writing about "dancing with other men," to their men.

The presence of United States troops in Britain is said to have changed the mentality of 17,000,000 women between the ages of 14 to 65.

More aggressive than the Tommies, the Canadian and American soldiers don't hesitate to leap off the Hyde Park bench to catch a pretty around the waist. The average forgiveness is nine minutes by girls in civilian clothes and somewhat longer by girls in uniform.

"How do you suppose they got their statistics?" wondered Kay. "Can't you picture a Domei newsman with gopher teeth, horn-rimmed spectacles, and a stop-watch in his hand, timing couples in Hyde Park?"

Margo's question and the vision of a Jap lurking behind a bench in Lover's Lane threw us into convulsive laughter.

Another whopper of a rumor had the optimists offering odds that we'd be out in 72 days. It was the news that twenty thousand of our men had landed in Aparri.

Laura gave me the following jingles on Rumorism, and it certainly summed up in verse the part rumors played in our lives.

Rumorism

If I sit on the ground a minute or two
And think of my house and feel sort of blue,
Along comes a newshound—now don't ask me who—
And tells me something too good to be true.
And when he walks away, I know not whither,
I find myself in an awful dither
Wondering if it's worth repeating.
But I simply can't resist competing
With the girls in my room, so without deleting
A single word, I spring my news.
And then each one begins airing her views
Until at last my original rumor
Is completely lost, and so is my humor.

I go in the patio and sit in a chair
Thinking I'll sit there and get some fresh air,
When along comes a man who looks very cheerful
And before I know it I get an earful—
Confidentially, you understand—
When suddenly, well I'll be damned,
There's my story dressed up anew!
Now, what's a poor dumb sap to do?

If I go to the taps to wash my clothes
Thinking perhaps that no one knows
The latest in rumors, then some chatty blade
Assures me the siren was not an air raid
But a truck with that kind of horn which got stuck.
Who am I to argue or pass the buck?

When a flying fortress turns out to be a star,
When bombs are not bombs—you know how bathrooms are—
When even our stay, supposed to be for three days,
Has turned into months I'm simply in a superdaze.
So now I swear I'll not make another bloomerism
Then perhaps I'll get rid of my darned old rumorism.

August 30, 1942

A sixteen-year-old mestiza girl of American and Filipino parentage left our room today. She was released permanently because she had one parent of native blood.

With her dark skin and Caucasian features, she had been an unhappy and emotionally upset girl, unable to adjust herself to either white or brown race. Always divided. Never knowing which side to claim as her own. She hated to leave us, and yet she wanted to join the fine Filipino family who had raised her.

After roll call, Rainbow, acting for Leslie, read her pitiful little note, and I noticed that she brushed a tear from her eye. "Dear girls: I am sorry to leave you all behind. You have been so nice to me and I have been so happy. Be good girls, Love."

September 2, 1942

Kay and Margo were in the depths of despair today. They had received notes from their husbands begging them to write and send money. No wonder the girls were depressed! On numerous occasions they had sent letters and money, but apparently both money and notes had gone astray. Filipinos who acted as messengers ran great risks in smuggling notes and money to the

118

military camps. Among the many honest messengers, there were
bound to be some crooks.

September 4, 1942

"What's so funny?" I asked Catesy and Henry, who were reading
and laughing as they looked at the classified ad section in the
morning *Nishi-Nishi.* They handed me the paper, and I read:

"The new feature of the Ipopi Charcomobile Ipopi Resuscitator,
which now enables you to stop your charcoal-fed engine several
hours and start it again without the necessity of further firing or
blowing—it is a product of our Ipopi Research Department."

"Hot diggety! Ain't that something?" said Henry with a grin.
"They won't ever need gas with a fine invention like that!"

Because it rained again, the corridors and rooms were cluttered
with people and the sound of their voices beat against the eardrums like the roaring of Niagara Falls.

The lucky people were the ones with rainproof shacks. They,
at least, could escape the confusion until curfew time.

September 5, 1942

Japan Does Not Covet P. I. Territory. Elimination of Western Ideas Is War Aim.

Grandma and I had just finished reading the headline, and she
remarked in a most belligerent and un-British manner: "Who are
they trying to kid?"

September 6, 1942

When Catesy told me that Mr. Nagy and Rags had been at the
front gate to see me, I was greatly disappointed, because the Japs
did not permit the visit.

New words were being coined every day. One of the most
colorful was telinum tarts, which referred to the hussies of the
camp who loitered in the telinum (native vegetable resembling
spinach) patch.

The shortage of ready-made underwear caused the women to
make panties resembling breech-clouts, and in camp parlance they
were called petate-pants.

We were stared at by another group of naval officers while
eating lunch in the corridor. They always managed to come at
lunchtime. Just like the telephone in pre-war days that always
rang just as one stepped into the tub.

Why did I become so upset when they passed by? I ought to be
used to them by now.

Cramps and diarrhea kept me up most of the night.

September 8, 1942

On tea and bananas today, but I hoped to be well by tomorrow.

In the Annex where mothers and young children were housed, one little fellow asked his mother:

"When I grow up, can I go and live with Daddy in the Big House?"

September 9, 1942

CLAIMS JAPANESE INTERNEES IN U. S. WERE MALTREATED.

"Even Americans would shudder in disgust if they knew of the barbaric and bestial treatment to which Japanese nationals were subjected in gross violation of all rules of humanitarianism and international law. Food given to the Japanese consisted of: For breakfast, corn-meal porridge, two slices of bread and coffee without milk-cream; for lunch and supper, hash made of left-over meat, navy beans, lettuce, and two slices of stale bread."

Mrs. Smith, who had just lost her son in a military camp, read us the article, and with a wry smile she remarked: "Such inhumanity!"

"I wish I had some of that stale bread and hash!" remarked her youngest daughter heatedly.

"Speaking of bread, have any of you noticed the large and lovely loaves of white bread bought for the Jap guards?" questioned Margo. We had all seen the bread. It sold in the camp at Pesos 1.50 or seventy-five cents, which was out of the reach of most of us. Our group bought the forty- and fifty-centavo loaf and sometimes it gave us severe cramps because of the substitutes used.

Bread at this time was made of practically anything the desperate baker could find. Cassava flour, ground from a native root, gave the bread an evil smell and a dirty gray color. Bread made of wheat, corn-meal and rice flour was the most expensive, and most **edible.**

This afternoon, Catalino, with tears in his eyes, told Catesy that his soldier brother had been released from one of the prison camps, and he was ill and in need of hospitalization. We were glad to help, but it meant dipping into our rapidly diminishing funds.

September 10, 1942

All the Dutch nationals, over twenty-one, were to receive an allowance of eighty pesos each month from their government. If only our government could have made the same arrangement for us, we could have bought and stored food for the time when all communications with the outside would cease. If the Dutch could do it with their country overrun by Nazi hordes, and with their government functioning from a foreign country, why couldn't our powerful government do the same? We heard this question asked over and over again, especially by those who were hungry and completely destitute.

September 11, 1942

Our jail within a jail was occupied by Poop Deck Pappy, nickname for one of our colorful characters, who had been caught appropriating a fellow internee's shaving kit. Our discipline committee had set the punishment. It was ten days in the local brig. But it looked like the lucky Poop Deck Pappy would never complete his sentence, as he and his jungle Princess, an extremely sloppy and dirty-looking native woman, were scheduled to leave on the ship sailing for Shanghai.

September 12, 1942

The people, bound for Shanghai, left this afternoon. Among those we knew, were a fine couple of *Life* magazine, an A. P. man from Japan, Jane, the very sick girl from my room, three nurses from Rockefeller Foundation in Peiping, a missionary nurse and several young Canadians who had been on their way to Persia to work for a major U. S. oil company.

Poop Deck Pappy, having been freshly sprung from the local clink, and looking more like a murderous pirate than an American internee, appeared very happy and smug as he climbed aboard the truck.

From the truck he motioned impatiently to his jungle Princess to get a "move on." But the Princess was not to be hurried. Her manner suggested that this departure was a common occurrence in her life. With her dark face, flat and languidly impassive, she shuffled to the truck in her worn-out shenalis in a most leisurely manner.

As a parting shot, Poop Deck Pappy gleefully said:

"My wife has never been out of the Philippines, so we might as well make this trip, since it won't cost us anything."

That night when we sat in the plaza, Poop Deck Pappy's name, crime and punishment were announced over the loud speaker, and everyone started to laugh. We all knew that by that time he and his Princess were safely on the high seas.

September 14, 1942

The boys surprised me with a lovely birthday lunch, and Mr. Nagy sent red roses and orchids.

In addition to the fine cooked meal, Catalino sent fragile ginger blossoms, tied together in clusters to resemble gardenias.

It was a happy birthday, and the tours by Cook were conspicious by their absence.

September 15, 1942

I was still in a happy glow over my birthday celebration, and the

121

morning headline didn't worry me a bit.

Tokyo Says: "U. S. Democracy Marching to Doom."

Old Mrs. Greenshoes cornered me in the bathroom to ask me if I believed the rumor that Germany had capitulated, and that Hitler had committed suicide.

"No, I don't. Do you?"

"Who starts these damned stupid rumors around here?" she asked me fiercely.

I sympathized with her. I understood her indignation. The crazy and fantastic rumors were the most exasperating aspects of our internment at this time.

September 20, 1942

Kay, Belle, Margo and I sat on my bed and listened to the church services in the Father's garden.

The Seminary building, which was about two hundred yards from us, also had four interested spectators. Four Dominican priests were leaning out of the window and watching the services.

We could see into their rooms and no doubt they could see into ours. Margo voiced my thoughts when she said: "Those poor padres are certainly getting a liberal education!"

"I'll bet the novelty of watching a bunch of women dressing and undressing has worn off by now," added Kay practically.

The chief nurse of Corregidor and I took a walk tonight in the rain in the front grounds. The rain seemed to add to the delicate flush of her pretty apple-blossom complexion.

We talked about old days and her friend who was somewhere in a military prison camp. Then we watched a Japanese soldier explaining the intricacies of the rhumba to an amused American. The word, rhumba, pronounced by the Jap, and repeated over and over again, seemed funny and unnatural, but when he executed the short mincing steps of the dance, we choked with suppressed laughter. He was a ridiculous and crazy sight with his thick, crooked legs, conspiciously exposed in khaki shorts.

September 21, 1942

After rereading *The Three Musketeers*, I started to write a war story. I read a few pages of it to Margo, but she didn't seem too interested.

The new rumor that some of us may be repatriated before Christmas, strangely enough, had saddened many.

"I don't want to leave my home!" declared a Scotchwoman in our room.

"What home are you referring to?" asked Kay.

"That's right! How do you know you have a home left?" asked another roommate.

"I want to be here when the Yanks come back!" Grandma's words were most emphatic and enthusiastic.

September 23, 1942

The husband of Leslie, our beloved room monitor, was dead! Everyone knew it but Leslie. Because of her weakened condition, it was thought best to postpone the dreadful news.

Two other wives whom I knew also received word that their husbands had died in Cabanatuan.

One of them received the official notice of her husband's death through the Commandant's office. When the Japanese handed her the slip of paper with the tragic news, she screamed hysterically, and threw the paper on the floor as though it had scorched her hand. The Japanese laughed, while the distraught woman, still screaming, was led out of the Commandant's office.

While we sat in the plaza tonight, listening to cowboy music, there was a break in the recorded program, and the names and punishment of three liquor violators were announced over the P. A. system.

Two men and a woman had been caught drunk by our internee patrol. The men were given thirty days in the jail within a jail, and the woman was confined to her room for twelve days. We were thoroughly disgusted with these incorrigibles, and most of us felt that, for the safety of the camp, they ought to be tucked away behind bars in a psycho ward outside.

September 25, 1942

There was nothing like a man to perk up the appearance and interest of a girl. Zest appeared with a bright Kelly-green scarf tied around her neck at supper tonight. The color was highly flattering to her clear white skin and black eyes, and I noticed that her curly black hair had been cut boyishly short.

Henry, with his blond hair slicked back like a choirboy's, straightened up in his chair the moment she appeared. These two were now a familiar twosome. They ate all their meals together, and they walked and sat together in the evenings, when their personal and camp duties were over.

September 27, 1942

Leslie was in the corner of her room weeping bitterly. A few minutes ago, several of her close friends revealed the tragic news about her husband.

"But I thought he was getting better!" She kept repeating the sentence in an anguished manner. There wasn't a dry eye among her roommates. If only her two grown sons were with her to lessen her grief, but they, too, were somewhere in the war! If only she could be alone with her grief.

123

The regular Sunday recorded music in the Father's garden had started, and fortunately it was sacred music, rather than gay Viennese airs. But the music could not drown out her heart-breaking sobs.

September 28, 1942

JAPAN READY FOR NEXT PHASE OF WAR—TOJO.
ALLIES WILL BE BROUGHT TO THEIR KNEES.

"Humbug!" declared Grandma after reading the headline.

Grandma, with her fiercely brisk manner and furious activity, was a great favorite of her roommates. To see her rushing about from one activity to another, it was hard to believe that she was a grandmother with grown grandchildren.

After the heavy rains and gusty winds had died down, Catesy and I took a walk around the Big House, the Education building, and then back to the front of the plaza for a rest on one of the tombstones.

With my nails, I scratched the moss off one of the stones, and I saw the year 1667, but I could not decipher the name.

"Only forty-seven years after the Pilgrims landed at Plymouth Rock!"

"I wonder who's buried here," I said.

"Look, honey! A turtle! How old do you suppose he is?" wondered Catesy. He picked up the small turtle and then he began to chuckle. A camp wit had carved on the turtle's back this information:

"I am not an internee."

September 29, 1942

The number five typhoon signal had been up since noontime. Since last night the wind had stormed and raged, and it had been anything but soothing to people crammed together in rooms and corridors. Many of the shanties had blown over and the owners' worldly goods were exposed to wind and rain.

Despite the heavy storm, Catesy and I kept our luncheon date at Don Juan's shack. Neither hail, sleet, nor typhoon would have kept us away for we knew that the food would be superlative, and that we would be entertained by Don Juan's racy dialect stories. Furthermore, my curiosity would be satisfied about his current blonde. She was a beauty! There was no question about that! Tall, shapely, and a natural blonde. She wore a perpetual smile, and she looked into Don Juan's and Catesy's eyes with the most disarming expression I've ever seen in a pair of blue eyes. She fixed her rapt and flattering gaze on the men as they spoke, but when I spoke, she ignored me completely. In fact, she deliberately set up a great clatter with the dishes, pots and pans that were stacked on the bungara to be washed.

The lunch was truly royal! Chicken Valencia with rice, fried eggplant, string beans, sayote, a native vegetable resembling a pear, chocolate cake and coffee with real canned milk.

Just as we finished our coffee, a sudden and violent gust of wind shook the shack, and the men rushed out and worked for more than a hour with stakes, ropes and canvas in an effort to anchor the shack more securely.

The gorgeous blonde and I were left alone.

"Let's do the dishes, while the boys are working outside!" I declared helpfully and energetically.

"That won't be necessary!" she said languidly. "There's a boy to do that. He gets three good meals a day for doing it!" Well, how about that? By shacking up with Don Juan, she not only had three sumptuous meals a day, but she was spared from getting dishpan hands.

October 1, 1942

With the gates still closed, hundreds of Filipino houseboys lined the outside fence with their arms loaded with boxes, large cans, and baskets containing food and clean clothing.

As we stood on this side of the fence, we could almost smell the cooked food. But the little brown men with the bayonets meant business. We stood around mumbling to ourselves, while our loyal friends on the other side of the fence watched us in bewilderment, until the Japanese guards roared at them to move on. Still clutching their undelivered bundles, they sadly looked at us before scattering.

October 3, 1942

With the gates still closed, we were compelled to rely on the vendors in camp. The stalls were mobbed, and fruit and vegetables were sold out every morning, despite the sky-rocketing prices.

Theoretically, only Mickey Mouse was the legal tender, but of course American dollars and Philippine currency were gladly accepted by the Filipino vendors. However, the transaction always took place under the counter, with one eye on the lookout for a Japanese guard.

I was still searching for someone who would give me a better rate than thirty per cent on my checks. They continued to support my arches, but by now both checks and arches were beginning to show signs of general breakdown.

October 5, 1942

Kay and Margo were half-hysterical with joy over the announcement that wives would be permitted to visit their husbands in military prison camps. Recently bereaved wives felt a fresh pang of pain over this new development.

The gates were opened today and there was great rejoicing among those who received bundles from the outside. Now that fruit and vegetables could be sent to us from the city, our vendors in the camp had lowered their prices.

Today, a group of us sat in Room 25 discussing the last war and the present one, when I thoughtlessly said: "But if the last war, which was a tea party compared to this present one, lasted four years, why do you think this one will last only a year?"

The girls were silent, and on the faces of some I saw fear and doubt. None of us could bear the thought of spending Christmas in this place, much less another year.

October 7, 1942

The bags of mail that arrived from our loved ones from all parts of the world were still in the Commandant's office. Unopened and undistributed. How cruel of them! How desperately we wanted to hear from our relatives! When the heads of our internee committee asked about the mail, the Nips talked about censoring it first, but weeks had passed and still nothing was done.

October 9, 1942

Grandma Britannica was sprightlier and happier than ever today! One of her granddaughters presented her with a great-grandson.

"I don't feel a bit different or older!" she explained.

October 11, 1942

Because of continued poor health, Sophie obtained a release to live outside, and my mess had shrunk to four.

With Zest always close by Henry's side, there was a new spring to his steps and his baby-blue eyes twinkled more than ever.

October 12, 1942

Six-thirty A. M. Though some of my roommates were still asleep, the camp was beginning to stir.

As I quietly crawled from under my net, I watched two of the Dominican priests cycling on the roof of the Seminary building.

In the Father's garden, a heavily bearded internee was busily fanning a charcoal stove on the ground, while his wife was fussing with pots and pans.

Another couple nearby had already completed their family wash and they were draping it over the barbed wire.

There was not a soul at the sink in our room! Now's my chance! Hastily, I grabbed a toothbrush, paste, towel and soap, but by the time I reached the sink, two of my roommates had sprinted ahead of me.

126

After making my bed, I reached under the bed to get my small wooden tray that Catesy had made for me, and which held my tin cup, plate and oversize soup spoon. Despite my efforts to keep quiet, I dropped my cup on the cement floor, and it made a fearful clatter. Immediately bejuca and Stateside springs creaked as heads raised to see who had created the disturbance.

The next obstacle was to get out of the room. With most of the mosquito nets still up, this was no easy matter, as the narrow aisles were almost impassable. But by good fortune and careful maneuvering, I reached the corridor without any further mishap.

When I reached the chow line in the back corridor of the Big House, the boys and Zest were already standing in line to receive our corn-meal mush, one banana, and muddy native coffee. With our breakfast on our trays, we joined another long line to buy coconut milk for our cereal.

Immediately after breakfast, Zest left for the hospital. While the boys did the dishes, I rushed to the fruit and vegetable stalls to get in line for my daily marketing for lunch.

When my shopping was completed, I dashed to my room to clean, dust and mop under my bed; and by then it was time to start my camp detail — cleaning and debugging dirty rice and cereal.

After showering and changing to clean clothes, it was time to start lunch. When the charcoal stove had been fanned into a red-hot blaze, I fried onion, garlic, and green pepper in my iron skillet, and I added left-over boiled rice. Over this, I cracked three duck eggs, which I swished over the nicely browned rice. With fresh cincamas, a vegetable between a turnip and a pear, thinly sliced and mixed with onions, garlic and vinegar, we had a good salad.

By 1 P. M. it was time for my camp vegetable detail. From two to three hours, I sat with thirty or more women, paring and cleaning squash and upo. The last was a monstrous-looking squash, a yard long.

By 4 P. M. it was time to get in line for our evening meal. After dishes were washed, we went to our rooms for roll call and important announcements, and after that came the best part of the day. Sitting outside until curfew time.

The editorial in the morning paper under the heading of "Beware of Contamination" was interesting. The editorial warned all Filipinos about believing false rumors such as the one about General MacArthur taking dinner at Manila Hotel in February, and that by April the skies would be darkened by American Flying Fortresses.

U. S. Admits Sinking of 3 Big Cruisers.

I brushed a tear from my eye tonight as I watched a mother preparing her three-year-old daughter for bed in the Annex. The child knelt by the bed, with tiny hands pressed together in supplication, and she ended her prayers: "God bless America, for Jesus Christ's sake, amen!"

I didn't know today was my name day until I received a fine bouquet of flowers from Mr. Nagy. Being a devout Catholic, he had naturally remembered St. Theresa's Day. Attached to the flowers was a tiny card, on which he had written that he prayed for us daily.

This place reminded me of a huge carnival or a country fair back in Butler County, Pennsylvania, rather than a concentration camp.

With the exception of harness racing, Ferris wheels, and merry-go-rounds, we seemed to be equipped with everything else.

In the evening, when all the work was done for the day, people in their light tropical clothes wandered about the grounds, while others sat on the grass or deck chairs, listening to recorded music.

Many took their daily constitutionals at this time. They walked back and forth in the long front driveway as far as the front gate, where a familiar sign greeted them: "Internees not allowed beyond this barrier." There was the walk past the Education Building as far as Santa Catalina, or past the Seminary building to the Gym, where, at present, over four hundred men were housed. To the right of the Gym, there was a small nipa shack where hot cakes, bacon and eggs, and coffee could be bought. To eat here, one had to have money, and those without it looked upon the fortunate diners in the same light as one would a Stork Club patron.

All the activity and lights were in the front of the Big House and the Education building.

While we listened to the recorded music, dozens of internee vendors shouted: "peanuts, homemade fudge, peanut brittle, and ice cream."

Two highly competitive groups in the ice cream business had rigged up pushcarts, festooned with lanterns made of a single candle encased in paper à-la-native style. They had added gaudy tinsel, paper and bells. The merry tinkle of the bells and their shouts of ice cream made us forget, for the time being, at least, that we were in a prison camp.

Tonight, one of the pushcart vendors did a more thriving business than his competitor, and for a good reason. In addition to all the gimmicks already on the pushcart, he had added a pretty blonde. Smilingly, she sat in the center of the pushcart, dishing up ice-cream cones until curfew time.

In the first-floor corridors of the Big House, there were a dozen or more stalls presided over by enterprising Jews, and here one could buy anything from bobby pins to ladies' panties. A professional candymaker dipped chocolate and other candies, but some of us could not afford to pay his price. But, apparently, there were many who could, for he kept busy all day. Nearby, the tattoo man, a former carnival freak, had a booth, and his wares were as picturesque and numerous as the designs tattooed on his scrawny body.

During the day, women vendors came to the ladies' rooms with their bundles and suitcases filled with lingerie and dresses. The prices of these garments were exorbitant and usually the material was cheap and sleazy, but if one was down to the last slack or sarong, anything would do — providing, of course, one had the money.

Last week I had a blouse and skirt made of a heavy cretonne chair cover and it should last me for years. But what was I saying?

October 17, 1942

The boys made hot cakes for lunch from left-over corn-meal, cassava flour, soda and coconut milk, and this time it was delicious. Zest and I raved over them and the boys were highly pleased with their cooking.

"With a little practice, we'll go a long way," prophesied Catesy.

October 18, 1942

Small groups throughout the camp were discussing the man who escaped a few days ago. What had happened to him no one seemed to know.

In my room, the girls with husbands at military camps were wondering if the Nips really meant their promises about wives visiting their husbands in the various prison camps.

"I don't believe anything will ever come of it!" declared Kay.

"Don't say that!" pleaded Margo, with tears in her lovely gray eyes.

October 19, 1942

The man who escaped a few days ago was caught! Fortunately for him, our quick-thinking and fast-talking American doctors convinced the Nips that the man was a mental case, thus saving him from the firing squad. He was shipped off to a mental institution and we all breathed more easily after that.

Who would be the next psycho to jeopardize our safety and the few privileges we enjoyed?

"If we had a staff of psychiatrists to give an individual mental test of all the people in this camp it might save us from further trouble."

Although Catesy laughed at my practical solution, he admitted that I might have something.

October 20, 1942

Grandma, Margo, Kay, Belle, and I sat on my bed while Grandma read the following article from the morning rag:

> Will Court-Martial Inhuman Enemy Airmen! Commenting on the ruthless and inhuman barbarity of the American fliers, military spokesman pointed out that the so-called American dare-devils only bombed hospitals, schools and civilian homes in Japan. He disclosed, it was confessed at the examination, that a group of schoolchildren were strafed "to give the Japanese kids a taste of bullets."

"Humbug!" declared Grandma. Then she read on.

> The spokesman declared that the American fliers looked upon the raid as a stunt and were only concerned with unloading their bombs regardless of where they landed and with full knowledge that civilians were the only ones endangered. He said that if enemy fliers in disregard of humanitarian principles persist in their cruel and inhuman "what the hell" attitude in the future, they will face death or some other severe punishment.

Grandma looked over her glasses and in an un-British manner she remarked delightedly: "So they can't take it!"

October 22, 1942

When it rained the Big House was a madhouse. Being built around two large patios, the hundreds of voices from the different floors came across the courtyard, from above us, and from below us. Voices came from everywhere. From our rooms, from the corridors on our floor, from the floors below and above us. Voices beat against our eardrums like the roaring of an angry sea pounding against the ragged reefs.

Catesy and I sat on the bedbug-infested bench outside my room. We talked, but we could not hear each other above the unbearable din.

October 25, 1942

The *Nishi-Nishi* always referred to the "degrading Western influence," and yet today there was a picture of the Empress of

Japan in trailing white dress. Grandma peered interestedly at the picture over her glasses.

"How degrading!" Her voice feigned shock.

October 27, 1942

Nazi Troops Control Most of Stalingrad. "Lieutenant General Summerville, head of the army service supply, said: 'So far, we have lost nearly every major struggle.' Donald Nelson of War Production Board said: 'Production lagged about 14 per cent in August.'"

After reading the dismal headlines, Leslie remarked: "If I were to believe the *Nishi-Nishi,* I just couldn't carry on through the day."

We heard tonight that U. S. planes raided Hong Kong.

October 28, 1942

3 U. S. Planes Downed in Raid of Hongkong!

The headline confirmed our rumor of last night, and most of us were convinced by now that a secret radio was in camp. Heaven help the brave fellow who operated it! If he were caught, it would mean the firing squad.

October 30, 1942

Jack-o'-lanterns carved from the native squash stared at us from shanty windows. Hard-working and conscientious parents tried to create an atmosphere of fun, festivity, and normalcy for their children.

In the city, just as in every part of the country, the annual visits to the City of the Dead began today, and would close tomorrow on All Saints Day. If the procession was as large as during former years, traffic to North and Paco Cemetery would be tied up for miles and hours.

All the graves, in all the cemeteries, from the tiniest and least impressive tombstone to the ornate marble mausoleums, would be gaily decorated by wreaths, flowers, ribbons, tinsel and bright lights.

Vendors of peanuts, popcorn, hot dogs, and soft drinks with carts garishly decorated, would be yelling their wares in loud and cheerful voices among the graves. It was just like a huge carnival or a fair.

The thousands of people, Filipinos and Chinese alike, who came to pay their respect and spend a day with their dead, were a happy and extremely congenial group. They brought picnic lunches and ate them on the graves. They brought their entire family and made a big day of it.

One such happy group, a few years ago, asked Catesy and me to join their party. We seated ourselves next to the ornate tombstone and joined the happy family. We ate their good food, and

131

we enjoyed the gay Spanish tunes that our host played on his guitar.

November 1, 1942

Room 25 was saddened by the news that the husband of one of our former roommates had died of malaria in Cabanatuan. The widow, a young mestiza of American and Filipino blood, had been tireless and fearless in her efforts to smuggle notes, money, medicine and food to men in military prisons. A few weeks ago, she had been released permanently because of her native blood.

November 2, 1942

No one had missed Tientsin Mary. And yet she had been out on a two-month pass. None of the women's rooms wanted her, so she spent the night in the local brig. The following day she was assigned to a room. With such a colorful character for a roommate, the rest of the ladies should never lack for entertainment and diversion.

We were riding "high" today on happy rumors.

The Japs had been pushed out of the Solomons, and Hong Kong was being bombed repeatedly. But the best of them all was the rumor that Clark Field had been bombed by the Americans.

November 4, 1942

Trouble seemed to pursue Tientsin Mary! This time, it was serious! Today, she became abusive with rough and profane language toward the Nips, and if our own internee guards hadn't intervened, she would have landed an uppercut on the Commandant's jaw.

Again our swift-thinking doctors came to the rescue by pronouncing Tientsin Mary crazy, and a few hours later she was hustled off to a psychopathic hospital.

Some of the congestion and eternal fussing with pots, pans, dishes and groceries under my bed had been eased.

The highly resourceful Catesy and Henry built me a cupboard with six shelves, which they nailed to the wall outside my room. Next to the cupboard was my bridge table, where we ate all our meals. Now I could park a few of my groceries and other kitchen utensils in the cupboard, as the boys had attached a lock.

Housekeeping problems continued to plague us. Today we worked over dry navy beans that the U. S. Quartermaster at Sternberg had given me almost a year ago. How many years the army had them, was something else again. We had tried cooking the first batch several months ago, but the beans had remained hard as marbles, though I had soaked them all night. Tonight, we decided to try something different. After soaking the beans in soda water all day, we set the huge pot of beans, plus soda water, on our charcoal stove in the patio.

When Catesy returned to check on the beans, he found stove, bench, and a large area of the patio ground completely covered by bubbling and frothy scum and beans. The pot was completely empty.

November 7, 1942

AMERICAN NAVY MET WATERLOO IN SOUTH PACIFIC — HIRAIDE. CAN NEVER STAGE COUNTER-ATTACK!

"If we believed that, there would be mass hara-kiri in here by nightfall!" declared Catesy.

When we were low in spirits or feeling ill, the Nips nearly succeeded in their psychological warfare and propaganda. At these times, our thinking and reasoning would be cloudy and unrealistic. A terrible fear would take hold of us, and we'd wonder if the Japs could ever be stopped. But when we were well and "riding high," especially after hearing a whopping rumor, nothing could rile or depress us.

Our cooking problems seemed to pile up on us as the months went by.

For the last few days it rained every day just at lunchtime, and Henry had to hold an umbrella over Catesy and the stove, as Catesy prepared the lunch in the patio.

November 8, 1942

When Catalino sent us an electric plate, I thought our cooking problems were over. After mixing left-over rice, coconut milk, sugar, and cinnamon in a saucepan, I placed it on my electric plate. Nothing happened. The pan remained cold, for the current went off just at lunchtime. We ate the uncooked pudding, which tasted like nothing we had ever eaten. But, at least, we had the satisfaction of knowing it was good for us.

Yesterday and today, the large museum was open to all of us, so that we could view the excellent display of hobby crafts and art work that our internees had made.

The rag dolls and stuffed animals could have been proudly displayed in any toy department back home, while the buttons and buckles carved from shells, coconuts, wood and native seeds were excellent in design and originality.

The sketches and cartoons of camp life were most realistic, and many an internee chuckled when he recognized himself as the subject hanging on the wall.

November 11, 1942

This was a sad Armistice Day! Those who came in from passes, reported that they had seen hundreds of our soldiers marching to the piers en route to Japan.

One young woman from my room out on a pass ran after the marching soldiers in the hopes that one of them was her husband. But he was not there, though she asked many of the men about him.

November 13, 1942

What a pleasant change for Catesy and me to spend several hours in Don Juan's shack! As we sat around in easy chairs drinking kalamansi (lime) juice, I was struck by the contrast of his easy life compared to ours.

"D. J.," I asked curiously, "do you ever start a fire, prepare a meal, or stand in line?"

It was a foolish question, for one look at him slouched in an easy chair with one leg over the arm, answered me. He was the epitome of relaxed ease.

"Tess," he said with a congenial grin, "Blondie, here, doesn't like me to work. She stands in line and fetches the water, and she cooks for me. It's good for her figure!"

November 16, 1942

A heavy explosion followed by dense black smoke aroused us at siesta time. Pulses jumped beyond normal, and when more loud detonations were heard, hopes ran high. Were our planes bombing the city? We rushed to the windows to search the skies, but we saw nothing but empty blue sky with billowy white clouds.

November 17, 1942

Naval Rattle Rages off Algeria. War Plants Are Opened to 16- and 17-Year-Old Girls, in U. S. A.

Today, I was dreadfully depressed, disillusioned and hurt. I had trusted Catalino and Adoracion; but my next door neighbor in the apartment had written that the servants were selling my canned goods, clothes, and furniture. Not satisfied with that, Catalino had been making constant demands on Catesy for more money to buy the weekly supply of food which he had been sending us. A few of the other internees had had the same experience with their servants.

An entire year of constant propaganda against us had shaken their loyalty and faith, and no doubt some of them believed that the Americans would never return.

November 18, 1942

Yesterday's news about my servants had upset me terribly. I was depressed all day.

In bed by seven, and because I had nothing else to read, I started to re-read *Lost Horizon*.

With Tientsin Mary safely tucked away in an insane asylum, we thought our troubles were over, but, alas, we had another troublesome female to take her place. This woman had been found drunk and disorderly on two occasions, and now her latest offense was going over the wall with one of her boy friends. The moment they returned late at night, they were seized by internee guards.

The man was placed in the camp jail, and he was made to cut grass for two hours daily, while the woman was assigned to vegetable detail.

When she came to clean vegetables this morning, she was met by icy stares from the women, and I could scarcely restrain a snicker when I saw her costume for this extremely dirty detail. She had worn beautifully tailored and freshly laundered white sharkskin slacks, and on her hands, so help me, she had snow-white string gloves.

In a disgusted stage whisper that was heard by all of us, one woman remarked: "By all means, protect those hands that were meant for jewels by Tiffany!"

Several Domei newsmen interviewed the army nurses to get their reactions on the fall of Bataan and Corregidor. When one of the nurses asked them about the possibility of an exchange ship, their reply was an unpromising "perhaps."

The Domei men complimented the nurses on their calm behavior when the Imperial Forces reached Corregidor.

"We were calm all right," said Zest to me after the interview, "We didn't know whether we'd be raped or machine-gunned!"

Thanksgiving was in the air! The kids in the primary grades were drawing colored pictures of turkeys, and everywhere one heard talks about the wonderful spread people planned to have.

People who had eaten poorly since internment planned to splurge and spend their last penny, if necessary, for a grand feast. Even the people who ate well daily, looked forward to the big day.

Although Catalino sent word that the money we had sent him was not sufficient for a Thanksgiving dinner, we were hoping that he'd send us something a little different from our usual rice, Babinka pies, and other ingenious messes we concocted.

After morning services in the Father's garden, we prepared our lunch. Besides Catesy, Henry, Zest and myself, I had asked two other army nurses and a bachelor friend of Catesy's to share our Thanksgiving dinner.

Our table, underneath the low-hanging palm tree in the Father's garden, looked festive, in spite of the cracked cups, tin cans, and dime silverware.

Catalino had sent roast chickens and pumpkin pies, and I cooked boiled sweet potatoes, gravy, and a vegetable casserole. We were a happy and congenial group, and we felt that we had much to be thankful for.

When someone thoughtlessly asked: "I wonder if we'll spend another Thanksgiving in here," there was a silence and our gaiety after that was forced.

November 27, 1942

Among the three men who returned from a mental institution a few days ago, there was one who was actually insane. His actions, since his return to the camp, proved conclusively to the doctors that for his own safety he should be returned to a psycho ward. Today he was taken outside to the same hospital he had left a few days ago.

The morning *Nishi-Nishi* was anything but cheerful. It filled us with fearful doubts and pessimism.

> INVASION OF U. S. AIM OF JAPANESE IN PRESENT WAR. Col. Nakasima told a gathering of Japanese and Filipino newspaper men at the Manila Hotel that "the Japanese were poised for an attack on Alaska and Canada, with the Imperial Navy in control of the Pacific and with the destruction of the American Fleet at Pearl Harbor and in subsequent battles off the Solomons, it is only a question of time when the flag of the Rising Sun is hoisted in America."

November 29, 1942

The rubberneck tours with shutter-happy Nips went on.

Today, just as I came out of my room in sketchy one-piece shorts, I ran into a horde of Japanese civilians. I was hardly dressed for a delegation of Nipponese. Looking neither to the right nor left, I concentrated on a straight line to the bathroom, and there I stayed until the coast was clear.

November 30, 1942

Just as our English teacher in adult education touched on the events occurring in Wordsworth's life, which included the French Revolution, the lives of Lord Nelson and Napoleon, another delegation of Nips walked in.

The teacher, somewhat nervous, continued with his lecture while the Japanese lingered. When they finally left, the teacher said that he expected to be called about his class, as no doubt to them the lecture had sounded warlike and incendiary.

December 1, 1942

Shanty-town owners were worried today as four of the owners

found their shanties completely stripped of furnishings, food, and cooking utensils. Though internee guards patrolled the shanty areas at night, they were scarcely equipped for a hand-to-hand combat with an armed Filipino robber.

Margo and Kay were also worried as they, too, had a shack, and it held all their worldly possessions.

About sixteen shanty owners were granted permission by the Commandant to stay in their shacks at night. The robber stayed away that night.

Grandma had her roommates in stitches today. She had been mimicking in a high falsetto voice the often repeated axiom seen in the daily *Nishi-Nishi*.

"Be Wise, Nipponize, Economize."

December 3, 1942

We had another problem female in camp. She was a pint-size Russian woman of forty with the mentality of a nine-year-old. In her shabby and dirty clothes and battered-looking tennis shoes, she was a familiar figure to all of us. Today, for no apparent reason, she announced to the camp that she was pregnant — and in addition to her present predicament she was a kleptomaniac.

December 4, 1942

U. S. BATTLESHIP SUNK. CRUISER AUGUSTA CLASS IS BLASTED BY NIPPONESE NAVY.

A November 16, 1942, copy of *Time* magazine was passed around in camp and read surreptitiously and gleefully by many people.

If this mazagine were ever found by the Nips, there would be trouble. Consequently, those who were privileged to read it were handpicked and considered absolutely trustworthy. The presence of this recent issue of an American magazine in the city raised delightful thoughts. It proved beyond a shadow of a doubt that our submarines were operating in Philippine waters, and that our guerrilla forces were organized.

In bed by eight to read a "Critical Essay on the *Rubaiyat* of Omar Khayyam" by Clarence Darrow — of all people. I was surprised to learn that this clever lawyer had other achievements besides grandstanding before an awestruck jury.

December 12, 1942

We were worried about the morning headline.

U. S. RETREAT IN SOLOMONS INEVITABLE — OBSERVER SAYS AMERICA NO MATCH FOR JAPAN.

We asked the people who came in for pass renewals for news, but they had no news. The radios were strangely silent.

AMERICAN PRESS CREATING ILLUSION THAT U. S. WON BIG VICTORY IN SOLOMONS.

The later headline cheered us. Perhaps we had won a victory!

The near approach of Christmas was evident in all the rooms, as women searched for scraps of silk and other materials to make dolls and dresses. When the supply of kapok and cotton to stuff the dolls was exhausted, rags, straw, and paper were substituted.

December 14, 1942

General Tanaka Issues Statement — Says Sacred War Must Be Led to Successful Finish.

For the last few days I've been trying to persuade Catesy to get a shanty. It would give us a place to cook our meals out of the rain and sun, and it would permit us to keep all our equipment under one roof. We could raise our own vegetables and flowers. But, best of all, we would be alone and away from the boiler factory, at least until sundown.

Another new subdivision called Garden Court was opened in the rear of the former hospital.

This morning when Catesy and I walked over to Garden Court to admire the orderly flower and vegetable gardens that surrounded the shacks, I was smitten with envy and longing to have a shack of our own. What bliss to be able to work in my own garden! What happiness I'd enjoy if I had a roof over my head, even though two sides of the shack were completely open to the elements!

Shanty people had somewhat of the same thrill and pride of ownership as a suburban owner had back in good old U. S. A.

Now that the Commandant had given permission to open this new subdivision, would-be owners were besieging the mayor of this area for a home site. Just as quickly as the site was chosen, one of the three internee contractors was consulted. The size, type and price of shanty was selected and ordered, and in about a week, the shanty was completely assembled and wheeled into camp. Everytime I saw one of these shanties being wheeled into camp, I was reminded of the song: "Did you ever see a dream (house) walking?"

At last Catesy succumbed to my needling, and late this afternoon we walked over to Garden Court, and with the help of the young mayor who used to be a neighbor of mine at the apartment, we chose a site next to the high stone wall and barbed wire that surrounded the rear section of Santo Tomas.

December 15, 1942

Because all the good shanty sites were already taken, ours was swamp land, and Catesy was anything but thrilled at the prospect of all the fill-in work he had ahead of him. However, Henry came to his rescue and for several hours a day they brought many wheelbarrow loads of dirt from another part of the camp.

December 16, 1942

NIPPON AIR UNITS DESTROY 54 PLANES, SINK 11 VESSELS.

The delightful prospects of owning a shack had given me a new interest, and I felt like whistling while I worked. I could scarcely wait until the shanty arrived.

The camp was in a jubilant and expectant mood. We were told by our room monitors that the long-awaited Red Cross kits from the homeland had arrived, and that a hundred of our men were asked to help with the unloading of the cases at the piers. This was wonderful news. When would we receive the kits? This question was on everyone's lips.

Catesy was busy with wheelbarrow, pick and shovel all morning, and his hands were blistered, despite the home-made mittens I had made for him.

I sneaked over to the contractor's shack to pay him for our shack, but he refused to accept my traveler's checks. It seemed as though I wouldn't be able to help Catesy pay for the shack after all, and it worried me, for I began to feel that perhaps I had been too persistent about something we couldn't afford.

December 19, 1942

I was greatly concerned over Catesy. He looked ill. What had I done? He refused to stop digging and wheeling the heavy loads of dirt to our shanty site, and now I wished that I had never started the shanty project.

In the evening, when we sat on the plaza, he remained silent and depressed, and my frequent questions about his health made him irritable and almost sullen.

December 20, 1942

Over a hundred tired and dirty-looking men, women and children, and several dozen priests arrived in camp with their luggage and cooking utensils. Just about the time they started to disembark from the trucks to register at the Commandant's office, a noisy rumpus broke out at the camp hospital.

One of the male workers went amuck from a combination of bad liquor, bad heart, and nerves, and after being subdued he was hustled off to the camp jail. Since the jail was directly behind the Commandant's office, the disturbance caused by his continual shouting and pounding on the walls brought two Japanese guards running on the double.

When he finally quieted down, we watched the new arrivals from Cebu get settled. The trip from Cebu, on a small Japanese boat, had taken five days, and the people had been crowded into a hold where they stayed for the entire voyage with never a bath or a change of clothing.

One of the most happy and touching reunions was between a three-year-old girl and her parents, who had been in Santo Tomas. The parents had been en route from Manila to Cebu over a year ago on the ill-fated *S. S. Corregidor,* which struck a mine and sank in a few minutes. They had been among the few who survived. Now, after a year of separation, they met their little girl, who scarcely knew them.

December 21, 1942

If I could abandon the shack idea, I would do it.

Catesy stubbornly refused to take a few days' rest away from the digging and hauling of dirt. He looked ill, and I knew that the work was too much for him.

December 22, 1942

The camp vendors had caught the Yuletide spirit, and for the last two weeks their booths had been displaying bits of last year's tinsel, ribbon, and wrapping paper.

Tonight the women's and men's chorus sang Christmas carols in the plaza under the stars. The beauty of the night, the Christmas carols, and our uncertain situation, made me feel sad and "weepy." If I could have found a private hole to crawl into, I would have liked nothing better than to allow myself the luxury of unrestrained tears.

December 23, 1942

There were happy smiles and joyous cries throughout this camp when internees opened their Red Cross kits. Cheese, chocolates, soups, powdered milk and cans of meat and dried fruit!

In the evening, we went to the movies under the stars. The Japanese had promised us movies more than nine months ago. The first picture was propaganda, "The Youth in Japan," and since we had been warned by our monitors to avoid demonstrations of any kind, we sat through the ordeal quietly and impatiently.

When the second propaganda picture, "The Backbone of the Japanese Empire" flashed across the screen, we fidgeted nervously. This was hardly the kind of movies we had been hungering for!

Finally, after what seemed like hours, a delightful comedy with Rosalind Russell and Don Ameche flashed before our eyes, and we were enchanted. Just about the time we were beginning to relax and enjoy the zany antics of the long-legged Rosalind, the picture stopped and the camp announcer reminded us that it was time for roll call, and that the picture would be completed after Christmas. Though we felt like weeping with vexation, we meekly

140

picked up our chairs and marched to our respective rooms.

December 24, 1942

In spite of prison walls, Christmas was evident everywhere. Packages beautifully wrapped and tinseled were being sent into camp every day.

By nine o'clock tonight, it was a well-known fact that some of the packages had contained liquor, for here and there one could see men who had guzzled a bit too freely. The Japanese guards, being sake-bent themselves, closed their eyes when they met an internee who had been drinking.

December 25, 1942

Christmas, 1942, was a day of joy and happy reunions. It was a day of sadness too! It was also the day when nearly everyone ate well!

The front, as well as the rear grounds of the University, had all the appearance of a mammoth picnic at a State Park back home.

More than seven hundred relatives from the outside with their children were permitted to spend a few hours in camp, and most of them were the families of Spanish-American veterans in camp. The visitors came loaded with huge baskets, boxes and bayongs filled with food, which they spread on the ground and ate picnic style.

The package sheds were jammed with baskets, platters and bundles of food. There were roast turkeys, ducks, and chickens galore! Huge layer cakes glistened with extravagant frostings decorated with "Merry Christmas."

The wide gates of Santo Tomas opened to permit a carromata with its driver to pass through. Stretched across the front and back seat of the carromata were four succulent roast pigs, barbecued to a golden brown and thrust through with long bamboo poles.

The heavenly odor of roast pig brought the saliva to our mouths, and we wished that we had been included in the lechon (roast pig) party. The Philippine Bureau of Mines had sent the pigs to about three hundred of their interned gold-mining people.

A husky six-foot American passed us with a long bamboo pole, to which was attached another mouth-watering lechon. A long red ribbon with a Christmas card dangled from the pole on his shoulder.

Greetings were scarcely over between the interned and the visiting relatives when the loud-speaker blared the sad announcement that all visitors had to leave within the hour.

In the back of the Big House, a large Christmas tree sent from the outside shone with its decorations in the brilliant sunshine.

The five hundred or more camp kids ran around excitedly,

141

red-faced, perspiring, and deliriously happy. The hand-made gifts
were distributed to the children by Santa, and by this time the
children were tired, and many of them were sick from the un-
accustomed rich food. While many of the kids rode their newly
acquired scooters and wagons, oblivious to the heat and the dense
crowds, other kids screamed and howled with fatigue and excitement.

Japanese photographers were everywhere taking pictures of
crowds and children.

Three other army nurses had shared our Christmas dinner of
roast chicken with all the trimmings, and just as we began to
clear the table, a blushing and embarrassed Henry and Zest
stood up to announce their engagement. After congratulations and
good wishes were over, we washed the dishes, and by that time
Henry had become ill and had to return to his room to lie down.

"It must have been the fruit cake!" he said weakly, as Zest led
him to his room.

I, too, had a proposal of marriage, and from a most unexpected
source. Mr. Nagy, my gallant Hungarian friend, had sent flowers,
candy, and a proposal of marriage.

In his censored note, he had been scrupulous in explaining that
he expected the war to last several years and that he could not
bear to think of a countrywoman of his in a concentration camp
for such a long period. By marrying a Hungarian national, I would
be permitted to live outside. He explained that our marriage
would be in name only, and that after the war, if I wished, I could
get a divorce.

Naturally, I was touched by his kindness and consideration for
me, especially by his ready consent to a divorce, as I knew him
to be a good Catholic. His reference to a long internment made
Catesy and me depressed. Somehow, we could not bear to think
beyond another six months of this life. As Catesy helped me to
compose a diplomatic letter of refusal to Mr. Nagy's proposal, I
wondered if any other girl had ever been helped by her fiancé
in a like situation.

When we reached the backstair landing, we kissed good-night,
and for a second my hand touched his forehead. His skin was
hot and dry! I became alarmed. "You must see a doctor right
away!" I insisted.

"I'm all right, and don't you send a doctor to my room, either!"
he answered me irritably.

December 26, 1942

There were many sick people in the camp today. The rich food
had been too much for them, and because of lack of refrigeration

142

many people gorged themselves rather than see the food spoil. Many attributed their illness to the lovely-looking cakes, made with musty flour and the hated cassava root.

The hospital did a rushing business with bicarbonate and castor oil, and many were so ill they had to be hospitalized.

December 27, 1942

People were still ill with dizziness, nausea and vomiting.

Many of the shanty owners had abused the rules about staying in their shanties until sundown, and others had completely ignored the rules about two open sides.

Tonight, our room monitors read us the following notice issued by our Internee Committee:

> The Commandant has intimated to us in no uncertain terms that the attitude of the Japanese authorities in regard to sexual relations under conditions of internment has not been changed, and if we are to avoid segregation of the sexes in this camp and retain other privileges such as the use of shanties at any time, as well as restricted areas after sundown, it is absolutely necessary that these privileges are not abused.

December 28, 1942

The movies were repeated tonight, and though we saw "The Youth of Japan" for the second time, we were happy as kids on Christmas morning when we were able to see the Rosalind Russell film to its frolicking end.

There was a Donald Duck and Popeye cartoon, and when the show was over the kids were still shouting and squealing with delight as they hashed over the antics of Donald and Popeye.

December 29, 1942

Now that we were back on our lean diets, digestions improved.

There was a great deal of gossip as to what couple or couples had precipitated all the sudden changes regarding shanty life. In all the rooms and on the bulletin boards, this notice was posted: "Shanties are to be used between the hours of 7:00 A.M. and 6:30 P.M. The construction of shanties must be such that they provide protection against sun and rain, but the interior must be open to view on at least two sides and at no time is it permitted for shanties to be closed when in use."

December 31, 1942

New Year's Eve! For the past week, people in the city had been shooting fire crackers, native bamboo cannons and modern guns in anticipation of the New Year. The noise reminded us of happier years when we had cause to rejoice.

The internee liquor patrol kept busy searching the shanties for liquor and carefully inspecting the packages at the gate. If, in spite of these precautions, an internee was found drunk, he received sixty days in the local brig, instead of the usual thirty days.

Only two drunks were thrown into jail to keep company with an old violator of several weeks ago. Three offenders among thirty-seven hundred or more people was a small percentage, and it spoke well for the character of our people and the discipline of our various committees.

1 9 4 3

January 1, 1943

A few months ago, Catesy made a bet with one of our more affluent friends that we wouldn't be out by New Year's Day. The prize, if Catesy was right, was a roast turkey, and today we were enjoying the beautifully roasted turkey.

There were eight of us to enjoy the delicious bird, but I wished that our feasts didn't come so close together. How much better it would have been to have this feast after a long period of lean rations!

The big event in the afternoon was the football game in the Telinum Bowl, named after a native vegetable, which was supposedly dripping with vitamins.

January 2, 1943

Just one year ago today, they had entered the city! To celebrate this great event, Japanese planes sashayed back and forth over our heads in parade formation.

The names of a husband and wife were publicly announced over the P. A. system because they had stayed all night in their shanty. The wife was confined to her room in the Big House, while the husband was given sixty days in jail with two hours out for exercise — cutting grass.

January 3, 1943

1943 Should Be a Year of Glorious Achievement.

We were fortunate to buy six cans of Carnation milk at P1.20 a can from a camp vendor, and we were surprised that the cans were shiny and the labels sparkled with newness.

U. S. — Britain Lost 7267 Planes Since the Outbreak of the War.

The rumor was being circulated in camp that sixty-five thousand Americans had landed in the Celebes. This was the type of news we loved, and it had many stepping on air!

When we questioned people who had been out on passes, who

145

might have had access to radios, we became angry when they informed us that they hadn't heard that particular news on the radio.

January 5, 1943

This date I shall never forget! We entered the camp just one year ago today — on my wedding day that never materialized.

At last I had a showdown with Catesy. Regardless of his angry protests, I marched him to see Dr. Fisher, an old friend, and well-loved civilian American doctor, who was now head of the camp hospital.

When I turned back, Catesy was meekly following the doctor into a small room that served as his office.

In about half an hour, Dr. Fisher and Catesy rejoined me. The doctor assured me that there was no cause for alarm which, of course, immediately threw me into a panic. He said that he would try to get permission from the Commandant and a Japanese doctor so that Catesy could get a chest X ray and fluoroscopic outside.

As I tried to mumble my thanks, the doctor put his arms around me in a consoling manner, and he promised to do everything possible for Catesy.

For many hours that night, I lay in my bed, sleepless and disturbed. I could not keep my mind off the fact that a year ago today I would have been a bride, if the Japs hadn't come. Now a year later to the day, I was still behind bars but — what was far more tragic — Catesy was ill, and I felt certain that he had T.B.

January 6, 1943

All the enthusiasm and delight about owning a shack were gone! When the shack contractor informed us this morning that our nipa house would arrive tomorrow, no doubt, he wondered why we remained silent and unenthusiastic, when a few days ago we had been pestering him daily about when it would arrive.

We met Dr. Fisher in front of the Education Building, and he told us that it had been arranged for Catesy to go out to the San Juan de Dios hospital for his examination. After we had thanked him, we traced our steps back to the Big House, and we felt almost lighthearted.

January 7, 1943

Catesy left this morning by bus, along with other sick people. Each of them wore a red arm band with Japanese characters signifying that the wearer was an enemy national.

As I watched the bus disappear through the front gate, the thought struck me that it was ironic that he should go through those gates for the first time since a year ago. Not as a free man,

146

but as a very sick man who wore the hated red arm band, symbolizing his servitude to an enemy.

It was also ironic that our shanty was wheeled in by six Filipinos an hour later. They immediately set to work by driving long bamboo posts into the ground, to support the house.

As I watched them working, I felt no elation over the clean and fresh-smelling nipa hut, for I knew that Catesy would not be with me to enjoy it.

A few hours later, the nipa house was all set up and I was ready to move in with my bridge table, pots, pans, iron skillet and tin cans.

When I met Catesy in the evening chow line, one look at his face told me what I had suspected. The well-known T.B. man, Dr. Gueverra, at the San Juan de Dios hospital, had found a spot in each lung and he had recommended a year of absolute rest, and Dr. Fisher had already made arrangements to admit Catesy to the camp hospital in the morning.

That night when supper dishes were washed, we sat in the plaza and planned how we would manage to provide supplementary feedings for him.

"I know the first thing we'll do is to stop sharing our rapidly vanishing food and money with others, now that it is so important that you have nourishing food. That's probably one reason why you are sick now. You've worried long enough about how you can feed and provide for others. Let them start worrying and scrounging for themselves!" I declared angrily.

"But, what will you do all by yourself, honey?"

"I'm going to break up our mess the first thing in the morning, and then I'm going to clean vegetables all morning and every day for the Annex—which means that I'll be provided with a fairly decent lunch and the money we've been spending for our lunch will be used for additional food for you."

"But it means paring and cleaning vegetables for four hours daily, and that's hard work under these conditions." He lifted my hands and looked at the broken nails and vegetable-stained fingers.

"My hands weren't meant for jewelry by Tiffany, anyway!" I remarked laughingly.

When I crawled under my net that night, I remembered that I had completely forgotten to tell him that our shanty had arrived and was ready for occupancy.

January 8, 1943

After breakfast, I walked over to the camp hospital to help him get settled for his long stay. The second-floor ward was filled with fifteen other T.B. cases, and like all patients suffering from this disease, they were smiling and cheerful, and I was happy to hear them give Catesy a noisy and enthusiastic welcome.

Before I left, I promised to visit him twice a day and bring him any extra food that I could buy or beg.

With a heavy heart, I went to my shanty and spent the rest of the day moving in with my pans, stove, and other gear.

While I labeled and scrubbed tin cans, which held such staples as pepper, salt, cassava flour, and brown sugar, a large pot of navy beans boiled merrily in the yard. If Catesy had been with me, this would have been a happy day.

Like a robot, I moved about my work, trying not to think. All the joy that I had anticipated with moving to a shanty was gone, with Catesy lying ill in a T.B. ward.

The handsome Mayor of Garden Court called to welcome me and to express his sympathy regarding Catesy.

After he left, three men came to plant hibiscus bushes around my shack, and they promised to come back to plant morning-glories near the unsightly stone wall that was only a few feet from my shack. On top of the stone wall there was barbed wire, also broken glass, and I thought that morning-glories would certainly enhance those grim walls.

Now I had seen everything! I could only marvel and admire the efficiency of our people. They had thought of everything! The shacks not only had to be neat and clean, but the tiny yards around each shack had to be planted with flowers and present an orderly appearance from the outside.

A friendly neighbor across the road brought me a slice of cake that she had just baked in a large tin can, placed over the primitive charcoal stove.

I visited my patient in the afternoon and took him a dozen bananas and three avocados which I had bought at the vendor's. He was not too unhappy, and had resigned himself to a long stay in bed.

January 9, 1943

Daring Reich Sub Goes up Mississippi. We refused to believe the nonsensical headline.

Henry built me some shelves for the swali wall, and when I placed some of my cracked but colorful California pottery on it, I was pleased at the change it had made. How desperately we all strove for a homelike atmosphere!

The neighbors to my right had two little children, a boy and a girl, and I heard the little girl asking her mother, "Mommy, why don't we go home?"

"But this is your home, darling!"

"I mean our other home!" said the child impatiently.

January 12, 1943

I watched the Military Police from Fort Santiago rounding up twenty-seven of our men who had admitted their connections with the army and navy.

They weren't given time to collect any of their belongings. Not so much as a razor. As the bus started to move down the long road to the front gate, several of the men threw their money out of the bus to their friends.

A wild-eyed and breathless young women with a baby in her arms arrived too late to say good-bye to her husband. Leaning against the side of the building, white-faced and distressed, she broke into heartrending sobs.

January 13, 1943

Catesy was a model patient. He obeyed all the rules and he ate everything that was set before him, and still had room for the bananas, avocados and other food I bought him twice a day. The lines on his face were less tense, and he seemed to be more cheerful.

The army nurses moved out of the long frame dwelling into the Big House. Their former dwelling was to be used as a kitchen for mothers and children.

The nurses gave me most of the plants they had planted around their former dormitory and I spent a happy and pleasant day puttering among my marigolds, gardenias, phlox, and hibiscus. I could scarcely wait until they were in bloom.

January 18, 1943

There was considerable talk and speculation in my room tonight as to what would happen to the women who were pregnant.

"Well, I'm going to bed," announced Great-grandma "I don't have to worry about anything like that!"

January 19, 1943

The following instructions were announced over the P.A. system followed by a written circular posted in all the rooms.

> The Commandant has issued the following order: "Confirming my verbal instruction of this morning, it is hereby ordered that all pregnant women, whether married or single, in this camp be transferred immediately to the Hospicio de San Jose. Further, those internees who have just given birth are to be transferred to the Hospicio de San Jose as soon as their recovery permits.
>
> All men involved in the above cases are to be placed under confinement in the building at the rear of the Commandant's

office with minimum essential equipment and no exercise privileges.

The Commandant has stated his dissatisfaction with the manner in which shanties are used and the lack of compliance on the part of some shanty owners with the orders providing that interior of shanties must be completely open to view at all times of occupancy with no suggestion of privacy.

January 20, 1943

Four of the "pregnant papas" — as the camp had named them — were starting to serve their thirty days of confinement in the camp jail. These men had been placed in the jail without the barest necessities and with no exercise privileges. Some of the women were chortling over the fact that the men, at last, were serving a term of confinement along with their women.

January 21, 1943

We had to clear out of our shanties! Only families with children under twelve, and married couples over fifty were permitted to stay in their shanties between the hours of 10 A.M. and 2 P.M.

I was crushed. Darn it! Why did the innocent always take the rap with the guilty? It reminded me of the time I was a student nurse. I had just been capped, and I could still remember the glow and pride I felt in my new pleated student cap, as I hustled around the ward.

One of the student nurses had thrown a patient's gown down the clothes chute, but she had forgotten to remove the patient's dentures, which he had carelessly left in the pocket.

We were all punished. Not only did we lose our beautiful new caps for two months, but we had to pay for new dentures out of our stipend of eight dollars a month.

Once again, my happiness was short-lived.

The grand exodus from the shanties started immediately!

After rolling the swali down on the two open sides of my house, I latched the door and gave my little home a last fond look. I had left everything in it, except my tin plate, cup, and large spoon. My sorrow at leaving my new garden was somewhat eased when my neighbor with the two little children promised to water my plants.

Though I realized that the pregnant women were the immediate cause of my leaving my shanty, I felt saddened when I watched them being hustled into buses that would take them outside and away from their husbands. Most of the women were red-eyed from weeping and some of their older children clung to them in a last desperate embrace. Since their men were already in the camp jail, they left without the consolation of a last farewell from them.

150

January 24, 1943

We had the dubious distinction of being visited by General Tanaka, the Number One man of the Philippines. The Commandant will be most unhappy when he learns of his visit, as he had been at a golf tournament at one of the country clubs.

January 25, 1943

Those without shacks had long ceased to gloat over our predicament now that they found they were directly inconvenienced by all the extra people in the dishwashing, clothes-washing, chow and other lines.

Daphne was in a terrific huff tonight. She and her husband had just settled themselves comfortably on the lawn when the guards informed them that sitting on the lawn after 6 P.M. was prohibited.

"Don't do this, don't do that!" chanted Grandma in a stage whisper that was heard by the entire room.

January 29, 1943

It was a happy day for shanty people! They smiled as they lugged heavy boxes, crates and other furniture back into their shanties. I felt absolute bliss to be back in my home, and away from everyone.

My morning-glories had been faithfully watered by my good neighbor, and they had grown over a foot. The other plants were doing beautifully, too.

January 30, 1943

Today I bought a large clay pot with a wide lid on top. This was to be my oven, and it proved to be a good one.

The first thing I baked was a banana spice cake. Talk about primitive baking methods! This had my mother's old coal range beat a mile!

After making a red-hot charcoal fire in my tiny native stove, I set the clay oven on top for pre-heating, while I mixed my batter of rice and cassava flour, duck eggs, bananas, spices, soda, prunes, and raisins. The last two items were from my precious Red Cross kit. When the oven was hot enough, I placed my batter in an angel cake pan and set it down in the oven.

Though I was completely exhausted after numerous stokings, fanning, removing, and replacing the oven back on the stove, the results were far beyond my expectations. The finished cake was high, light, and had a delicious aroma.

When Catesy complimented me on the cake, he remarked, "Why, you get better results on that native stove than with your electric range at the apartment! Remember that four-layer birthday cake you baked for me about two years ago?"

How well I remembered! Catesy would never stop teasing me

151

about it as the four layers stacked together scarcely had been higher than a single pancake.

January 31, 1943

Something in the evening chow upset many people and I was among them. After my afternoon visit to the hospital, I went to bed and stayed there.

February 2, 1943

Five Enemy Warships Sunk off Solomons.

Our Commandant spoke to us tonight in the plaza and he reminded us repeatedly that his job had been a particularly hard one, to please the military and to serve the internees. We appreciated his position. He made one slip when he said, "We can afford to be magnanimous as long as we are victorious." Now we knew what to expect when the tide turned!

February 3, 1943

"Here comes your convoy!" shouted Catesy's wardmates when I walked into the ward with my arms loaded with bananas, avocados, or cake.

Besides the three rather sketchy hospital meals for a T.B., he ate a dozen and a half bananas and three avocados daily. Though his afternoon temperature was still up, he had gained a little weight.

February 4, 1943

The strain of this unnatural life was beginning to show on people with highly nervous and volatile temperaments. For the second time this week, Margo had an attack of hysterics followed by periods of depression and uncontrollable weeping. One of the camp doctors finally had to give her a sedative.

We had women in the camp hospital who lay in their beds motionless, and staring into space.

February 5, 1943

Mr. and Mrs. Mack never seemed to lose their optimism and faith that the war would be over in a few months. Were they kidding themselves, or did they really believe it? I wished I had their optimism.

Mrs. Mack's pretty blonde hair was generously sprinkled with silver, and I noticed that Mr. Mack had lost considerable weight, but they had their usual sparkle and cheerful smile.

February 7, 1943

A heavy rain came suddenly this afternoon and old Sunshiners remarked that it had been the first rain that they recalled during February in thirty years.

I spent the evening with a group of old Shanghailanders during the musical broadcast. It was interesting to note that all of them believed that after the war business would once more boom for them in Shanghai. They firmly believed that the white man's star would shine again.

February 9, 1943

How fortunate we were to have such gifted professional and amateur entertainers!

Tonight some of our talented internees broadcast the old Broadway hit *Arsenic and Old Lace,* and it was enjoyed by everyone.

February 10, 1943

The headline had us jubilant, smiling, and walking on air.

ORDERLY RETREAT OF JAPANESE FROM SOLOMONS AND NEW GUINEA. JAPAN SET FOR NEW DRIVE IN PACIFIC.

My patient had gained a pound and, because of the headline, he and the rest of his wardmates were as cheerful as a spinster in a convention of bachelors.

As I worked around my shack today, I felt at peace with the world.

February 14, 1943

From the money I saved from disbanding our mess, I bought two cases of canned milk at forty-one pesos a case. From now on, I hoped to build up a reserve of canned food.

Since I received my noonday lunch at the Annex, I no longer had to spend money for my food except on rare occasions when I felt especially hungry.

My hands were bruised and blistered, and blood oozed from the cuts inflicted by paring knife and hard-skinned vegetables, but each day I was becoming more practiced and swift.

Early to bed to nurse a terrific cold.

February 18, 1943

The sun baths, which I started to take daily after lunch, were good medicine. There were times when I felt that I had never known any other life, and the thoughts of changing my present routine filled me with dread. The despised restrictions, walls, and chains had become familiar, and many of us were afraid of a change.

February 20, 1943

U. S. WAR SECRETARY ADMITS DEBACLE ON TUNISIA FRONT.

One of Grandma's old friends died of a heart attack last night. "What a fine way to go, especially now!" remarked Grandma.

There was a picture of the Archbishop of Manila and other Catholic priests standing beside Lieutenant General Tanaka, Commander-in-Chief of the Imperial Japanese Army in the Philippines, on the front page of the morning paper.

Underneath the picture were these five words: "The Sword and the Cross."

February 22, 1943

FOUR CHUNGKING DIVISIONS ANNIHILATED. ROOSEVELT ADMITS DIFFICULTY OF SENDING AID TO CHUNGKING.

Margo and Kay hadn't heard from their husbands in months. Kay was tense and quiet, while Margo was nervous and extremely despondent.

The entire camp was turned inside and out in searching for a four-year-old boy. Just as the hysterical mother's weeping had reached the uncontrollable stage, the prodigal returned. With eyes sparkling with excitement, he told about his wonderful ride in the ambulance to the Philippine General Hospital, where the nurses had given him a good lunch and fed him "lots and lots of peanuts!"

February 24, 1943

IMPERIAL BENEVOLENCE MAKES P. I. INDEPENDENCE POSSIBLE.

"What bunk!" remarked Grandma in disgust after I had read her the headline.

The names of two women and a man were announced over the loud speaker. They had been caught drinking by our internee patrol.

These irresponsible nitwits were the worry of the entire camp.

Our Recreation Committee had arranged to have boxing tonight. The boxers included four-year-olds and up to the professional class.

There'll be no wormy cereal for me in the morning! Tomorrow I'm going to splurge and serve pancakes to six of my army nurse friends. My two charcoal stoves were laid and ready for the match, and beside them were two new palm-leaf fans. The other two fans had long since worn out from frequent use.

Two days ago I had prepared a pancake starter from left-over mush, coconut milk, sugar, and crushed bananas. It now had a frothy and mildewed scum on top, which assured me that the pancakes tomorrow would be light as a feather. To this starter, I would add rice and cassava flour.

February 28, 1943

These little special feasts helped to make life livable! What fun, to be with old friends and to eat something different from the scurvy cereal!

The pancakes were high and light, and the syrup made from the brown sugar tasted like honey, while the bacon from my Red Cross kit — well, words failed me completely.

154

We would have lingered and chatted over a second cup of coffee, if we had had it. The memory of this delightful breakfast will stay with us for many days to come.

En route to the hospital, I stopped to chat with Harvey Jones, our hard-working emcee. He stood around guarding a clothesline sagging with theatrical costumes and wigs of all shapes, sizes, and colors.

"But surely, no one would swipe anything like that!" I remarked.

"A kleptomaniac isn't too particular!" said he with his infectious grin.

At the hospital door, two men were carrying a handsome young priest on a stretcher. He was my favorite batter, and he had been injured on the ball field.

March 1, 1943

I candied the thick skin of a pomolo, which is a native fruit much larger than a grapefruit, but less juicy. Standing over the hot stove in the tropical heat was like working in front of an open-hearth furnace in a Pittsburgh steel mill, but the candied peel was good, and well worth the effort.

I started to read *Kabloona* tonight. Excellent tropical and prison-camp reading.

March 3, 1943

Enemy Shipping Losses Heavy. The pretty Dutch and Spanish girl in my room received a note from her fiancé after fourteen months of silence. He had been transferred to a military camp only a few blocks from ours. He wrote that he had been ill with dysentery, pellagra, beri-beri, and that he had lost sixty pounds.

In the good old days when I had lived in the sixth-floor apartment, high enough to get the breeze from Manila Bay, I had hardly noticed the heat. In here, most of us were covered with prickly heat as we stood in the broiling sun for long periods to get near the chow, the vendors, the sinks, and other lines.

Today I bought peanuts from the vendors, and after roasting them, I made a pitcher of kalamansi, lime juice, and took them to my patient and his neighbors.

March 6, 1943

There was a great deal of air activity over our heads day and night, and many of our people were ready to swear on a Bible that the planes were American. They were certain that the planes were ours because they were larger, a more brilliant silver, and there was a different sound from their motors.

More humbug, as Grandma would say. But wouldn't it be wonderful if it were true?

The picture in the morning *Nishi-Nishi* would strike terror in a heart far braver than mine. It showed a fierce-looking Japanese soldier in full war regalia with bayonet thrust toward the viewer. Underneath the picture were these words: *Uitesi Yama!* "Crush Anglo-Saxons!"

An impressive-looking delegation of high-ranking Japanese officers, all of them tall and well-built, came to look at us. Their chests were lavishly decorated with medals and campaign ribbons, and I would have given a sound tooth if I could have snatched off a ribbon that represented the conquest of Corregidor.

March 8, 1943

The rumor that Tokyo had been bombed for five hours had us stepping on pink clouds, though many of us wondered if it was just more humbug.

March 9, 1943

P. I. BUSY GETTING RID OF FLIMSY AMERICANISM. LOCAL AMERICANS ENJOY WHAT JAPANESE IN U. S. ARE DENIED.

Not by the wildest stretch of the imagination would I call the treatment received by our fellow Americans at Fort Santiago enjoyable. One of the victims, a fellow American, who had gone through the Spanish Inquisition handed out at Fort Santiago, returned to us today. The startling change in this man shocked all of us. Though still comparatively young, his hair had turned completely white and he was crippled and shockingly emaciated. The "enjoyable" treatment that he had received at the Fort in nine months of imprisonment had turned him into an old and broken man.

March 10, 1943

Another large group of weary and dirty-looking men, women and children from the southern islands entered our camp. They carried their possessions in sacks, baskets and bundles, and they looked like hoboes from a jungle town rather than respectable folks.

We gave these people a royal welcome and we helped to get them settled in their new surroundings. Many of the people were old and feeble and some of them could scarcely walk. Just as quickly as they had registered in the Japanese office, they were whisked off to the camp hospital.

At the hospital, there was another upheaval. Old patients who hadn't quite recovered had to be discharged to their rooms to clear the beds for the new arrivals. Fortunately, the T.B.'s were not disturbed.

March 11, 1943

Several of the newcomers were assigned to our room, and we

lost an inch or more of precious space. Dolefully, we wondered how many more would be squeezed into our room.

Repatriation rumors were in the air, and those who took the news seriously were already packing.

I sat outside for an hour to watch the boxing matches. The boxing between the professionals was good, but the highlight of the whole evening was between the seven-year-olds.

My little seven-year-old shack neighbor was one of the contestants, and after he had won, he said confidentially, "You know, I thought I was a goner when I started to cry in the second round!"

March 13, 1943

GUERRILLA CHIEF SURRENDERS UNIT. It was rumored in camp that the Major's wife had been kept as a hostage in Fort Santiago until he surrendered.

Floor and room monitors went from room to room armed with tape measures and, of course, we knew what that meant. Could we stand any more crowdedness than already existed? At roll call tonight, among other problems, we discussed our cramped quarters.

March 14, 1943

Don Juan and his current blonde were sitting on Catesy's bed when I arrived this afternoon. The blonde was wearing suggestively abbreviated shorts.

All the men in the ward fixed their fascinated gaze at the long expanse of beautifully proportioned tan legs. She would wear those skimpy shorts in a men's ward, I thought wrathfully, and a bit enviously, while I had on my misshapen and faded slacks. The white turtle-neck sweater, which she wore, hugged her exactly where it mattered.

Catesy was enjoying himself immensely, while Don Juan, the picture of relaxed ease, with one arm resting lightly on the blonde's shoulder, was telling a naughty story in a thick Scotch brogue.

March 15, 1943

Kay and Margo heard from their husbands today, and it was good to witness their joy. Their men were at Billibid, only a few blocks from us, but they might as well have been in Manchuria for all the good it did them.

Most of the wives of military prisoners had given up the beautiful dream promised them by the Nips — that they would visit their men in prison camps. That promise had come many months ago and, so far, nothing had come of it.

March 19, 1943

The primitive cooking facilities and lack of proper ingredients should have driven us to babbling idiocy; instead, it challenged

our ingenuity. We were always trying out new recipes with new
substitutes, and if we discovered something that was halfway
edible, by nightfall, everyone in camp had the new recipe.

Even Fanny Farmer, with her wealth of experience, would
have had moments of despair.

Today I baked a lime meringue pie, and it was a horrible mess!
But no wonder! Nearly every ingredient in the pie was a substitute never found in cookbooks. In a few days, I'll try again, but
I'll compare notes with other women and perhaps from their
combined experiments with substitutes, I'll strike pay dirt.

March 22, 1943

ENEMY POWERLESS TO COMBAT U-BOATS.

About thirty of our fellow nationals, out on passes and releases
were picked up on the streets of the city by the military police.
The Japanese claimed that most of these people had no legitimate reason to be out, and I was told that they were fined fifty
and a hundred pesos apiece. Two of the men in the group were
given ninety days, to be served in the infamous Fort Santiago.

I planted a papaya seedling outside the door of my shack, and
I was told that in less than a year it would bear fruit. I wondered
if I would still be here.

From my Red Cross kit I produced a can of cocoa, and I decided
to use some of it today to make a devil's-food cake. Cassava and
rice flour, duck eggs, brown sugar, coconut milk, soda and, *Voilà*
—there was my cake!

Stuffing my patient with avocados, bananas, and cake started
to pay off. He gained ten pounds, but he was still far below his
prewar weight and his temperature remained elevated.

While Catesy was gaining steadily, I was losing weight, but
thank goodness my lungs were sound and I could afford to slough
off more avoirdupois. In fact, the less I ate, the better my tricky
stomach felt.

March 28, 1943

The health of the camp, as a whole, continued to be fairly good
if one discounted the many deficiency cases that we already had.
The hospital census fluctuated between eighty and one hundred
patients, and most of them had T.B., bacillary and amoebic dysentery, diarrhea, dengue, and flu.

April 1, 1943

There was another happy and tearful reunion between parents
in camp and their children who had been brought from the Brent
School in Baguio. It was their first meeting since December, 1941.

House-cleaned my rat hole, pared vegetables until I was dizzy, worked in my garden, and made a brown-sugar and coconut-milk syrup for my hot-cake breakfast in the morning.

Another Saturday night! No fancy dressing to dine under the stars at the Polo Club.

In bed by seven to read *Mr. Skeffington.*

April 4, 1943

If only we had some rain to settle the dirt and dust, and to decrease this intense heat. By noontime, people who had completed their camp duties were in the shade of their shacks or in the buildings.

With a thick straw coolie hat on my head, I weeded, watered, and pottered around contentedly until it was time to shower and clean up for my afternoon visit at the hospital.

April 8, 1943

A sprinkling shower that lasted for about an hour blessed us today with its grateful coolness.

Every day there were more native carts outside the Japanese office. The carts were piled high with household belongings of fellow nationals who had moved permanently into the camp. After they had registered, they scampered around to see a mayor of a shanty subdivision, to choose a homesite, and to order a shack from a contractor. However, homesites were becoming scarcer and the price of shacks had doubled and tripled.

Those who had never been interned had to learn the "ropes" just as we had, but if they had the wherewithal, it was surprising how quickly their path was smoothed out. Money talked in here, just as it did outside.

April 9, 1943

The brave and lonely women whose husbands died in other prison camps showed a splendid courage.

Leslie went about her personal, camp, and monitor duties with a patience and courage that won the admiration of all her roommates. She always had a word of comfort for Kay and Margo. These two never gave up hoping that they would be permitted to visit their husbands who were so near—and yet so far.

April 10, 1943

2 Enemy Warships, 10 Transports Sunk. Nippon Airmen Blast Force off Florida Island.

Our energetic emcee, Harvey Jones, led a Quiz Program in the plaza tonight, and many of our people participated.

If the Japanese propaganda boys had heard the loud laughter of the audience, they would have been convinced that we led an exceedingly gay life in here.

April 14, 1943

My old friend, Mr. Nagy, sent me a small box of locally made coconut candy and a bouquet of flowers. The note in the box assured me that Rags was frisky, companionable and lovable as ever. He had added that "without her, I would be a lonely man!"

Because I worked like one driven by demons on my vegetable detail, the American dietician in charge promoted me to a fore-woman. This rather dubious distinction increased my speed and output with the paring knife, and it made me impatient with the gals who dallied or gabbed too much. I was eager to get the messy work over with so that I could go on to pleasanter tasks about my shack.

April 16, 1943

I lost my lovely jade ring that I bought in Peiping so long ago, and I was most unhappy about it.

Though the morning paper gave the impression that Manila was a boom town with business as usual, we, of course, knew it was a lie. Those who had been out recently told us that the city came close to resembling a ghost town. There were very few people on the streets. There were no streetcars, and very few buses and automobiles. Carretelas, carromatas, and bull carts were the only means of transportation.

But, of course, the high-ranking Japanese still enjoyed our cars as long as they had alcohol and the queer-sounding charcoal contraption to run them with.

April 18, 1943

Our Commandant returned from Tokyo.

A written message from him regarding repatriation was read to us over the P. A. system.

The Commandant stated: "Due to our shipping losses, repatriation would not be possible, at least, not in the near future."

Those who had never taken the repatriation talks seriously were considerably buoyed by the Commandant's admission of shipping losses. This was good news! Wonderful news, and straight from the horse's mouth!

Those people who had already pictured themselves landing in San Francisco were utterly crushed.

April 21, 1943

Because we kept busy with our personal and camp duties, the days passed quickly. But the idle women who did little or no work were far from contented. Fortunately, they were in the minority.

One of these idle women was under the care of a doctor. When I looked at her manicured and well-kept hands, I wasn't envious, I only marveled that her doctor hadn't told her to get a little grime under those shapely nails. A little dirt and a daily battle with a charcoal fire and hauling water would have been the best medicine in the world for her.

But not for this spoiled and pampered gal! She had a hired girl to do her dirty work! The maid of all work was the destitute wife of a captured American soldier in a military prison nearby. She worked to earn money for extra food for herself, an ailing mother, and two teen-age sisters.

My prescription to cure the pampered darling's neurotic aches and pains was simple and practical. Dig in and do her own work, and donate the money she was paying now to the overworked soldier's wife. She could well afford it.

April 22, 1943

Two U. S. Army officers were brought into camp a few days ago. One of them told us that he had been in the Philippines only two weeks when the war broke out, and he readily admitted that he knew nothing of the country or its people.

He described how effectively the Japs infiltrated into our lines, wearing the uniforms of captured Filipinos.

"I wasn't able to distinguish between a Jap and a Filipino! And there were many others like me!" said the captain.

The dictionary should change the definition of war to four simple words: stupidity, blunders, inefficiency, and waste.

April 23, 1943

Good Friday! The Catholics were happy to attend mass at the Santa Catalina chapel, which was opened to them only a week ago.

The Protestant services were held in the Father's garden, and the familiar hymns, the portable organ, more wheezy than ever, took me back to childhood days in Pennsylvania.

It was an earnest and devout congregation and, no doubt, as we bowed our heads in prayers, most of us prayed that we would be free before another Good Friday came to pass.

April 24, 1943

Since school was out, the kids ran wild, happy and carefree as the hundreds of pigeons that roosted in the tower of the Big House.

Because movies were expected tonight, people rushed to the plaza with their chairs, petates and cushions as early as two in the afternoon in order to get a good spot.

The P. A. announcer begged the people to disperse and remove their chairs, but the movie-starved people refused to budge. The announcer spoke again. This time he said that duck eggs would be sold immediately at the canteen. The crowd wavered for only a second. Then they were off like a herd of stampeding buffaloes.

In the twinkling of an eye the plaza was deserted and the line that formed to buy duck eggs stretched twice around the Big House. In half an hour the eggs were all sold, and I was among the four or five hundred who walked away with a duck egg in each pocket and four in my hands.

April 25, 1943

I boiled the duck eggs and dyed them in boiling water that had contained onion skins, just as I had seen my mother dye eggs when I was a child. The dyed eggs turned out a high-yellow brown, different, and quite pleasing to the eye.

Lining a cardboard box with tissue paper, I filled it with bananas, avocados, eggs, a slice of cake, and a half-dozen cookies that Mr. Nagy had sent me for Easter.

Catesy was pleased with his Easter box, and when I received my present from him I was pleasantly surprised. It was a pencil sketch of me, secretly drawn by one of his ward mates, a talented Chinese. I prized the sketch, though I thought it was a poor likeness of me. I looked more like a glamorous and designing night-club hostess in a plush Shanghai night club, than the tired and weary-looking girl that I really was.

As I walked back to the Big House, carrying my sketch, I was as happy as the carefree children who romped on the grounds, proudly displaying their home-made baskets filled with eggs and home-made cotton bunnies.

April 26, 1943

Margo left today to work at the Holy Ghost Convent where internee children were quartered. As we embraced, she whispered that she was wild with joy. She was happy to leave Santo Tomas, though she knew she was only changing prison walls. At the convent she would help the sisters to care for the orphans and other internee children.

We were line-happy! I stood in seven different long lines today! No wonder we all complained of exhaustion at the end of the day. Many times, I'd join a long line though I had no idea what it was all about, or what was being sold. Whatever it was, I reasoned to myself, it must be good, or the line wouldn't be as long. There was always the possibility that something worthwhile, like canned meats, canned milk or vitamins would be sold.

May 4, 1943

With the typhoon season so close, shanty dwellers uneasily eyed their homes with the two completely exposed sides, and they pressed our Internee committee to get consent from the Commandant to make their homes waterproof. Many shack owners had already put up wide mediaquas (overhanging eaves) to keep out the rain, but it would hardly protect the occupants and their property from the violent wind-swept storms that could level a nipa house in a matter of seconds.

The Macks and I spent a pleasant hour or more in the plaza reminiscing about some of the interesting trips we had taken in years gone by.

Mrs. Mack spoke nostalgically of her life in Hawaii. As a young woman, she had gone to teach school there, and there she had met Mr. Mack shortly afterwards. When his firm transferred him to Manila, she followed him, and they were married a month later.

"I knew a good thing when I saw it!" she said laughingly, as she reached for his hand.

Now, after thirty years of happy marriage, they seemed closer than ever, and their devotion to each other was beautiful to see. As I watched them holding hands, a feeling of loneliness came over me, and I fervently wished that Catesy were sitting beside me.

May 6, 1943

General Tozyo (tojo) Speaks at Luneta Today. 100,000 Welcome Premier.

"Wouldn't you love to see the great and distinguished man today at the Luneta?" I teasingly asked Grandma.

"I'd rawther see a dogfight than him!" The tone of her voice was more than convincing, and she slapped the mop around her bed in a violent manner, as though she were slapping Tojo.

May 8, 1943

A state of uneasiness hung over us when the news spread that we would be transferred to another camp. We knew from experience how much work, time, and money it took to establish ourselves in this University campus that had not been equipped to house such a large group of people.

We knew the long hours of conferences that were spent between our Internee committee and the Nips to persuade them to permit us to buy and install plumbing facilities, kitchen, and hospital equipment.

The hard-working and conscientious heads of our camp, like Mr. Grant and many others, were directly responsible for everything that we had received in the line of plumbing, extra buildings, and other facilities. Theirs was a thankless and difficult job. When we passed the outside of the Japanese office, we could hear the shouts of the Japanese as they argued with our men, and it was anything but pleasant. Yet these men spent hours with the Japanese daily, to argue and coax for more food and equipment. Just now, they were working on our jailors for permission to make our shanties rainproof.

May 9, 1943

PREMIER TOZYO BACK IN JAPAN. GENERAL GIVEN WARM SENDOFF IN MANILA.

We heard tonight that the entire camp was to be moved to Los Banos about 70 kilometers south of us, where we were to continue to enjoy Japanese hospitality, fresh air, and tranquil surroundings.

The first group to leave will be eight hundred men, and it will be their job to build barracks, dig ditches, start vegetable gardens, install plumbing, and to lay the groundwork for a new city of thirty-five hundred or more people.

May 10, 1943

The camp buzzed with restlessness and speculation about Los Banos, while women were worrying if their men would be on the first list of eight hundred men to be sent to the new camp.

Surely, they wouldn't send Catesy to Los Banos! It was my last conscious thought before I fell asleep.

May 12, 1943

BOMBING OF U. S. MAINLAND COMING.

Added to this threatening headline was the worry and uneasiness about moving to Los Banos.

Since the number of men who volunteered to go to Los Banos never went above two hundred, our heads chose unattached and married men without children between the ages of eighteen and fifty-five.

Hammering, pounding, packing, and preparations for leaving were in full swing from morning until night. Men painted beds, boxes, wash pails, and other luggage with their names, and made other last-minute preparations.

The package sheds were closed for the last few days, and people were wondering if they would ever open again.

May 13, 1943

The twelve navy nurses and several of our doctors will accompany the eight hundred men to Los Banos.

It was pathetic and yet amusing to see to what sly, conniving men and women would resort to, to escape from going to Los Banos. Men who had posed as bachelors suddenly sprung a full-fledged family on our surprised internee committee. Their families were supposedly living outside. Others rushed to the hospital to obtain certificates from doctors to prove that they were unfit for the rugged life expected at the new camp.

One healthy young man-about-town, whose career of amorous escapades had been as extensive as that of a *Decameron* character, tried to bamboozle the doctors. After having played a strenuous game of football, he collapsed and was rushed to the hospital.

164

The examining doctor, a bit dubious about his collapse, began to question his patient. Finally, he revealed that his current paramour had administered a liquid-soap cocktail, which had brought on the acute stomach cramps. He was told to pack and be prepared to leave for Los Banos in the morning.

May 14, 1943

At 5 A.M. we were awakened by the loud music of "Time to Get Up" trumpeting throughout the entire camp.

By 7 A.M. the eight hundred men and twelve navy nurses were Mustered for roll call in front of the Big House, while the rest of us stood around to watch their departure.

A few minutes later, the trucks rolled into camp, and in a very short time men and nurses had climbed aboard. As the loaded trucks started to move toward the front gate, we waved, cheered, laughed and cried, while the loud-speaker blared the music of "Anchors Aweigh" and "The Stars and Stripes Forever."

May 16, 1943

Tape measures were dusted off again, and room and floor monitors were in a huddle to prepare room for an additional four to six hundred men; women and children. Many of the expected arrivals were old people who were unable to climb stairs, so the present younger occupants of the first-floor rooms were being transferred to rooms on other floors.

May 17, 1943

Again this place had the appearance of a Grand Central Terminal as trucks filled with men, women, and children, with their belongings, passed through the front gates. They deposited their worldly goods in front of the Big House, while Japanese soldiers and civilians rummaged through their crates, suitcases and beddings. They rattled pots and pans like noisy children at play. They lifted and peered at objects nearsightedly, and when they turned the pages of books and magazines, it was difficult to keep from laughing as we knew they couldn't read English. One goggle-eyed soldier picked up a large and beautifully dressed doll. The four-year-old little mother shot out her arms to snatch it from him, but not before he had lifted and peered under the doll's dress and numerous petticoats.

May 18, 1943

The chow and other lines which had been noticeably shorter since the Los Banos exodus were now stretched again. There were new faces everywhere.

Our sugar ration was cut and we now received one tablespoon per day. Those who had money were starting to buy additional sugar to store away.

Many of the new arrivals were plentifully supplied with money, and shacks were changing hands daily, and the prices were fantastic.

There was always the possibility that Catesy and I would be shipped to Los Banos in the next group, so we decided to sell our shack to a couple who had three young children. When I left my cozy little shack with the lovely flowers that I had tended so faithfully, my eyes clouded with tears. But it was no time for sentimentality, for with the money realized from the shack, I bought canned food, sugar, and other supplies at the canteen today in preparation for the move to Los Banos.

More and more people came into the camp. Old people, crippled men and women, and other invalids. It was pathetic to watch these old people. They were tired and confused by the crowds, and the yelling of hundreds of kids scampering over the grounds and through the long corridors.

With eight hundred of our younger men gone from the camp, the burden of heavy camp work fell on the shoulders of the remaining men who had already been overworked. In many instances, women were doing the work that had been formerly done by men.

Food prices continued to climb steadily as imported food items became scarcer. I was still trying to buy canned milk, but there was none to be had.

A small native bar of laundry soap sold for fifty centavos today and after a few lathers, disappeared into thin air. Toilet paper cost six pesos a roll. Fortunately, we could still buy fresh fruit and vegetables, but the prices were extremely high

Dr. Roberts, in charge of the T.B. ward, stopped to talk to me today, and he commented on Catesy's steady gain in weight. "What's your secret?" he asked me.

"A dozen and a half bananas a day and one avocado tid!" (three times daily.)

"But how do you keep him in bed? I notice that the others sit on each other's beds to play cards and checkers, but your guy never does!"

"He doesn't dare! I have my spies to report to me. I threatened to stop coming to see him if he ever got out of bed!"

"Well, I sure wish I could put some bacon on the other T.B.'s!" He shook his head in discouragement and continued his rounds.

Parents with children in camp were greatly worried when a girl of thirteen was sent out to San Lázaro with polio. They trembled at the thoughts of a polio epidemic like the one we had a few years ago. At that time I had specialed six polio patients, one after another. Three had died. When my last patient, a young soldier, had died, I already had pain and leg cramps, and I was in a state of nervous collapse.

After six weeks of total bed rest, I was back at work with scarcely any ill effects. Apparently, immunity acquired the hard way had miraculously paid off in my case.

Flying ants descended on us tonight as we sat in the plaza and the front grounds. When they crawled into our eyes, ears, and mouths, we took refuge under our mosquito nets.

May 25, 1943

The young girl with polio had a partially paralyzed throat, but it was believed that she would recover.

May 30, 1943

Memorial Day Services were held in the Father's garden, for the men and women who had died since the outbreak of the war.

I watched and listened from my window. Mrs. Smith, who had recently lost her son at Cabanatuan, stood near me, weeping quietly. Leslie sat on her cot with her back to us, and she too was grieving for her dead.

June 1, 1943

CHITTAGONG BASE RAIDED. ATTU DEFENDERS MAKE HEROIC STAND. *Japanese Garrison of 2,000 Fights to Last Man Against Odds 10 to 1.*

This was the type of news we loved! We were excited and happy today. As far as we were concerned, our American forces were just outside the city.

June 2, 1943

One of Catesy's close friends died of dysentery today, and because Catesy couldn't go to the funeral, I was going in his place. It was to be my first glimpse of the outside world since a year and a half ago.

June 3, 1943

We gathered outside the Commandant's office this morning to get our passes and red arm bands, and to await the bus which was to take fourteen of us to the funeral parlor and church.

Just before we climbed into the bus, we were given our red arm bands with the Japanese characters that signified "land of many rice."

As we moved toward the front gate, one of the men in our party remarked that it was the first time he had ever worn a red arm band at a funeral. No one answered. Everyone seemed to be busy with his own thoughts. For most of us, it was our first glimpse of the outside since internment. I expected some sort of emotion. Sadness or depression. Instead, I felt nothing.

The familiar streets were the same, except there were very few cars and buses, and the latter were filled with grinning Japanese soldiers. When we passed familiar public buildings with the Rising Sun flag waving in the morning sunlight, we quickly averted our gaze.

Filipinos on the streets looked sorrowfully at the Americanos with the red arm bands, and one could read loyalty and sympathy in their expressions. When we walked into the funeral parlor, all the windows on the outside were jammed with Filipinos looking in. I sat next to the young widow, whose beauty was apparent through the heavy and ugly black veil which she wore. Sitting on the other side of me was a middle-aged white woman, whose face appeared strangely familiar. When she whispered my name, and asked if there was anything she could do for me, I recognized my former Russian dressmaker. I reached for her hand and squeezed it gratefully. Then I felt a gentle nudge from behind, and when I looked back, I recognized my former Filipina hairdresser.

The tears that I shed in the next half hour, while we stayed in the funeral parlor, were not for the dead. I wept because I was overcome and touched by the loyalty of these two friends. Before I left the funeral parlor, the hairdresser had coaxed me into accepting a permanent kit. "It will do so much for your morale!" she whispered, and the dressmaker promised to make and send me a pair of slacks.

From the funeral parlor, we went to the Cathedral of St. Mary and St. John, where after a short prayer, we said our condolences and farewell to the family of the deceased.

As our bus pulled away from the church, several prominent Spaniards, all of them pro-American, waved at us from a carramota, and they continued waving and shaking their own hands energetically and enthusiastically in the air for several blocks. It cheered us considerably. They, too, hadn't forgotten us!

A few months later, one of the Spaniards was executed because of his pro-Americanism.

In about ten minutes, we were back among the familiar scenes of Santo Tomas. As I walked slowly to the hospital to see Catesy, I wondered if another eighteen months would pass before I went outside again.

June 5, 1943

There was no news, not so much as a rumor about the young woman who disappeared from the camp a few days ago.

June 6, 1943

Commissioner Jose P. Laurel Shot at Wack Wack. (A local country club.)

Because we considered him a collaborationist, everyone was of the opinion that he got what he deserved.

June 7, 1943

Tonight I took a walk with an old friend in the front grounds, and later we sat in the plaza to listen to the recorded music. It must have been the lovely night and the music that made my friend reach for my hand, but I jerked it away impatiently and crossly.

"Why don't you bring your wife into the camp? Her place is with you!" I was cross because I hated myself for not giving him even the comfort of a handclasp. I knew that he was desperately lonely — with that empty loneliness that filled one in the midst of crowds. It was the same intolerable loneliness and longing for companionship that once overwhelmed me in congested Times Square on New Year's Eve. I shall never forget that moment!

"But she couldn't stand the crowds, the confinement, and the hard work."

"Nonsense! If she loves you, she should be here with you!"

I wanted to add that if she didn't soon come in, he would be holding hands and playing games with another woman. With eight hundred men gone from the camp, predatory females, lonely females, and hungry females were on the lookout more than ever before for a single man who had a shack, well-stocked with food, and it wouldn't be long before one of them nabbed him.

June 8, 1943

I can remember how our hospitals in the States were thrown into a nervous tizzy when a case of impetigo was discovered among their patients. It made me smile when I thought of the strict asepsis and isolation they practiced with these cases.

Here, many of the children and adults were peppered with impetigo and other skin diseases brought on by filth, malnutrition, and nervousness, and of course, isolation was out of the question.

June 9, 1943

There was still no news of the young woman who disappeared from camp.

One of the new patients in Catesy's ward was the Italian who had written *Secret Agent*, which I had read only a few months ago. We hoped that the Nips would never discover his identity.

June 10, 1943

It rained daily and the ground was covered with mud and water, ankle deep. Boots, umbrellas, wooden bakias, stateside and native

169

grass raincoats, and the heavy straw rain hats were sold at the canteen.

Shortly after supper, the rain stopped, and I took my chair to the Father's garden to hear a reading of Shakespeare's *Tempest*.

June 11, 1943

81 More Enemy Planes Bagged. Raiders Downed by Nippon Anti-Aircraft.

Every domestic chore irked us because it was done in the hardest way possible. Though our camp details took much of our energies, they kept us from becoming drooling idiots.

June 12, 1943

Reich Ready to Launch Final Drive. Hitler Masses 70 Divisions. Moscow Is Goal.

Our morale was exceedingly high today as we had heard that Sicily had been taken by the Allies.

June 13, 1943

After five months in bed, Catesy had gained twenty-eight pounds, and he looked like a new man. His moody silences and frequent spells of depression were completely gone, and the doctor thought that if he could eat as well as he had been doing, he would recover.

But a fear that was distressingly real gripped all of us. What happened when we could no longer buy extra food?

June 14, 1943

Heavy rains, deadly routine, boredom, and occasional spells of depression were all a part of my daily existence. The only bright spots in the day were my two visits to the hospital.

June 15, 1943

Nippon Wild Eagles Down 33 Foe Planes over Russell Island.

The women's choir gave us some fine music tonight and I sat with the Macks as we listened to them. The Macks were in high spirits, and I wished that some of their optimism would rub off on me, but tonight I was more wooden and lacking in faith than a drugstore Indian. Only the return of our forces could have snapped me back into life.

June 16, 1943

Foe's Return Impossible! General Says — Enemy Has No Chance with Japan in Control of All Southern Bases.

The *Nishi-Nishi* didn't reach me today with its calamitous predictions and boasting. I took a day off from my vegetable detail and had a machineless permanent from the kit that my good Filipina friend had given me at the funeral. Then I bought myself a pair of hand-painted wooden bakias, which I immediately wore to visit Catesy. He was happy to see how cheerful the freshly corrugated wave had made me.

170

"It's time you bought yourself a good carabao steak dinner!"
he ordered.

Though a great many people ate at the camp restaurant daily, it
was my first experience and I felt like I was really "living it up."

There was an empty stool next to Henry and Zest at the tiny
restaurant near the gym, and it was like old times sitting beside
them. They appeared well and completely happy with each other.

The dinner consisted of steak, fried sweet potatoes, and rice
pudding. Though the carabao steak was extremely tough, I chewed
each bite with the intense joy of a dog with a large, juicy bone.
When I completed my elegant and expensive meal, I was sitting on
top of the world.

What a difference a full stomach and a fresh permanent made on
a gal's morale!

June 17, 1943

P. I. INDEPENDENCE IN '43. PREMIER TOJO GIVES ASSURANCE.

Could it be that the Japanese were trying to save face and ease
out of the country prior to the return of the Americans? At least,
that was what we wanted to believe.

June 18, 1943

Mr. Nagy sent me a tiny little box of candy with a cheering note.
From his pitiful little gifts, I could tell that he was having a difficult time outside.

June 19, 1943

GERMANS PREPARING ALL-OUT INVASION OF BRITISH ISLES.

Long before it became dark, we sat waiting patiently for the
movie that was promised tonight, but it was postponed because
of rain.

June 20, 1943

At the movie tonight we watched seemingly endless reels of
Japanese propaganda. The might of the Japanese Empire was depicted in the schools, the ricefields, the factories, shipyards and
steel mills.

The main feature was a football story, a grade below a B
picture, but how we enjoyed it!

June 21, 1943

LAUREL HEADS NEW COMMISSION.

We thought that the collaborationist, Laurel, had died from the
gunshot wound he had received. Too bad! We had him dead and
buried long ago.

June 22, 1943

Room and floor monitors were in a confidential huddle as they
fiddled with tape measures. It meant more roommates.

Late this afternoon, a hundred and nine men, women and chil-

dren arrived from the southern islands. The younger ones seemed
to be in fairly good condition, but the older people were weak
and exhausted. With a little extra squeezing, we made room for
another woman in Room 25.

June 23, 1943

When two internees met on the campus, the following conversation was typical: "What's the dope? Do you believe it? Are
you getting enough chow? I can't understand why I'm always so
tired. When do you suppose we'll go to Los Banos?"

June 24, 1943

One of my friends received a smuggled note from her husband
in Cabanatuan, and it only increased her worry about him.

He had written: "Here is an idea of what we have to do,
including all officers up to Lieutenant Colonels and on half rations
of food that our dog wouldn't eat. Haul gravel in five-gallon cans,
work on the farm without shoes, make rock paths for the Japs,
bring in trees for Japs' houses. Yesterday 25 officers, including
myself, loaded dirt from the city garbage dump. The worst feature
is the beatings we get from them. Yesterday an American captain
had five stitches taken in his head as a result of a beating with a
bayonet."

June 25, 1943

We forgot the walls, the barbed wires and shuffling boots
when our talented Harvey Jones gave us another show tonight. It
included dancing, clowning, and plenty of singing.

June 26, 1943

Our present census was 3700. The youngest was three weeks
old, and the oldest was ninety-two.

The women in camp had good news today. Due to the shortage
of materials and the subsequent cloth rationing which had been
in effect in the city for several months, our camp buyers planned
on buying materials to sell to us. Those without funds would be
given the material free.

Starting tomorrow, shorts for women would be legal, but they
must be four inches, no more, and no less, from the knees.

The P. A. announcer, an Englishman, summed up his news
about shorts in the following manner: "Owing to the shortage of
materials, there will be an increase in exposure."

June 27, 1943

I read another smuggled note from a prisoner at Cabanatuan,
and the writer told of short rations, beatings, and hard labor.

The frantic and worried recipients of these notes, who had their
own problems in here, were half crazy with fear and concern over
their men.

June 28, 1943

There were many comments, crude and otherwise, when the women blossomed out in shorts today. The more timid girls wisely refrained from wearing them the first day or two.

Catesy remarked, "In another year, even a fig leaf will go unnoticed."

June 29, 1943

Australia Heavily Raided.

The Australians in camp were saddened by the headline, though many of them would not believe it.

June 30, 1943

I spent an hour in the corridor talking to Zest and Henry, and it made me happy to watch the warm interchange of glances that passed between this engaged couple. Henry now had a monthly allotment from his boss outside, and they were able to buy a good supper every night at the camp restaurant.

July 2, 1943

Another jail had to be built in back of the Jap's office to accommodate a few more of our irresponsibles. The new addition was built entirely of nipa and swali, and any prisoner with the strength of a nine-year-old could have easily brought the house down on himself if he wished to escape. But there was no escape. Devil's Island had nothing on our camp jail.

July 3, 1943

We sat through more propaganda hogwash, which puffed the might of the Japanese Empire. But it was a small price to pay for the highly entertaining Ginger Rogers and James Stewart picture, *Vivacious Lady,* which followed.

July 4, 1943

We spent another glorious Fourth under the protective custody of the Japanese, but we were all cheerful and smiling as we felt that victory was near.

Catching a greased pig was the highlight of the afternoon's entertainment, and the squeals of the pig and the shouts of the people watching pleasantly intermingled in this hot, sunny day.

On the blackboard outside the main kitchen, someone had written "pork and beans" as the menu for the day, and underneath he had added: "God Bless America." Later in the day, this had been erased and the initials "G.B.A." had been substituted. It had been a wise precaution, for late in the afternoon a delegation of Japanese officers visited the camp.

July 5, 1943

I made a blouse from an old slip of mine. It was my first attempt

173

at sewing for a long time, and the blouse certainly looked home-
made.

Women were making slacks, shorts, and dresses from cretonnes,
sheets, tablecloths, and evening dresses. Sheets that used to sell
for four pesos were now selling for forty. Towels that sold for
fifty-nine cents at Macy's now sold for ten pesos. The woman who
had a sheet to cut up for a dress or shorts was lucky indeed.

July 6, 1943

Nearly every patient at the camp hospital was stricken with
ptomaine poisoning, resulting in severe cramps, acute diarrhea,
and vomiting.

Catesy lost seven pounds overnight. Another T.B. lost nine, and
it was feared that he would not recover.

July 7, 1943

Eight hundred more people were to be drafted and sent to Los
Banos. The eight hundred would include wives, mothers, and
sweethearts of men who were already there. Men and women
with essential jobs in camp would be exempt from the draft, and
those who had been reluctant to devote so much as an hour to
camp work were now clamoring for jobs in order to evade the
Los Banos draft.

July 8, 1943

Four Warships Sunk in Solomons.

The morning paper never failed to reprint the Imperial Rescript
declaring war on U.S.A. and Britain on the eighth of each month,
and by now, most of us knew it by heart.

July 9, 1943

Japanese Attack Foe in New Guinea. Nassau Bay Bombed.

I've just finished reading a gem of a book with plenty laughs:
Pamela — Virtue Rewarded.

I ought to loan it to Don Juan's blonde just to get her reaction.

Twenty-four more cases of food poisoning at the hospital, and
again all the T.B.'s were affected. Catesy lost nearly half of the
weight he had gained in six months, and he lost this poundage
within one week.

The weakest T.B., with the most weight loss, was on the verge
of collapse from acute diarrhea, and his chances of surviving were
now lost forever.

If I still had the shanty, I would have started working on Dr.
Roberts to release Catesy to my care. But without the shack it was
hopeless. I hoped that the shake-up caused by the last poisoning
would jar the hospital kitchen workers and make them more
careful.

174

July 14, 1943

Enemy Loses Three Cruisers in Night Battle in Solomons.

Catesy was still extremely weak and on liquids, but by tomorrow he would be able to eat bananas.

July 15, 1943

Domestic Crisis Forces America to Launch Drive. Growing Difficulties. U. S. to Start South Pacific Offensive One Year Ahead of Time.

Happily, we read the above headline, and we felt like we ought to start packing.

Two of the habitual souses, the bad boys of the camp, raised the nipa roof of their jail, and they were found lying on the street outside the camp walls. Both were taken to the camp hospital. One was suspected of having a T.B. spine, while the other had several broken ribs which he could not account for.

July 17, 1943

The lonely and hard-working women with children, and with husbands in other prison camps, had a difficult time. Not only did they try to eke out a daily existence and look after their children under turbulent and impossible conditions, but they had to raise money to feed themselves and their children, and, if possible, to send money and supplies in secret to their men in other camps. They raised money through friends and business firms on the outside, or they borrowed money from friends in camps. Many sold their jewelry to raise money, and in some cases the money and supplies they sent their men never reached them. It was a dreadful pity, for the money could have been used to feed and buy essentials that they themselves needed desperately.

July 18, 1943

Since some of our men had been caught and taken outside by the Japs because they had been found with written radio transcripts, it was extremely dangerous to read typewritten transcripts. But in spite of that, transcripts of radio broadcasts were passed from room to room with one eye on the alert for a Jap.

July 19, 1943

The heavy rains had flooded out the shanty people, and as a result the corridors were jammed with tables, chairs, baby cribs, strollers, and screaming children.

The barbed wires and clotheslines were filled with wet wash that had hung there for the last several days.

A bearded, six-foot giant had just passed my window in a child's Red Riding Hood raincoat, and everyone who saw him smiled or laughed out loud. An artist and a photographer looking for unusual subjects would have found them in this crazy place.

July 20, 1943

Mr. and Mrs. Greenshoes still occupied the large university museum on the second floor. Mr. Greenshoes, many years younger than his wife, was her devoted slave. He was the most overworked husband I had ever met. He cooked, washed, and climbed the high stairs many times a day. He queued up in endless lines, while the old lady sat in the corridor reading, writing poetry, or discussing Buddhism with anyone she could corral.

July 21, 1943

We were fortunate to have reading matter. At the rate I was going, I'd soon have all the seven hundred books in the library read.

I started to read A. J. Cronin's *Three Loves.*

July 22, 1943

HITLER AND DUCE HOLD VITAL WAR PARLEY.

So he's still alive! We had the Fuehrer dead and buried several months ago.

July 23, 1943

The British were in a state of twittering anticipation as several of them had been placed on the repatriation list. No one knew when this great event would take place. Some were openly envious, while others had no desire to leave now that the Americans were about to return. I wondered, sometimes, if that great event would be as soon as the Macks and other equally optimistic people had predicted.

July 24, 1943

Thieving was on the increase now that food, money, and other supplies were scarce. One of the thieves, a white-haired veteran of Dewey's days, was apprehended, and today he was sentenced to ninety days in the local brig.

July 25, 1943

More than forty-eight Americans were to be on the repatriation list.

"We'll be out for Christmas!" This was the most beautiful and promising phrase that we had heard in months. It was also the most repetitious phrase we heard these days.

July 26, 1943

Though we were confined to the buildings because of the rain, we were cheerful because it was rumored that Mussolini had resigned and that the Fascist party had dissolved.

July 27, 1943

BADOGLIO IS NEW PREMIER OF ITALY. SUCCEEDS MUSSOLINI WHEN HE RESIGNS POST DUE TO ILL HEALTH.

The headline made us happy and it gave us faith in the news that we had been receiving. We expected Munda to fall next.

July 30, 1943

The women in the camp had their first shopping spree when they purchased two yards of Indian head and three yards of poplin. This was our quota for the year.

When I showed Catesy the material, and I told him that all the women had bought the same design and color, he said, "This place will look like the home for wayward girls, when you gals decide to wear your dresses on the same day!"

July 31, 1943

From reliable sources — how I hated those ugly words — we heard that Italy had capitulated, but several hours later our hopes were scuttled when it proved to be just another rumor.

August 1, 1943

A young mestiza with her four-months-old baby was placed in the camp jail and then taken out of camp. No one seemed to know what it was all about, except that she was the wife of an American.

How I missed my shanty with its tranquil solitude! I could not bear to go near it, or even look at it from a distance.

August 2, 1943

A contribution was raised today for American soldiers and officers who were imprisoned at nearby Billibid. We heard that the men were without shoes, clothing, food, and medicines.

August 3, 1943

Burma Declares War on the United States and Great Britain.

Margo sent us a cheerful note, and it appeared that she was happier at the Convent where she helped to care for children.

August 4, 1943

Nippon Wild Eagles Raid Port Rendova.

The wife and two children of an American guerrilla commander who had surrendered a few months ago were admitted to Santo Tomas, and there was a possibility that her husband might join her.

August 5, 1943

We again had movies tonight. During the first hour we were shown a nauseous and malicious propaganda picture, and we were all thoroughly disgusted.

When pictures of Roosevelt and Churchill flashed on the screen, we forgot all caution about demonstrations of any type, and we broke into wild and enthusiastic clapping.

August 9, 1943

The food was becoming poorer in quality and quantity. The cooked stew and hamburger had an evil smell and, though we feared it, we ate it because it was food.

Long before the canteen opened, there were long queues of people standing in the blazing sun or drenching rain in the hopes of buying food.

The overworked and harassed internees who acted as buyers and clerks tried to limit the food purchase so that each person could buy something. It was the same every day. In a short time everything was sold out, and those at the end of the line walked away hungry, disappointed, and with pockets bulging with Mickey Mouse currency.

August 13, 1943

On the days when I stood in line for several hours, only to learn that there was nothing left to buy, my disappointment almost made me ill.

But today was a lucky day for me! I bought a tin of corned beef and ten kilos of extremely dirty and old rice. After I spent several hours trying to exterminate the worms, webs, and weevils, I was more than ready for bed. Though some of my friends laughed at my rice purchase, as they felt that we would always have all the rice we wanted, I was glad that I had bought it.

August 14, 1943

IMPERIAL NAVY AIR ARM SCORES HEAVILY AGAINST ENEMY IN SOLOMON ISLANDS.

Saturday night and no place to go, and so to bed to read Emil Ludwig's *Cleopatra.*

If I were a literary critic, I'd sum up the review in three words: "What a gall!"

August 15, 1943

The sermon, the familiar hymns, and the benediction at church in the Father's garden, acted as a balm. It eased my anxiety about our future. It gave me hope.

As I hurried to the vendor's after church, I passed the front east corner of the Big House, and when I heard children's voices singing, I stopped. Sunday school was in session, and they were singing "Brighten the Corner Where You Are." Sunday school, church, and familiar hymns! There was an air of normalcy everywhere. Yet we were all jittery and worrying about tomorrow. The constant fear and worry of what's coming next was ever present with us.

August 16, 1943

Blue Monday lived up to its name in here, especially when it rained.

There was not so much as a juicy rumor to divert our conversation from food and high prices.

One of my dear friends, an attractive Filipina citizen, and married to an American officer imprisoned at Cabanatuan, was finally released after more than eight months of wire-pulling by her prominent Spanish father. We wept as we kissed good-bye, and sadly, I wondered when we would meet again.

August 18, 1943

It seemed as though we had every type of mental and physical sickness found in the medical books. Several nights ago a young married woman suffering from a mental disorder made several attempts to crawl in bed with a frightened and startled male internee. Naturally, there was a great deal of commotion, ribald nonsense, and excitement over this incident.

Tonight the young woman was in a serious condition at the hospital. She had drunk iodine, and it was her second attempt at suicide.

August 19, 1943

This was a big day for Catesy and me! He was allowed in the hospital garden for half an hour because of his birthday. I baked a spice cake for the occasion in a friend's shack, and there were ten of our friends in the garden to share it with us.

After almost nine months in bed, Catesy's delight at being up was indescribable, but I noticed that he was completely exhausted after the half hour was up.

August 20, 1943

Cholera! There were several cases of Japanese soldiers who had this dreaded disease in the city.

The young woman who tried to commit suicide was removed to an outside hospital.

August 21, 1943

Due to the cholera scare, there was a noticeably short line of buyers at the carabao milk stall.

August 22, 1943

Five cholera immunization stations were set up, and after vegetable detail I joined one of the stations to give shots. Four hours of vegetable detail and two and a half hours of swabbing and jabbing long lines of anxious people had me completely exhausted, as my own cholera shot had made me ill and faint.

August 23, 1943

Old-timers who had survived several cholera epidemics told us to stay away from fresh fruit and vegetables. Those who came from India told us to drink plenty of kalamansi juice. We drank vast quantities of the juice and we stopped buying fruit and vegetables.

August 26, 1943

I continued to give shots with pounding headache and rising temperature. By evening I was so weak and ill that, in desperation, I went to see my old friend, Dr. Fisher.

It was a consolation to know that I was in better shape than some of my fellow internees. Though I was weak and ill, I was well enough to keep on going.

August 27, 1943

This was another big and profitable day for me! I was able to buy ten kilos of dirty rice and ten pounds of raw peanuts, which I shoved under my bed for safekeeping.

August 28, 1943

Repatriation became more than just a word to a lucky few hundred. It was a certainty that over two hundred American, British, Dutch and Canadians would leave on a neutral boat to a neutral port.

Many claimed that the list did not include the aged and the ill, and loud were the lamentations among those who felt that they should have been on the cherished list.

August 29, 1943

I read *Guilty Men,* and according to the author, Baldwin, Ramsay MacDonald and Chamberlain head the list of guilty Englishmen who were responsible for the unpreparedness in England, France, and America.

Thank goodness, I felt a little stronger. The best remedy for illness and weakness was to keep on going with one's work.

August 31, 1943

It wasn't easy for Catesy to be a helpless vegetable all these months, but his good conduct paid off. He was allowed to spend ten minutes in the garden twice a day. How we looked forward to those twenty minutes of happiness!

September 1, 1943

JAPANESE INFLICT HEAVY LOSSES ON FOE IN NEW GUINEA!

"What a treat!" exclaimed Catesy, as he stretched his arms high above his head. "Green grass, trees, and away from the sick and pale faces of my wardmates!"

As we sat close together on a metal bench in the hospital yard, our hands touched. There was no need for words.

September 2, 1943

JAPANESE DAMAGE TWO FOE WARSHIPS, DOWN 31 PLANES. ENEMY RAIDS NIPPON ISLANDS IN PACIFIC.

The young woman who swallowed iodine was improving and would be back in camp shortly.

180

September 3, 1943

No truer words were ever said than "idlesness is the devil's workshop." It certainly applied to the few men and women who refused to do any type of camp work. They were in and out of the camp jail for quarreling, drinking, or other violations.

September 4, 1943

I was touched and worried by the pitiful little packages that Mr. Nagy sent me occasionally. Being outspoken, and anti-Nazi, I had a feeling that he was having a difficult time under the Japanese regime.

Catesy and I spent a wonderful ten minutes in the garden tonight as we made plans for our wedding and future home — if and when we got out of here.

September 5, 1943

The morning *Nishi-Nishi* was filled with the approaching Independence, and we wondered how this would affect us.

September 6, 1943

"Billibid is only a few blocks away from here. Why can't we visit our husbands?" The empty loneliness and yearning in Kay's voice misted the eyes of her roommates.

Why wouldn't the Japs allow these wives to see their men? If only for ten minutes. Soon it would be two years since they last saw their husbands.

September 7, 1943

Included on the repatriation list were the three young women who had made themselves conspicious by fraternizing with the Nips, and for the last week their names were tossed about in ribald jokes and puns. Every day, a new verse was composed about them, and I wondered if these women realized or cared that they were gossiped about. They had paid a big price for their repatriation.

September 9, 1943

Though the optimists annoyed me with their home-for-Christmas drivel, the extreme pessimists and realists annoyed me more.

There was one man in particular who upset me. He was a tiny, beetle-eyed, and serious-looking professor of mathematics. His manner and appearance reminded me of a mummified Egyptian. When I asked him if he thought we'd be out by Christmas, he looked at me pityingly, and started his lecture with, "My dear, let's be realistic." Then for half an hour I listened to a learned discourse on wars, starting with Alexander the Great down to the present war. Names like Kiska, Attu, Rat, Munda, Solomons, Bougainville, and New Britain dropped from his lips in a most knowledgeable manner. Surely, this man was another Napoleon! His logic

181

was so convincing that I felt I was in the presence of a great
strategist.

"I'll bet MacArthur and Eisenhower could have used you!" My
admiration was sincere.

His narrow and concave chest puffed like swelling bread dough,
and he added confidentially, "You know, I keep a map under my
mattress, and I know exactly where our forces are and where they'll
strike next."

September 10, 1943

NIPPON NAVY SINKS 13 SUBS DURING MONTHS OF JULY AND AUGUST.

At the movies tonight, we were delighted with Mickey Mouse and
Popeye, and then came the main feature — eight reels of a Japanese
war epic.

The hero of the picture was a flannel-mouthed, bespectacled and
gopher-toothed Nip, who looked more like a peaceful collector of
beetles than the skipper of a Nipponese gunboat. When the American guerrilla, portrayed by a brutish and coarse-looking white man,
nearly killed our mild-mannered Mr. Hase, our sympathies were
entirely with him. We wanted him to live, and we didn't care what
happened to the apish-looking American guerrilla.

Such was the power of slanted propaganda!

September 11, 1943

Don Juan had a new girl friend. She was another blonde, and a
beauty.

I stuck my head in his shack today en route to the hospital, and
the cozy and tranquil scene which met my eyes gave me food for
thought for many days to come.

Don Juan lolled in a long easy chair, reading a book, while his
blonde was stretched out in another chair beside him. She was the
picture of serenity and domesticity. She was knitting a pair of
socks for Don Juan.

September 14, 1943

Today was my birthday, and I was invited to a friend's shack for
cake and coffee. Just as I was about to cut the cake, Catesy walked
into the shack, and for a moment, I was overcome with surprise
and delight. He had been allowed to leave the hospital for an hour.
No other present could have pleased me more.

After escorting Catesy back to the hospital, I walked back to the
Big House loaded with birthday presents.

September 15, 1943

Several of the girls in my room wept when they heard that our
Allied forces were having reverses at Salerno.

September 16, 1943

The news that our Allies weren't doing as badly as the *Nishi-Nishi* claimed had cheered us tremendously.

September 17, 1943

When the repatriates leave, we'll settle down to daily existence. Since it was beyond our grasp, the thoughts of freedom, home, and normalcy were more than most of us could bear.

September 20, 1943

I thought this day would never end. Everything went wrong today because I was depressed and ill. I cut my finger at vegetable detail and after that my clumsiness with the paring knife irritated me. I had a bad cold, and I had worms.

When I stood in a canteen line that snaked twice around the Big House for more than an hour and a half in a burning sun, I became weak. Every time I thought of my worms, waves of nausea made me feel like a spinning top, and the hot sun increased my vertigo. By the time I reached the canteen counter, everything was sold out, and if I hadn't been so angry, I would have burst into tears of disappointment.

Rushing to the vegetable stalls, I saw a woman coming out of the Japanese stall, carrying a can of sardines and milk, though I despised the boastful and sneering Japanese girl behind the counter, I shot into her store. If she had anything to sell, I was willing to eat crow. Her shoe-button eyes pierced me with a less-than-the-dust glance. "Well, what do you want?" she asked me insolently.

Though my blood pressure leaped, I smiled sweetly and asked for sardines and milk. As she handed me the last two cans, there was a smirk on her putty-like face. When I started to pay from my wad of soiled and crumpled Mickey Mouse money that had been bunched in my slacks pocket, I dropped the bills on the dirty ground at my feet. My enemy laughed spitefully.

This time my temper could not be leashed. I held out my hands with the hateful money and spat, "One of these days I'm going to paper my Chic Sale with this!"

It was fortunate for me that her knowledge of our vernacular was limited.

September 21, 1943

The repatriates were packing feverishly and happily, and disposing of their excess baggage.

"I'll be glad when they're gone!" declared Grandma, rolling her eyes ceilingward. Grandma's voice and expression left no doubt in our minds that she too was heartily sick and weary of the word, repatriation.

183

September 24, 1943

Our Commandant gave a speech for the departing internees and more than one person remarked that his speech was subtly conciliatory, or as Catesy aptly expressed it, "It sounded like he was suing for a separate peace."

September 25, 1943

The trunks and luggage of the repatriates were in the front plaza, while a group of military police went about their inspection. Nothing was overlooked. Rolls of toilet paper were unwound and Kotex was torn apart. But the biggest laugh came to the interested spectators when the Nips confiscated a woman's knitting instructions. The K3 and P1 looked like a secret code to them.

September 26, 1943

Amidst tears, farewells, and best wishes, the repatriates left at 5 A.M., and the Commandant accompanied them to the pier. The moment they left, some of the tension left us, and we settled down to await the next boat or the war's end.

September 28, 1943

How stupid I was to allow the Japanese female to irk me! Every time I bought something from her, her crowing and superior airs were more than I could take.

Today she boasted that the Imperial Japanese Army would soon be in Chicago, and for a moment I thought I'd bash her over the head with my bayong. In my most doubtful and scornful voice, I said, "This I have to see!"

There was a look of hate in her eyes as she hissed, "Fool, keep on daydreaming!"

September 29, 1943

Kay and other wives of army men were happy today. They received notes from their husbands from nearby Billibid. Most of the men were hopeful that the end of the war was near.

Apparently, the much discussed visit of wives to see their men in military camps was just a cruel promise of the Nips.

September 30, 1943

After leaving Catesy, I passed the women's ward, and I heard a snaky hiss. I turned around and looked into Tientsin Mary's bold, black eyes. She was in the first bed next to the door. Her eyes expressed warmth and friendliness.

"When did you get back?" I knew that she had been shipped off to a psycho ward some months ago.

"I came back yesterday, and now these damn doctors are trying to tell me that I have dang-gay-u!" (dengue.) "What the hell! I'm all right!" To demonstrate, she leaped out of bed with a violence

184

that shook the ward. The other patients turned to look at us, while Mary turned a shade of pea-green.

As I helped her back into bed, she said weakly, "Ain't this place the hell?"

"You ain't just a-kiddin'!" and I meant every word.

October 2, 1943

This was a red-letter day for us! Catesy was discharged from the hospital after nine months in bed. He was still weak and far from well, but the hospital needed his bed for patients sicker than he.

If only we had our shack now, so that he could stay there all day without having to climb three flights of stairs three and four times a day. Six months ago, when we had sold our shack, we thought we were to be shipped to Los Banos. That possibility, of course, was still present. When we sold our shack, we had made a hundred per cent profit, and now shacks went as high as six and eight times the original price. If we only knew how much longer we would be here, we could borrow money to buy and store food more systematically and intelligently for the months ahead.

As Catesy repeatedly said, "It isn't the internment, it's the uncertainty."

October 4, 1943

It was wonderful to have Catesy back with me! Though most of the time he rested in bed, we saw each other at mealtimes, and in the evenings. But to see him walking slowly and carefully like an old man, while his breathing was labored when he climbed the stairs, made me infinitely sad. He was only thirty-one, yet he acted like a man more than twice his age.

October 5, 1943

Trouble always comes in pairs. An elderly American with diabetes, who faced the possibility of losing a gangrenous leg, heard today that his son had died in a nearby military camp.

October 6, 1943

This was my day off from vegetable detail and I put my free time to good use. I washed clothes, scrubbed my bed, and wrestled with suitcases, baskets, crates, pots and pans under my bed, as I dusted and mopped.

October 7, 1943

Sending Catesy to Los Banos in his present weakened condition might well prove fatal, and I was determined to keep him off the next list of men being sent there, even though I had to resort to a soap cocktail. I was most fortunate to be well at this time, as I was able to save him as much exertion as possible.

October 9, 1943

At last, I received a letter from home. It had been mailed seven months ago. What a relief to know that my mother and the rest of my family were well! The envelope was passed around in my room like a precious heirloom and the postmark and stamps were carefully inspected.

To complete a red-letter day, Catesy and I went to the restaurant and we thoroughly enjoyed a tough carabao steak.

October 10, 1943

The wives and sweethearts of men in Los Banos had definite word that in a few weeks they would join their men, and they were in a frenzy of pleasurable excitement.

October 11, 1943

The price of food and other commodities was still climbing, but there was an abundance of Mickey Mouse in the camp among those who had contacts with wealthy Filipinos, Chinese, and neutrals. These people on the outside were happy to loan huge amounts of the occupational currency, especially now that the war tide had turned. The prospect of being paid back in good American dollars and Philippine currency after the war was very good. It was as safe as putting money in the bank.

October 12, 1943

Japanese Intensify Air Attacks. U. S. Positions in Solomons, New Guinea Battered.

Flying Eagles ceased to torment us by their low flying and buzzing in the last month. Were they busy elsewhere, or better still, were they all destroyed?

October 13, 1943

Our wishful thinking regarding the Flying Eagles was blasted today when dozens of them flew over us in parade formation in preparation for the big day tomorrow.

October 14, 1943

Republic Born Today!

The celebration of this great event went on from early morning until late at night. Planes roared over us! Church bells rang! Bands played spirited and triumphal marches, and thousands of soldiers marched to the accompaniment of screaming sirens!

October 16, 1943

Mr. Nagy remembered my name day today. He sent a pathetically half-withered bouquet of flowers with a tiny box of rice cookies. He wrote that his health was poor, and that his inseparable companion, Rags, was also sick. I could read privations and other hardships between the lines, and from friends who had seen him on the outside I learned that he had been reported twice by the Nazi Germans for being too outspoken regarding the present regime.

Two men tried to escape last night! One was taken to Fort Santiago, and the other was confined to the camp jail for the duration.

October 16, 1943

Shanty people who looked forward to living in their shacks in the near future had a disappointment today. Because of the drunken behavior of a female dipsomaniac, and the attempted escape of the two men, the hours spent in shacks were to be lessened.

October 17, 1943

All the drudgery and dreary loneliness of the past nine months was forgotten tonight, when Catesy and I sat outside in the plaza, holding hands surreptitiously, and listening to the canned symphony music.

October 19, 1943

We invested in a small four-by-eight portable lean-to, which we placed in the west patio. It had a roof and one closed side. When weather permitted, we planned to cook and eat our meals there.

October 20, 1943

Twelve of the High Commissioner's staff, who had been living on the outside in an old mansion, came into the camp.

It was understandable that they would be bewildered by all the activity and confusion found in here.

October 21, 1943

Instead of eating wormy and dirty cereal this morning, we treated ourselves to a good breakfast of scrambled duck eggs and the last of our Red Cross bacon. In the afternoon, I baked a banana spice cake.

October 22, 1943

I met my general of strategic warfare at the sink this morning. When, in answer to my question of how much longer we would be here, he started with, "Let's be realistic, my dear," I felt like bashing him on the head with my tin plate. I was tired of being realistic.

October 24, 1943

"Virtue is its own reward," remarked Grandma piously, after we had discussed the easy sentence that had been imposed on one of the camp's bad girls. Because she had been drunk and out of bounds at curfew, she was given a month in the camp jail and two hours of camp detail, while the decent and well-behaved men and women did three, four and six hours of camp work a day.

October 26, 1943

The unusual personalities that surrounded us acted as a conversation piece when rumors, news, and gossip were scarce.

All eyes bugged out like a frog's when a middle-aged man with loose and flowing white pajamas floated around on the grounds. His unusual garb, held up by a heavy clothesline, was worn in the style of a Roman senator or a devotee of Isadora Duncan. He wandered through the campus like a disembodied spirit, and he peered at his fellow internees through rose-colored spectacles that were always parked on the tip of his nose.

Then there was a likable, but extremely pathetic punch-drunk relic of the ring. He shadow-boxed, jumped, danced, grimaced, and muttered continuously as he shuffled around the camp.

A more cheerful sight was our entertaining and happy emcee, Harvey Jones. He had a friendly word and a grin for everyone. With his bean-pole tallness, and prominent Adam's apple, I was reminded of Ichabod Crane, without a horse.

October 27, 1943

The handsome young Mayor of Garden Court was stricken with polio today and he was taken outside to the San Lázaro Hospital. Some of our medical men assured us that polio would not reach epidemic proportions in the midst of filth, poor food and overcrowded conditions.

What better place than this to test out the theory?

October 28, 1943

We paid $2.50 for a half pound of sausage at the canteen, and it tasted wonderful. In the afternoon I baked a spice cake for a dear friend's fourth wedding anniversary.

October 30, 1943

Everything was being done to make the children's lives as normal as possible. There was a party for them in the playhouse, and judging from their squeals and laughter that reached us in the Big House, they were having fun. The children were getting better food than the adults, but soon they, too, would be on our poor diet.

October 31, 1943

The young man with polio died today in an iron lung, and his young wife was with him until the end.

November 1, 1943

Our long months of internment were not altogether wasted. We learned many practical things. We learned to eat native vegetables, fruit, and other food, and we learned to build a fire faster than a Boy Scout. We learned to make clothes out of seemingly impossible garments, and we learned to cook with garlic. We put garlic into everything. Not one clove, but an entire head, for it was one item that we could always buy, and there was always the chance that an important vitamin lurked within its smelly cloves. Most

188

important of all, we learned that freedom, the most precious thing in life, and which we had taken for granted, was not ours.

November 2, 1943

It was good to see Catesy puttering about our lean-to as he prepared fried rice mixed with onion, gobs of garlic, and dabs of fresh pork. For the last item, we paid a king's ransom.

November 7, 1943

We were in a state of glorious exuberance over the news that Red Cross shipments of food, medicine and clothing had arrived for us and the military camps. We talked of nothing else.

When a hundred of our men, who had gone to the piers to help unload the ship, came back, they reported that the cases bore this beautiful greeting: "Greetings from U.S.A. to all Americans in the Philippines."

November 8, 1943

The unloading of the supplies at the pier went on and we worried that some of the precious supplies would fall into Nipponese hands.

November 12, 1943

Japanese Land Additional Forces on Bougainville. U. S. Marines Hemmed In at Beachheads.

The women going to Los Banos were leaving in a few days and they were in a state of tremulous excitement. Seventeen of the women were engaged, and it was believed that they would be permitted to marry their men in Los Banos. They reminded me of the famous Casket girls, so called because the King of France gave each girl a small dowry to marry the early settlers of Louisiana. Instead of Caskets, our girls would be toting bayongs, tampipis, petates, suitcases, and wooden crates filled with food and tin cans. This would be their dowry!

November 13, 1943

If I don't soon cash my traveler's checks, the letters will be illegible, for by this time the constant friction of my arches had worn them to a ragged and dog-chewed appearance.

November 14, 1943

The number four typhoon signal was up, and we braced ourselves for a severe typhoon. A violent storm arrived during the night with a fury that leveled many shanties. Other shanties leaned in a crazy and lopsided way, swaying back and forth with each fresh gust of wind. During the night, children who slept with their fathers in shacks, were carried to the safety of the buildings.

In the Annex where mothers and children were housed, there was mind-sundering bedlam. While excited children screamed,

frantic mothers and fathers scurried around to shop for food at
the canteen and vegetable stalls, and to find a sheltered spot to
set up a stove to cook.

November 16, 1943

The typhoon continued with its savage devastation. There was
no gas or electricity, and candles, coconut oil and kerosene lamps
faintly illuminated the funereal gloom of the corridors and rooms.
All the shanty towns were covered with two, four and six feet of
water.

When the gas failed, our hard-working kitchen men built large
improvised stoves made of dobe stone under the dining sheds, and
the enormous cast-iron containers on top of the stoves were filled
with cooking mush, stew, or tea.

With several thousand shanty-towners flooded from their homes,
the meal line, the laundry, and dish-washing troughs were jammed.

November 17, 1943

The typhoon was over and the water that covered much of the
campus was receding. The camp was like a busy anthill as we
went about our work with a joke and a smile. Shanty dwellers
waded, swam, or went by raft to check on the damage done to
their homes and supplies.

There was a scarcity of food in the canteens, and we were unable
to buy bread or peanut butter, two of our most reliable fillers.
The fruit and vegetables were of poor quality, and the prices
were higher than usual because of the flood. The two restaurants
did a thriving business. Lunches were two and three pesos, and
dinners were three and four pesos.

By late afternoon the water was nearly gone, and strange objects
were seen in the oozing mud — bamboo poles, baby cribs, boots,
shoes, pots, pans, and various types of marine life. A five-foot baby
python was also discovered.

November 18, 1943

When the sun came out for a short time, we rushed outside to
enjoy its welcome rays, and we set to work dragging out our
musty and soaking possessions.

Shanty owners worked all day to clean off the mud and slime
that covered their homes. During their absence, huge armies of
ants had moved into every corner and crevice of their shacks
to escape the flood.

November 20, 1943

Grandma rushed into our room today, breathless and excited,
with the news that there were two fresh apples in Santo Tomas.

Two fresh apples in the Philippines? How could that be? For
we knew that no apples were grown in this country. Immediately,

190

these delightful questions filled our minds. Were they apples from Formosa or America? If from America, how did they get here? Could it be that our forces were that close?

November 23, 1943

Tropical ulcers, boils, deficiency diseases, and bacillary and amoebic dysentery, and low blood pressure headed the list of ailments among the adults, while most of the children had bacillary dysentery and respiratory ailments at the children's hospital.

November 24, 1943

From our camp buyers and Filipino Red Cross doctors, we learned that there were many food riots in the city. Apparently, the Co-Prosperity Sphere for all Asiatics had hit a snag.

November 25, 1943

As the shortage of purchasable food in the canteen became more marked, our thoughts turned to the Red Cross kits. When would they arrive?

My cold hung on. The cramps in my legs nagged me like a toothache and I seemed to be tired all the time.

Via the bamboo wireless, we heard that our captured soldiers had already received their Red Cross supplies at Cabanatuan, Bilibid, and other military camps.

November 28, 1943

Former U. S. Army trucks rolled into our camp all morning loaded with our precious Red Cross supplies. While young and older men helped with the unloading and storing, the rest of us stood by watching, drooling, and wondering when the distribution would take place. With sacks of mail still undistributed and collecting dust in the Nip's office for months, we were naturally worried that our jailors might act the same way with the Red Cross food.

November 30, 1943

While we watched a basketball game tonight, Catesy and I held hands. When several Nips joined us and stood directly behind us, we snatched our hands away as though we had touched a hot stove.

December 1, 1943

Nip Wild Eagles Score New Victory off Makin Island.

All the room monitors asked us to show more respect when we encountered the Commandant. It seemed that most people just rudely went about their business and failed to recognize him on the campus but, worse still, many ignored him. We were asked to bow, nod or stop, until he passed by.

December 3, 1943

Because of ill health, a group of Los Banos men were permitted to come back to our camp, and there was great rejoicing among the families of these men. The men reported that food at Los Banos was a little cheaper and they verified the rumor that husbands and wives would be permitted to live together in small cubicles partitioned off in the long wooden barracks.

December 4, 1943

Over the P. A. system, we were informed that we could no longer buy sugar, lard, soap or rice at the canteen. I thought of my fifty pounds of scurvy rice under my bed, and I wished I had bought more.

We had a good breakfast of hot cakes made from my starter batter and an egg apiece. Next week, we planned to have the same treat.

December 6, 1943

There was good news for the people who expected to leave for Los Banos. It would happen any day. The canteen was crowded with these people as they tried to buy ropes, bayongs, and other supplies to take with them. The seventeen Casket girls were in a state of twittering joy and nervousness, as they expected to be married when they reached Los Banos.

December 7, 1943

1 Battleship, 2 Cruisers, 4 Aircraft Carriers Sunk off Marshall, Bougainville Islands.

Five wretchedly emaciated American priests, who for the last six months had been confined at Fort Santiago, were admitted to camp. Because of their pitiful condition, they were admitted to the camp hospital.

December 8, 1943

The Nips never allowed us to forget the day. "The Imperial Rescript Declaring War on U.S.A. and Britain" was again reprinted in the morning *Nishi-Nishi*, and during the evening an impressive display of fireworks blazed against the dark sky. We watched almost indifferently. Only two years ago! Yet it seemed like centuries.

December 10, 1943

At exactly 3 A.M. the entire camp was awakened to the music of "It's Three O'clock in the Morning."

By five, large army trucks driven by Japs and armed with guards, rolled into the camp to park in the front plaza. We stood around like sleepwalkers in the gray dawn and made jokes about the 17 Casket girls who planned to marry at Los Banos. As the heavily loaded trucks started slowly down the long driveway toward the gates, the P. A. system went into action and blared out the "Mendelssohn's Wedding March," and "There Will Be a Hot Time in the Old Town Tonight."

December 11, 1943

As enormous piles of Mickey Mouse currency were smuggled into camp, many an internee went deeply into debt in an effort to feed his family. Employees of large Stateside concerns like Standard Oil, Business Machines, International Harvester, and Singer Sewing Machines had less to worry about as they were able to get all the Mickey Mouse they needed from wealthy Chinese and neutrals. Transients and those who had been self-employed had more difficulty in raising money.

Catesy and I took an inventory of our food supply under his bed and mine, and we decided that it was imperative, if we wanted to survive, that we start adding still more food to our supply. But what could we buy? There were no more canned foods, sugar, lard or rice in the canteen. However, we could still buy fresh duck eggs, so today we bought a hundred duck eggs at eighty-five centavos apiece and stored them in huge clay crocks and slack lime. As our neighbors around our lean-to watched us, most of them were skeptical that eggs would keep in this humid climate. One outspoken neighbor said he thought we were crazy. Crazy or not, we had to take the chance, and in a few months from now we'd know how efficacious the slack lime would be.

If counterfeiting hadn't been punishable by death under the present regime, this would have been the time it would have paid off.

If I had only had a bayongful of Mickey Mouse, I could have bought twelve cans of milk today. A twelve-cent can sold at ten pesos Mickey Mouse, or ten Philippine pesos, or five American gold dollars.

December 12, 1943

Shacks were still being looted by natives from the outside despite the fact that Japanese guards were supposedly patrolling the outer wall of our camp. Last night one of our internee guards caught a Filipino in the act of looting a shack. But since looting was punishable by death, our men released the Filipino. But before they let him climb back over the wall, they took away all his clothes.

December 13, 1943

Thieving also went on in the buildings among our own people. A can of milk was reported stolen from one of the rooms, and clothes from wash lines continued to be lifted.

A young American woman was escorted into camp today by six Japanese guards. Until September of this year, she had been in the mountain regions with her guerrilla husband, and loyal Igorots had risked their lives to hide and shelter the couple. Since their capture, they've been in six different provincial jails. After reaching Manila, the woman's husband was taken to Bilibid and she came to our camp. After the solitude and loneliness of the wild Bontoc mountains, she found the furious activity and congestion of the camp overwhelming.

"It's like spending your days and nights in a madhouse!" she explained.

December 14, 1943

There were ten worried kids in the isolation ward with measles. They were afraid they would miss all the Christmas excitement.

December 15, 1943

The joyous news that the Red Cross kits would be distributed spread like a grass fire, and hundreds of us rushed to the east side of the Big House to watch the distribution. But when a half dozen Japanese soldiers started ripping precious Borden and Kraft packages of cheese with their bayonets, a cry of horror escaped our lips. Corned beef cans and powdered milk were punctured and their precious contents were strewn on the filthy ground. A speechless and hate-filled audience looked on, helpless and powerless to stop them. An emaciated and anguished-looking mother with her two skinny kids by her side burst into tears. Other women started to weep and murmur protests, but our watchful men of the internee committee hustled them off to prevent an incident.

It was believed that all the rumpus and stupid rage of the Nips had been caused by the patriotic and innocent verse found on all the wrappers of Old Gold cigarettes: "Our heritage has always been freedom — we cannot afford to relinquish it — if we do our share to preserve it." They had found this verse in the first kit they had opened, and after it had been translated to them, they had gone into a rage.

As we watched their imbecilic and wanton destruction with hate-filled eyes, we hoped that they would soon tire of their childish game. After a few hundred kits had been inspected, ripped open, pawed over, and the Old Golds along with other brands of cigarettes had been removed, they became more careless with their inspection, and many packages of cigarettes were overlooked in the kits. Among the first thousand kits that were distributed today, many a person was overjoyed to find cigarettes. Those who found Old Golds with the patriotic verse were jubilant. When we had our first close peep into one of the kits, we could scarcely believe our eyes. In our wildest dreams, we had never imagined anything as complete, and filled with the type of food that we

194

hadn't seen for many months. Bars of chocolate and cheese were opened immediately and eaten. It was a glorious and happy day for everyone!

December 16, 1943

Swapping on a grand scale had already started! Cans of dry milk were swapped for canned beef, spam, or vice versa. The current price of a kit was six hundred pesos, or three hundred dollars. Catesy and I swapped all of our cigarettes for powdered coffee.

December 19, 1943

11 Enemy Vessels Sunk, Damaged off New Britain.

In addition to our kits, the Red Cross had sent thirty packages of cigarettes to each internee over eighteen. Because nurses were considered "worthy workers" according to the Commandant, each of us received an additional thirty packages.

"It would have to be you!" said one of my friends. "And you don't even smoke!"

I gave Catesy my cigarettes and, by nightfall, he had traded nearly all of the packages for powdered coffee. I was exasperated and almost in tears, for I wanted him to have the cigarettes.

"And I wanted you to have the coffee. It means a lot to you!" he said.

December 20, 1943

The American public, through the Red Cross, had surpassed themselves in generosity, for today we learned that we were to receive still more gifts. Trucks poured into the camp loaded with huge packing cases. Printed on each case were these delightful words: "Wearing apparel and toilet goods for men and women."

December 21, 1943

Brutal Attack on Nippon Hospital Ship Condemned. Foe's Strafing of Helpless Victims Bared. Japan Files Strong Protest With U. S. Through Spain.

Christmas preparations absorbed the time of mothers and fathers in camp. Fine-looking handmade toys were being secretly made in the tool shops, while in the rooms and shanties mothers were busy making and dressing dolls.

Tonight, in the theatre under the stars, we listened to a mixed chorus singing Handel's *Messiah.*

December 23, 1943

There was another stampede to place chairs in the theatre under the stars for the expected movie tonight. Young and old enjoyed Clark Gable in *Honky-Tonk,* and for the first time we weren't forced to sit through hours of stupid progaganda.

December 25, 1943

Our third Christmas under wartime conditions would have

been bleak and hungry if it hadn't been for our Red Cross kits. Though about three or four hundred of our people still received cooked food from the outside, the remainder ate in the chow line, or they opened one or two of their precious cans for this big day. There was a noticeable difference in the packages that were sent from the outside. There was less food, and less of everything.

December 27, 1943

I read the headline "Nippon Army Firmly Keeping Offensive Position — Tozyo!" loudly and dramatically to Grandma, who sat on her bed stitching at her crazy quilt. She looked at me over her glasses and declared, "That damn Tojo is a liar!"

December 28, 1943

A *Time* magazine that escaped the Japanese inspectors was found by a joyful internee in his Red Cross kit. The magazine was slowly making the rounds of the camp, and we could hardly wait until it reached our room.

December 31, 1943

P. I. Honors Rizal Today. There was no music in camp nor in the entire country in commemoration of the national hero, Rizal, who was executed forty-seven years ago by the Spaniards.

December 31, 1943

Cinderella, with a cast of over a hundred and fifty internees, was presented tonight under the guidance of our energetic emcee, Harvey Jones. The footlights and the lighted arch on the stage were cleverly disguised by Lactogen cans covering the bulbs. It diffused a soft glow on the actors and the makeshift costumes, creating an illusion of a real theatre stage on Broadway.

1 9 4 4

January 1, 1944

The past year had left its mark on us. Although we were more optimistic and cheerful, as we felt that liberation was extremely close, we were in poorer health and we suffered more from deficiency diseases.

January 2, 1944

Two hundred seventy-nine men, women and children arrived today from the southern islands. Among the group were nuns, priests, missionaries, and several army nurses. All of them were ragged, dirty, and emaciated. Three of them had to be carried by litter to the hospital. One was in an advanced stage of T.B., and the following day twenty more had to be hospitalized. One of their members, an old man, died on the ship, and he was buried at sea.

We witnessed many happy reunions today. One of the most joyful and tear-jerking was between a mother, her husband, and three young children. They had been separated for over two years. The mother had come to Manila to do her Christmas shopping in December '41 and had never been able to return to her family. She was a complete stranger to her two younger children, and when they failed to recognize her, she wept bitterly.

There was no time for pow-wows. The new arrivals were assigned to crowded rooms and we made them welcome. Four of the women whom I knew in the group had lost their husbands. Two of the latter had been beheaded by the enemy.

January 3, 1944

The newcomers were left pretty much alone so that they had a chance to get settled in their new surroundings. They were amazed at the size of our camp and the efficiency with which it was run. They marveled at our well-groomed appearance which, of course, made us laugh, and, at the same time, pleased us immensely. We rushed to our mirrors, fiddled with our hair, and applied a fresh coat of lipstick. Perhaps we weren't the scarecrows that we had imagined ourselves to be! To the tattered and dirty newcomers, we were well dressed though we wore handmade and crazy-looking creations designed from sheets, bedspreads, curtains, and chair covers.

January 4, 1944

Each person received a bottle of vitamin tablets and one towel. This was also a part of the Red Cross shipment. When the southern island people received their kits today, they were speechless with wonder. They hurriedly opened the chocolates and cheese and ate them immediately. They also received shoes, clothing, and other articles. Toys that had been made by our people and laid aside for southern island kids were passed around today, and blue, brown, and gray eyes grew round with delight as grimy little hands lovingly clutched homemade dolls, scooters, and gaily colored stilts.

January 5, 1944

Two years ago today, we would have been married if the Nips hadn't shown up. A year ago today, we learned that Catesy had T.B., and he started nine months of slow convalescence in a T.B. ward. Now, a year later, he still walked and puffed like an old man, and he could not regain his strength on our poor diet.

January 6, 1944

The depressed young woman who tried to jump out of a third-story window was removed to the camp hospital where it was hoped that, with a little attention and strong sedatives, she would be straightened out mentally.

Encouraging radio transcripts regarding American gains and heavy Japanese losses were sneaked from room to room. A copy of President Roosevelt's Christmas speech was read as intently as though we were reading the Scriptures.

January 7, 1944

Japanese Down 41 Foe Planes over Rabaul.

Fear and anxiety had touched us again because there was a possibility that the canteen, fruit, and vegetable stalls would be closed. If we were hungry now, what would happen when we could no longer buy our reliable fillers?

January 10, 1944

Excitement ran high among our Australian and British people! A survey of these nationals was taken just in the event there would be another repatriation ship. These nationals were tingling with pleasurable anticipation, and so were the people who would be left behind. For with five or six hundred less people in camp, we believed there would be more food and more space for those left behind. What a delightful thought!

January 13, 1944

As I removed the freshly baked apple pie from my native oven, a crowd of my neighbors stood by to admire and sniff the heavenly aroma of apples and cinnamon. For two years, the gallon can of apples had gathered dust under my bed, and today I opened the can. After giving a third of it to a delighted roommate, another third to a friend, I used the remainder to make a pie.

January 14, 1944

Last night the news was circulated that Rabaul had fallen and that our country was jubilantly celebrating the occasion.

For two years I had tried to get my good inner-spring mattress from my apartment. Finally, after all that time, a mattress was sent to me today. I gazed in horror and surprise at the filthy mattress. It was as thin as a worn-out tea towel, and it looked as though it had been dragged by a string through the gutters of Manila.

January 18, 1944

Because we had been warned by our room monitors that General Homma, the Number One man, and the Butcher of Bataan, was going to visit the camp today, we made ourselves scarce, so we wouldn't have to bow to this great personage.

January 20, 1944

The mentally disturbed young married woman who had tried to commit suicide by drinking iodine returned from an outside hospital. Though considerably improved, her sad eyes had a far-away look, and she rarely smiled. A medical man and a minister-psychologist were trying to solve her problems, and today the latter asked me if I would talk to her occasionally and help her as much as possible.

The earnest young minister-psychologist and I sat on the tombstones in front of the Big House to discuss her case. He spoke of the unnatural segregation of husbands and wives and of repressed desires that brought on frustration and melancholia.

As I listened to my companion, I wondered how he would have reacted had I launched into a series of laments about my repressed desires and frustrations. More than two years had gone by and I was still a long way from the altar! Just give me time, I thought grimly, and I, too, would be eligible for a padded cell.

January 21, 1944

ENEMY BASES ATTACKED INCESSANTLY — U. S. ADMITS HEAVY CASUALTIES IN NEW GUINEA AND NEW BRITAIN.

Every time we passed the Nip's office we gazed longingly and wistfully at the tremendous pile of mail and packages sent to us from our homelands, but the Nips were in no hurry to distribute them.

January 22, 1944

The melancholy young woman's eyes never changed expression as we talked about the weather, food, clothes, and places we had visited.

"I hate kids!" Her answer was listless and there was no change in her voice to denote dislike.

When I left her, I probably was more depressed than she, and I felt I sadly lacked the mental and physical strength to cope with her inertia and melancholia.

January 24, 1944

The isolation ward was jammed with extremely sick kids who had measles and chicken pox. T.B. among the adults was increasing and so were the bacillary cases.

January 25, 1944

The men were just as thrilled as the women over their gifts of wearing apparel. Swapping of play suits and other items started on a grand scale and everywhere there were people walking around gingerly as they broke in their new shoes.

January 27, 1944

Today, the sad-looking young woman sat with her husband, and I stopped to chat with them. As I watched her applying red nail polish to her well-kept nails, I quickly hid my chapped hands and broken nails in my slack pockets. I complimented her on her lovely hands, and I asked her if she would like to knit, as I still had some yarn and knitting needles that she could have.

"No, thanks. It would make me too nervous. Besides, it's such a bore." Still no interest, no dislike, no inflexion, absolutely nothing in her voice.

January 30, 1944

The morning *Nishi-Nishi* continued to beg guerrillas to return to normal life and all of them were assured amnesty.

Today, one of our American internee electricians, who had business outside, encountered a group of Filipinos at a bus stop. In a low voice, he asked them if there were any guerrillas in that part of the country.

Oh, yes, sir! I am also a guerrilla, and I already surrendered three times!" answered one of the Filipinos.

February 2, 1944

Our new pint-size Commandant, an ardent baseball fan, and somewhat of an eccentric, was a dynamo of energy. He appeared daily at sundown, armed with gardening tools. He was setting a good example to reluctant internees, who hated to exert more energy in starting new gardens because of the fear that the Nips would declare them out of bounds, just as they had done on previous occasions. When no enthusiastic gardeners appeared, our internee committee drafted men from various buildings.

February 3, 1944

Our census increased daily. Four of the outside institutions, where the sick and elderly people and children were housed, were dissolved and all the inmates returned to Santo Tomas. Our rooms had never been as horribly and alarmingly crowded.

February 4, 1944

Grandma picked up the *Nishi-Nishi,* and in an impressive voice read the headlines.

"Raspberries!" said Grandma, and her roommates laughed delightedly. Her extremely British accent and her American slang tickled our funny bone.

February 6, 1944

The hectic tempo of our lives was accelerated by new people moving into the rooms and by news that outside contact would cease.

The long lines at the canteen became longer, and people stood for hours waiting to get near the counter in hopes of buying staples for future use.

February 7, 1944

Short measure seemed to be a characteristic trait of our friends, the Nips. In addition to the short measure today, we were given putrid fish. We were sorry for the hundreds who had to rely solely on this food.

February 8, 1944

The Commandant was unhappy about the cooking that went on in all the shacks and lean-tos, and we were nervous and fearful that this privilege would soon be taken from us.

The mountainous piles of mail which arrived months ago were still in the Nip's office collecting dust. If this was their idea of effective punishment, they had succeeded. Nothing could have been more depressing and demoralizing than to see these stacks of mail day after day with little hope of ever receiving it.

February 13, 1944

All the children from the Holy Ghost Convent, with their American and British staff members, returned to the camp.

Otherwise all outside contact had ceased! A week before the gates were closed, many of the Filipino wives of Spanish-American veterans in camp moved to houses near Santo Tomas. From the second and third floors of the Big House, we watched these faithful wives waving to their husbands who were housed in the Education Building, the Gym, and the Big House.

February 16, 1944

A little girl of three had diphtheria, and the Commandant allowed the child to be moved to an outside hospital. Those who had come in close contact with the child were in strict quarantine, which, under the circumstances, was a farce.

February 17, 1944

The morning rag was our only contact with the outside. In spite of its lies, there was some comfort in knowing that we weren't completely shut off from the rest of the world. Those closest to the secret radio reported that our forces had landed in Truk.

No more meat and charcoal could be bought! Fortunately, Catesy and I had several sacks, which would probably last six or seven months.

February 21, 1944

No more food packages! All contact with the outside world had ceased!

No more *Nishi-Nishi* was to be sold in camp. Despite its lying propaganda, it had given us plenty of laughs. Those in the know, and of course that included all of us, believed that the paper had been giving out too much information.

February 22, 1944

According to reliable sources (which made me smile), our forces were only five hundred miles from Philippine waters.

Iucluded in the last Red Cross shipment of a few months ago was a large supply of sulpha. Without this wonder drug, the children and adults in camp would have died like flies from bacillary dysentery and respiratory ailments.

February 24, 1944

Bacillary dysentery, respiratory diseases, and thirty cases of measles in the Isolation Ward. The children with measles, at this time, were extremely ill and it took them a long time to recover.

February 25, 1944

Every few days the nerve-shattering rumor cropped up that there would be no more individual cooking. Charcoal fires were frantically and hastily started and there was a pathetic last attempt to cook enough food to last for the next few days.

Today I boiled a pot of vegetable soup and added two strips of our salted pork. To us, it was wonderful, but I daresay a dog back home would have turned up his nose after taking one sniff.

202

February 26, 1944

The "no cooking" rumor proved to be only a rumor, but the damage was done, with nerves in a jittery state. Precious food was spoiled, and upset stomachs followed.

February 27, 1944

Hot plates, irons, electric razors, toasters, percolators, and extension cords, which we had long given up using, were confiscated, and we were surprised it hadn't been done long ago.

February 28, 1944

The news and rumors being circulated were good. They had never been anything else.

We chatted with the Macks tonight in the corridor and, as usual, they were bubbling with optimism. Poor darlings, I thought pityingly. How thin and emaciated they were! Mr. Mack's hair had turned completely white, and Mrs. Mack's skin was sallow and wrinkled, but her lovely brown eyes were smiling. They had never once lost their faith and optimism. From their cheerful manner, one gathered that the American forces were just outside the gates of the camp.

March 2, 1944

When weather permitted, we had soft-ball games in the evenings, and one of the most interested and enthusiastic spectators was our eccentric and pint-size new Commandant. He never missed a game. Several of the teams played excellent ball, but our favorite team consisted of French-Canadian and Irish priests, who came to this country only a few weeks before the war to fulfill missionary assignments. All these young priests were well-liked by everyone. They worked hard, and they were good sports on the ball field.

March 3, 1944

The Japs were still tearing the camp apart in search of the renegade radio. They searched for transcripts, diaries, or anything that was incriminating. Who could foretell what was incriminating to the Oriental mind?

The tension and anxiety that gripped us when the dreaded Military Police from Fort Santiago searched our rooms, shanties, hospitals, and various parts of the camp were fearful. We all had something to hide and worry about. Money, jewelry, diaries, transcripts, and maps. While we worried about our own problems, we prayed for the safety of the brave man who operated the renegade radio. All around us, people buried their money in various spots, and they burned their diaries.

My diary had become so bulky that it would not fit into a Lactogen can, which I had planned to bury. Instead I sneaked out to the balcony one dark night and brought in my bundle of old rags. And I unwrapped the rags and oilcloth, and carefully added the many pages that I had written in the last year to the already thick stack of sheets. After rewrapping it, I took this bundle and again secured it to the drainpipe next to the brooms and mops. Then, for a while, I stopped making a daily entry in my journal, as the snooping went on all the time.

March 31, 1944

The last few weeks had been a nightmare! It all started when two Americans, former camp buyers, were taken to Fort Santiago. Then another camp buyer, after a great deal of questioning and inhuman beatings, was confined to the camp hospital with a broken leg and back injuries. From time to time, he was carried by litter to the Nip's office for further questioning. Another American, a lovable old man, who for the past few months had trimmed the wicks and filled all the coconut-oil lamps in the corridors, was taken outside and no one knew what had happened to him.

The radio still hadn't been found, and the Military Police were on a rampage. When they searched the Big House, a cordon of soldiers encircled and froze that area and no one could leave or enter the building. The other buildings and shanty areas were worked the same way. Nothing was overlooked. The Nips searched under mattresses; they examined the wires that held up our nets, and they looked outside the windows and balconies. When the squatty but powerfully built member of the Military Police went out on our balcony, I died a thousand deaths. When he returned without a bundle of dirty old rags in his hands, I died again—this time from pure joy and relief.

A young American who, prior to the war had been a radio expert, was on the suspect list. His shack and belongings had been searched many times, and although they didn't find a radio, he was taken outside. Who would be next?

As the days passed, restrictions became tighter and this place had all the earmarks of a concentration camp, as depicted in books and movies. We had roll call twice a day. We were made to line up in double rows to face the Rising Sun in the east. With hands behind our back, eyes straight ahead, we stood at respectful attention while an arrogant Japanese lieutenant in a dirty and ill-fitting uniform shuffled by to count us. To show him and his cohorts respect was difficult, as perhaps only a few hours before we had seen several of them in the doorway of the Commandant's office picking their noses or bare toes.

The pattern of the Nip's behavior was inconsistent at times. Leniency and kindness alternated with inconsideration and marked brutality. Today, they displayed leniency when they permitted three U. S. Army doctors from military prison camps to help the civilian doctors at the hospital.

The Japanese displayed further kindness by distributing the mail. There was nothing for Catesy and me.

The feeling of optimism that the end of the war was near had disappeared.

Now that no one left for outside hospitals, major surgeries were done in the camp. An enucleation and hysterectomy were performed the other day.

Added to our food problems and the tension brought on by the snooping, we were facing another hot season and, as a result, boils and unsightly skin eruptions were on the increase.

The loud speaker blared at midnight last night that: "By order of the Commandant, no internees were to leave their rooms or shanties."

Immediately, lights were turned on in all the rooms and corridors, and the buildings buzzed with talk. It could mean only one thing: someone had escaped, and they were taking roll call. A few minutes later several Nips started to count noses. Since no one could leave any of the buildings, I was unable to relieve the night nurse at 3 A.M. But, instead of getting a good night's sleep, I lay awake until daybreak, listening to the shouts and rifle shots in and around the camp.

April 1, 1944

An alert, which continued all day, and blackout at night, created a tiny hope in our hearts. Were our planes preparing to bomb the city? However, those people who had lived in Japan for years told us it didn't mean a thing.

April 2, 1944

Another exodus to Los Banos would take place in a few days. Now there were many volunteers, as they felt that conditions at Los Banos could hardly be worse than here. Only a few of the draftees tried to keep from going. Two of them were women. One of them, in a last desperate attempt to evade the draft, shammed a beautiful fade-out on the hospital floor, and the doctors and nurses, wise to her tricks, left her lying there. Another woman, at the eleventh hour, with a little more originality, developed a pain in her side.

April 3, 1944

The traffic of Flying Eagles over us went on day and night. During the day, the show-offs always flew low enough for us to see the familiar orange dot. How oppressively tired we were of that hated fried egg! If only we could see a beloved star!

It was twenty-eight months ago when I last saw an American plane, and it seemed more like twenty-eight years. I had been sitting by my window in my sixth-floor apartment, sadly watching the flames and dense smoke which blanketed the ruined city. Suddenly, I heard the roar of a plane close by. Startled, I looked up. The plane was so close that I could have touched the star on the plane with the end of a broomstick, and I could plainly see that the pilot was very young. By that time, the Japs had already landed at Lingayan Gulf, and most of our planes had been destroyed at Clark Field and Iba. I remember how I had thought about that lonely pilot. It seemed as though he was fighting the war singlehanded.

April 4, 1944

We've had an excellent opportunity to see the power of the Military Police. Though our present, eccentric Commandant was a colonel in the reserves, an arrogant, and young lieutenant of the Military Police bosses him around.

The present "no cooking in shanties" came as a thunderclap and we were hungrier than ever now that we had nothing but the mouldy rice and evil-smelling fish that was served in the line.

Another five hundred men, women and children left for Los Banos today.

April 10, 1944

Again the Japs shifted their pattern of behavior to leniency. We were allowed to cook on our native stoves and we each received a box of matches from them. On the cover of each matchbox, graphically depicted in brilliant colors, was the Rising Sun flag shining over the Stars and Stripes and the Union Jack.

Twenty high school students graduated, and many of us attended their Class Day ceremonies with mixed emotions. The young girls wore evening dresses made in the camp, and they carried tiny bouquets of flowers grown around the shacks. This was a strange and sad graduation, and as we watched these young people receiving their diplomas, our eyes were blinded by tears.

April 15, 1944

There were eighty cases of measles among the children in the Isolation Ward, besides chicken pox and whooping cough.

Two babies were born in camp last week, and because of the food situation, the parents received considerable criticism. The "pregnant papas" no longer served a term of confinement in the local jail, and the mothers were no longer cruelly separated from their husbands and other children.

April 24, 1944

The Japanese presented our Internee Committee with this prepared oath: "I, the undersigned, hereby solemnly pledge myself that I will not under any circumstances attempt to escape or conspire directly or indirectly against the Japanese Military Authorities, as long as I am in their custody."

Our Internee Committee tried to prevent this further humiliation and they filed a protest concerning our starvation diet, our crowded living conditions, and the brutal treatment of some of our fellow prisoners. But all our protests and yakamashi regarding the signing of the oath came to nothing. Everyone over fifteen was made to sign. There was one exception. He was a quiet and eccentric Chinese who was born and raised in America. When he refused to sign the oath, the Nips threw him into the camp jail.

May 30, 1944

We attended Memorial Day services in the Father's garden and we remembered those who had already passed on. We prayed for our men in the military camps nearby, and we prayed for ourselves.

June 5, 1944

It was rumored that our eccentric Commandant was suffering from shell shock, or that he was just "plain nuts."

Because none of the garden workers showed up today, the little man went into a tirade. He screamed, pounded his desk, and pushed his subordinates around. He shouted at our men of the Internee Committee, and then he ordered that all athletics in the camp would cease.

The following day, he spoke before a monitor's meeting, and Leslie reported that his pantomiming was more hilarious than Charlie Chaplin's in *The Dictator*. Scarcely five feet tall, and weighing less than a hundred pounds, he strutted back and forth before his audience, with arms waving like a windmill. He removed his hat and sword with a businesslike flourish and placed them on a chair beside him. Then he started his speech in rapid Japanese, while the confused interpreter groped around for words. Under the stress of watching the Dictator's gyrating arms, and trying to keep up with the machine-gun rapidity of words, the interpreter's English bogged down completely. There was an exchange of glances between the Dictator and the interpreter. The Dictator's was furious, and the latter's frankly bewildered.

But the Dictator didn't give up easily. He switched into broken English, and then Japanese. The interpreter, having regained his second wind, began to interpret again. The pointless and rambling speech went on with more ludicrous pantomiming. Suddenly the Dictator seized the interpreter's head and pushed it roughly against the microphone. The audience scarcely breathed. They were near bursting with suppressed laughter.

He continued with his speech and no one could follow his rambling words. After he had exhausted his favorite subject, baseball, he changed to dancing. The climax came when he demonstrated the benefits of aesthetic dancing by kicking his legs back and forth in the manner of a chorine. Not content with this demonstration, he lifted his short leg, and executed a high kick accompanied by groans and fearful grimaces. The room monitors could no longer bottle their mirth. They burst into laughter and then thunderous applause.

The applause was sweet to his ears, for he continued to talk and strut back and forth. Having pulled out his shirt from his breeches, his shirttails flapped around him as he pranced before his awestruck audience.

"Why don't you like baseball?" he asked suddenly.

"We can't play baseball on the food we get, and besides, you have just forbidden all athletics," answered someone in the audience.

"The food is good. It makes you strong!" On the last word, the Dictator flexed his puny deltoids to show his manliness, and to further emphasize his point, he pounded his concave chest in the manner of Tarzan.

"We have only twenty-five sick out of each thousand internees. Very good! Very good! (This was a gross misstatement as the number of ill in the rooms and shanties ran into the hundreds.) "I would like to give you one egg a day, and two eggs for the weak and sick, but I cannot now; this is wartime!" Then, concluding his speech with both arms raised as though in benediction, he added, "You may have baseball and athletics again!"

June 9, 1944

More landings in France! What a change in camp morale! There were happy smiles among our people and there was less talk of hunger. Maps were dusted off and surreptitiously consulted while camp strategists planned the next move. Of course, the burning question was: How soon would the blitzkrieg start out here! The wise guys said that no major offensive would take place in the Pacific until after election. Wagers were made, and many of the optimists bet we would be out by Christmas.

Our old friend, the lying *Nishi-Nishi*, was distributed in camp today, and this was the headline:

GENERAL MACARTHUR'S FROG-JUMPING FROM ISLAND TO ISLAND IS PROVING VERY COSTLY AND FAR FROM SUCCESSFUL.

According to our bamboo wireless, our forces were 350 miles from Mindanao.

We've had four deaths in the last two weeks.

We were plainly worried. Our pint-size Dictator left us. Whatever his faults, he was not unjust, cruel, nor anti-white. Who would his successor be?

By evening, our worst fears had been realized. Our new Commandant's helper was the arrogant young Lieutenant Tamura of the Military Police, whom we already knew. He ordered all able-bodied men to build a ten-foot barbed-wire fence in the front entrance of the camp. Our men refused. They stated that the food was insufficient for hard labor of this type, and that our camp would in no way benefit by such work; furthermore, they stated that the Japanese violated a Geneva agreement by forcing labor on civilian prisoners.

The Commandant issued a statement that the Japanese Military did not recognize any Geneva agreement and that if the men did not start work immediately, he would be forced to call on outside help, and that he would in no way be responsible for the consequences. So the men went to work.

A long stream of large and dilapidated trucks filled with men, women, children, nuns and priests crept into the camp. They were the much-discussed missionaries who had signed a pledge many months ago which read: "to cooperate with the Japanese through religion," so that they could live outside. Some of our internees believed that these people had lived in comfort and in the privacy of their homes, while the rest of us had been caged up like animals and fed slop. They probably had lived better outside than we had, but at the same time they had carried on their work in orphanages, hospitals and schools as long as the enemy permitted them.

The following day, all the missionaries were shipped off to Los Banos.

One of the cruelest things the Japanese did to a group of desperately hungry people was to refuse to accept the carts of food that were sent to our camp by Manila organizations. Day after day, fruit, vegetables, and eggs were sent in pushcarts, which were left standing outside the gates, while representatives of charitable organizations pleaded with the Japs to permit them to give us the food. But our benevolent jailors told them that we had sufficient food, and we sadly watched them wheeling away the carts. For this cruelty and falsehood, we hated them. Our hate was intensified when we saw the listless children and the old men and women in advanced stages of beri-beri and other deficiency diseases.

Catesy was in the hospital with bacillary dysentery and I was

worried about him. With his chest history, he could not afford to
lose much more weight.

July 17, 1944

Just as quickly as patients were able to creep around, they were
dismissed to make room for more sick people. Because the doctor
knew I'd take care of Catesy, he was discharged today, and the
following day I was sticken with bacillary.

Headache, backache, leg cramps, abdominal distension, diarrhea,
and high fever. I had them all, and it left me as weak as a day-old
babe. There was no room for me at the hospital, so Catesy looked
after me. Though still weak and shaky, I was back at the children's
ward in five days.

July 18, 1944

The Philippines will be retaken in sixty days! This rumor had
many in an emotional tailspin. The people who were moved by
these rumors were either in a state of short-lived elation, or when
the rumor proved false, they sank into a pit of despair.

No more ups and downs for me! It took me a long time to learn
not to be touched by rumors, and now my emotional graphic chart
was always the same dead level. Subnormal.

Two of the hardest-working women in camp were Holy Mary,
a religious worker, and Polish Mary, the wife of a prisoner in a
military camp.

Polish Mary had worked all these months doing odd jobs, such as
washing, ironing, and other equally menial tasks for people who
could afford to have their work done. The money she earned from
these jobs, and all of it paid in good Philippine pesos or dollars,
went into a small bag around her neck. Though she went hungry,
the pile of money in the bag became larger as the months went by.
Some day, when the war was over, and her husband returned from
a military camp, her nest egg would come in handy. But, alas, one
of the Japs, noticing the string around her neck, yanked it off, and
that was the end of her many months of hard work and self-denial.
Poor Polish Mary! All her work for nothing! Her eyes were red
and swollen from weeping.

Holy Mary was a good Christian. She practiced what she
preached. All the money she had earned from doing odd jobs was
shared with those who were penniless.

Every time I thought of those two hard-working women, I was
reminded of the Biblical parable of the "seeds that fell on good
ground."

July 20, 1944

My little dog, Rags, had died, and Mr. Nagy was very ill. The
local Nazis had been hard on him, and he had been forced to move

several times to escape their prying and persecutions. His note had been smuggled in by a priest who had been in the missionary group that left for Los Banos. The priest had given it to the first internee he encountered, and I received the note only today. Several years ago, I would have wept at the news of Rags' death, but now it seemed that nothing could move me.

Several long wooden barracks were constructed by the Nips to house the additional soldiers that were added to the camp garrison, and additional floodlights were installed to illuminate all of the camp.

"Manila will be retaken in sixty days! Just wait and see!" Mrs. Mack's voice was as confident as her husband's, and she patted me on the back before she left.

"Good! Wonderful!" My voice was devoid of any elation and my pulse rate remained the same. Time enough to go berserk when the Yanks opened the gates of our prison!

July 22, 1944

It rained all the time.

The Nips were photographing every man, woman and child in groups of five. Like Sing Sing inmates, we posed with numbers printed on a placard tied to our chests.

Just as I was beginning to feel a little stronger from my bacillary bout, I became ill from plague shots. The shots were ordered by the Nips. And who was I to argue with a guy who carried a gun?

July 24, 1944

Five A.M. at the children's hospital was a lonely hour. The children were asleep and all my fellow internees were asleep in buildings quite a distance from this isolated spot. Only a few internee guards patrolled this large campus and, of course, the Japanese guards, and that's what worried me.

Thank goodness, the children were quiet, and I was able to sit at the desk for my head felt as large as a pumpkin and I was weak and nauseated.

Suddenly, I heard the shuffle of oversize boots coming on the walk nearby. My heart started to pound and fear glued me to the desk. I couldn't move. Who would hear me if I screamed? The shuffling steps came closer. The Jap hawked, expectorated, and blew his nose, while I sat glued to the chair. Where could I hide? My eyes searched the darkened ward wildly. In the dim light of the tiny office, perhaps he wouldn't see me. Noiselessly, I left my wooden bakias at the desk and tiptoed in my barefeet to the ward, and there by the bedside of a little boy, I crouched and watched.

The Jap came through the door and stopped at the desk to rummage through my charts. Then, taking a few steps toward the darkened ward, he peered inside. Could he see me? I could see *him* perfectly. Peaked cap, rifle, sloppy uniform, with bare chest and huge belly exposed. As in a nightmare, I watched him, terrified, and cold with fear. I dared not breathe—not until he walked through the front door to the outside. Not until I heard his shuffling gait a long way off did I leave the darkened ward. When I finally stood up, I was so weak I could scarcely walk. Two more hours before my relief came on. How could I bear it?

July 25, 1944

People were opening cans recklessly, and trying to buy anything that they could from other internees in order to dispose of excess Mickey Mouse. All because of the choice rumors that Hitler was dead and Tojo had committed hara-kiri.

"If we believed all the scuttlebutt today, the Yanks should be coming through the front gates by sundown!" Catesy grinned as he built a fire in preparation for our daily lunch of boiled rice.

Our enemy again did the unpredictable. One of our Number One guerrilla leaders, whose name had frequently appeared in the *Nishi-Nishi* as the most wanted man, was brought into our camp to join his wife and children. After months of cat-and-mouse existence, he finally surrendered, and now his family occupied private quarters in the Big House.

August 2, 1944

Beri-beri was another queer sounding word like Tiki-tiki, a native formula, for this serious vitamin B deficiency. I had studied about beri-beri in my nursing course, but I had never actually encountered any of these cases in my daily nursing.

Here in this large prison camp, most of our people suffered from this dreadful disease in various stages, from beginning symptoms to the last mutilating stages when death came.

Its symptoms were gastric irritation, emaciation, swelling of legs, chest and even the face, neuritis, polyneuritis, burning pains, muscular wastage, paralysis, inanition and disturbance of the heart's action. These people, with their extreme dropsical condition, literally drowned in their own fluid, just as I had seen pneumonias of the fatal type dying in Pittsburgh, before the days of the wonder drug.

A few months ago, one of our friends had stopped at our lean-to to announce gleefully that he had gained eight pounds. I looked at the poor deluded man standing before me, and saw obvious beginning signs of a puffed face, edematous hands and eyelids. That was three or four months ago! By now, we all knew the symptoms. Each day, we examined our faces, hands and legs for the telltale signs. Most of us had some symptoms, but what we feared most were the edematous legs that resembled useless and dead stumps of wood. Worse still, were the distorted and large faces that resembled grinning Halloween pumpkins.

The faithful spouse of Mrs. Greenshoes continued to wait on her though he was already in the last stages of beri-beri. His legs, face, and hands were puffed, and the skin over his bones was taut, and it glistened like the white belly of a toad. His respirations were labored, and as I walked behind him on the back stairs today, I marveled that he didn't collapse before my eyes.

August 9, 1944

The Nips were digging air-raid shelters in front of the Commandant's office. Something was in the wind! What a thrill to watch them dig and sweat! Standing at a discreet distance, we made facetious remarks in an undertone, as we watched them digging.

August 10, 1944

I was sick again with bacillary, and the huge doses of sulfa made me dizzy, ill, weak, and my eyes bothered me. Watery rice, tea, and kalamansi juice was my diet, and occasionally I had a ripe banana for which Catesy paid a fortune.

Fortunately, the children were good and I didn't have too much running to do. While I sat at the desk, I placed a wide bandage underneath the cramped toes of both feet. By pulling upward on my reins, I was able to keep my toes from pushing down. My toes behaved in this annoying and nerve-wrecking manner most of the time. It was worse than a toothache, for in addition to cramps, the toes stubbornly pushed downward. By pulling on my reins, I kept the toes in position, but it didn't relieve the cramps. This, too, was a part of beri-beri, but I was fortunate; my face was thin as ever, and I hadn't gained any excess fluid pounds. Too miserable to feel hunger or to fear shuffling boots.

August 11, 1944

Several priests and a very old man, who had worked with the lepers at Culion for more than thirty-five years, were brought into the camp and placed in the crowded jail.

The air-raid shelter that the Japanese dug a few days ago was covered with about twelve inches of water. If only the Yanks would come now! It would be such a treat to see our jailors hit the flooded trenches!

Our hospitals, clinics, and first-aid stations were prepared, just in case of bombing. Outwardly, we went about our work calmly, but we thought of only one thing. How soon? How soon would our boys start bombing the city? Excitement and expectancy had reached the boiling point.

213

The leper worker was released from the camp jail and we learned that many of the lepers had starved to death. The leper island of Culion had always depended on food and other supplies being brought to them by boat once a week, but since the occupation their supply had ended. They ate cats, dogs, rats, and leaves off the trees, and those who tried to escape from the island were machine-gunned by the Japs.

The Nips were dreaming up a new form of torture. Enforced labor. Ropemaking for the men, and making envelopes for the women. They believed that there was too much idleness in the camp.

Holy Toledo! We never had an idle minute, what with camp duties, cooking, washing, gardening, marketing, standing in lines, and taking care of the sick, the aged, and children. What's more, we did it on half rations consisting mostly of rice and vegetables flavored with tainted fish.

Today's joke was a bit grim, but it brought a cackle every time it was repeated. "If MacArthur didn't soon come, he'd get here in time to bury the last internee."

Because it was Catesy's birthday, we celebrated by opening a can of corn and a can of corned beef which we added to boiled rice and many cloves of garlic in the iron skillet. Garlic was one item which we could still buy at the canteen, and people ate it raw, like apples, in the hope of deriving some nourishment from it.

While the rest of the city was brilliantly lighted, we were in complete blackout. Why? We wondered.

It was difficult to work in such a poorly illuminated ward, and I continued to stumble as I went from one child's bed to another. Added to the pneumonia and bacillary cases, we had one extremely sick child, a typhus suspect. The child was in delirium, and I kept sponging her to reduce her high temperature. I was so busy and worried about the sick child that I failed to hear the shuffling boots until I saw the soldier, with shirt unbuttoned and bare chest exposed, silhouetted in the doorway of the ward.

My heart raced madly. Could he see me? Where could I hide? I dared not move to another bed for fear he would hear me. Quietly, I lifted the covers of the little typhus suspect, and just as quietly, I crawled in bed beside her.

Like a motionless statue, he stood peering into the darkened ward. The filthy cummerbund around his abdomen was sloppily wound and it exposed the upper part of a fat and repulsive abdomen. He probably stood in the doorway for only a minute, but to me it seemed like hours. When he finally went away, I was shaking with fear and rage. I was determined that it was the last time that I would be left alone in this isolated spot.

August 23, 1944

What a difference to have someone to share these lonely hours of nursing with me. My aide was a lovely young matron from India, whose husband was fighting somewhere in the Pacific. When the children were quiet, we sat in the tiny nurse's office and whispered about our dreams and future. She planned to have a baby as soon as the war was over. The hours went by quickly, and now that I had a companion, my fears of shuffling boots had completely disappeared.

Only my toes misbehaved with their usual stubborn dropping and cramping. When I applied the bandage to my bare toes, and pulled on the reins as with a spirited horse, my aide watched with fascination. When she started to giggle, I joined her. Our giggles turned to laughter, and we laughed so long and hard that we were afraid we had awakened the children.

August 24, 1944

Blackout. Rain. Upset stomach. Another recurrence of bacillary and another course of sulfa. Dizziness, weakness, distended abdomen, and tenesmus were with me day and night, but there was no one to take my place at the hospital. When I crawled out of my bed at 2:45 A.M., I felt I was only half alive. Fortunately, my aide was well and she did most of the running. The tiny typhus suspect was still delirious and I stayed by her bedside all night.

August 27, 1944

Like a shadowy zombie, I moved around at the hospital, and every opportunity I had was spent sitting down with my head resting on the desk.

The little typhus suspect was rational and her temperature was normal. When I relayed the wonderful news to her parents, they broke down and wept with relief and joy.

August 30, 1944

I tried to eat the mushy boiled rice, but was unable to retain it. It gave me cramps and severe distension. Catesy was greatly concerned. I lost so much weight that my faded slacks hung around my hips like a pup tent. The generous hips, that I jokingly called a congenital deformity, had melted away. Under normal conditions, I would have been wildly elated. Now, nothing was important, except to retain the mushy rice.

September 3, 1944

Thrilled and excited groups of people were seen around the

campus discussing the rumor that Germany had surrendered. Surely, the Japs couldn't fight the world alone!

Tonight, we watched the giant searchlights spread wide ribbons of light over the heavens. The lights danced across the sky like long streamers around a Maypole. Was the enemy expecting a visit from our bombers? Delightful thought! We talked of nothing else!

September 4, 1944

The people who had believed that Germany had capitulated were a little less enthusiastic today. In fact, they felt let down, and they wondered if, perhaps, they hadn't been a bit reckless in opening several cans of their small hoard of provisions. Perhaps liberation was still a long way off.

September 6, 1944

The understanding and kind lady doctor at the children's hospital gave me a short holiday and she told me to stay in bed as much as possible. Catesy was my nurse, and he brought all my pitiful meals to me. As soon as I regained a little strength, I went outside to the corridor for our meals. In addition to my muscular cramps, abdominal distension, gastric disturbance, and lassitude, I had a desire to weep. I've always detested weepy and weak women, and now I was weak myself.

September 8, 1944

Blackouts and searchlights combed the sky nightly, and we were keyed to a highly expectant mood. When would our bombers show up?

September 12, 1944

"What's wrong, honey girl? You look like hell!" Tientsin Mary's frank though sympathetic comment about my looks was so like her.

I explained about my bacillary.

"How are you, Mary? Do you get any extra food besides the line chow?" We always asked that question when we met a fellow internee. Then I remembered her friendliness with the soldiers, and I felt my face getting hot.

"Awww!" she retorted with a harsh laugh. "I never have to worry about food. All I worry about is when we get out of this damn place!"

September 13, 1944

We were looking forward to tomorrow. It was my birthday, and we planned to open four three-ounce cans of food.

September 14, 1944

I had never been more discouraged and depressed than I was today. Because I was too ill to eat, Catesy refused to open any cans until I was well enough to share them with him. How we had looked forward to this day! How we had talked about the food we would eat! When I urged him to open at least one can for himself, he stubbornly refused, and it made me more miserable than ever. For the first time since internment, I began to wonder if I'd live to see the Yanks return.

Then something wonderful happened! The air-raid siren went into its banshee wail, and we could scarcely believe our ears. We were electrified into one beautiful hope. Were we to see our bombers today? Food was forgotten, as we waited tense and expectant. Though the alarm went off and then on again for the second time, nothing happened. But we were convinced our boys were near. Already the optimists predicted that we'd be out by Thanksgiving!

September 15, 1944

Our rice ration was cut again and Catesy and I were fortunate to still have some of our own reserve supply of dirty rice. I was still sick and spending most of my time in bed, and I had lost five pounds in two days.

Because typhoid was prevalent in the city, we were boiling our water.

September 16, 1944

The air-alert was off, and we were sunk in despair! Were our forces getting farther away from us?

The new cut in our rice ration was a bitter blow. Our people were desperately hungry. They looked like scarecrows with their scrawny bodies, listless manner, and with that anxious mask that we all wore these days.

Our arrogant young Commandant issued instructions that we were to show more respect toward the Japanese, and that if we failed to make the proper bow of respect, he would teach us how it was done. This constant yakamashi regarding bowing and respecting them certainly added up to one thing—their feeling of inferiority.

September 17, 1944

Still on sulfa every fourth hour and on a strict diet, which of course would be laughable if it weren't so grim. Catesy opened our last can of powdered Klim, and he brought me a glass twice a day.

September 18, 1944

The Commandant insisted that we dig more air-raid shelters, "since the war had been intensified out here." We were cheered by his admission, but we wondered why all the concern over our safety? How eagerly we listened for an air-alarm! How desperately we searched the sky for our planes!

September 20, 1944

The three- to six-year-old kids in camp couldn't remember any other life but this, and their vocabulary consisted of a jargon of Santo Tomas words, such as telinum, pechay, teen-age line, chow line, Issue Tissue, rollcall, beri-beri, and many others. They were naturally war conscious. They imitated the blood-curdling wail of the siren, and they flourished toy pistols, swords, tin helmets, and blank cartridges. They jumped into half completed trenches and crouched in several inches of mud and water. To many of these young children, the Japanese soldier was the hero, the top man; consequently, they wanted the role of head man when playing war.

Today, I saw eight American kids fall in line with twelve marching Nips. They imitated their swinging arms and exaggerated goose step with considerable enthusiasm and hilarity, while internees looked on a bit worriedly.

September 21, 1944

The day started quietly and monotonously like any other day in the past two and a half years.

Since 5 A.M., the enemy had been firing their guns in target practice. A lone Japanese plane pulled a long snakelike target which kept sashaying back and forth in the clouds. The guns kept firing, but they consistently missed the target.

Then suddenly the heavens were darkened with planes! Why were the Nips using all those planes for target practice, I wondered curiously? Just about that time the anti-aircraft guns started to pop furiously, and a joyous shout came from hundreds of throats throughout the camp.

"They're American planes!"

Men, women, and children ran out of buildings and shacks shouting like maniacs. Others, with eyes cast heavenward, stood rooted to the ground. They could not believe their eyes! A few of the bombers flew low enough to give us the thrill of a lifetime! We saw, not the familiar and hated orange circle, but a flash of blue and a white star. It was like a beautiful dream! We watched with wild joy and fascination.

Kay, Margo, and Leslie joined us at the window, and for an hour or more we saw a show that could not be duplicated on Broadway.

There were so many of our bombers that it was impossible to count them as they flashed rapidly back and forth across the sky. We watched, entranced and jubilant. A large Japanese transport plane had tried to reach safety, but our bombers literally blew it from the sky. Like bits of burned paper carried by a high wind, we saw the plane fall and drop.

Meanwhile, all the internees had been herded into the buildings, and we were warned about looking outside as the Japs had threatened to shoot anyone found at a window. Though the risk was great, no one wanted to miss the wonderful show.

By placing bath towels on the head of the cross bars of my bed, we had excellent peepholes and Grandma, Margo and I were on my bed, lying on our stomachs. We had a complete view of the Bay area. The others crouched by the window. The show lasted for more than an hour and throughout the room there were cries of admiration. Look at that one dive! See that bomb dropping! Now listen! Just like clockwork! Isn't it beautiful?

We pounded each other until we were black and blue, and we shouted until we were hoarse. We behaved like pagan Romans watching the lions devour the Christian martyrs.

When we saw a Japanese soldier in camp camouflaged with large banana leaves, darting out of his air-raid shelter to shoot at one of our bombers with his rifle, we laughed so hard that the tears gushed from our eyes. How stupid! How very, very funny!

The first-aid stations were prepared, and although considerable shrapnel fell around the camp, there were no casualties.

After we ate our simple lunch of boiled rice and fish water, most of us had to lie down and rest. The joy and wild excitement had left us weak but deliriously happy.

They came again at 6 P.M.! This time, our bombers came in waves of thirty-six. Enemy aircraft popped furiously, but thank God, their many weeks of practicing hadn't helped their aim. Our audacious bombers circled, dipped, swooped, dived and dropped their bombs, and they literally thumbed their noses at the enemy aircraft.

When our bombers left, there were three great fires in the Manila Bay area, Neilson airport, and Grace Park. The mammoth conflagration illuminated the heavens.

Like excited and pop-eyed kids on Christmas Eve, we went to bed filled with quivering anticipation of more good things to come.

September 22, 1944

We dressed hurriedly and excitedly, and choked down our wormy mush. As soon as our plates and spoons were washed, we rushed back to our rooms to our ringside seats. This time, Kay, Margo and I lay on my bed, while Catesy crouched under the window.

We were just in time! For, no sooner did we get settled, than our bombers came again. In the beginning, we counted fifty-four of them, but as the sky darkened with planes, we lost count. The bombers separated, converged, dove one by one, and the bombs dropped like baskets of groceries. Because we didn't want to miss any of the furious activity, our heads jerked from side to side as at a three-ring circus.

That night we celebrated! Cans were opened recklessly. We expected landings very soon.

September 23, 1944

Blood plasma and vitamin shots couldn't have done as much for the morale of the camp as the spectacular bombings we had witnessed in the last two days. We talked of nothing else.

September 26, 1944

Could it be that our jailors were trying to be good to us?

For quite some time, our persevering Mr. Grant had been clamoring and coaxing for cornmeal to supplement our inadequate and insipid rice mush. Today, the Nips sent us several tons of cornmeal and we had cornmeal mush. What a treat!

Had our bombers visited the city, it would have been a perfect day.

September 27, 1944

"Lover Come Back to Me!" How we chuckled when we heard this popular song blaring out its appropriate lyrics over the P.A. system. We dressed hurriedly, breakfasted, and rushed back to our rooms in anticipation of more good things to come. When our boys didn't show up, our disappointment was like an acute pain.

September 28, 1944

The reckless opening of precious cans had somewhat abated, now that there was a possibility that our small reserve had to last a few more months.

The leaders of our camp estimated that more than twenty-five hundred of our people depended solely on the breakfast mush and the supper of rice with a tiny scoop of watery gravy. With their sallow skins, ulcerated and swollen legs, and emaciated bodies, it was not difficult to differentiate them from the internees who had a little extra food to supplement the starvation diet.

It was only a question of a short time before the rest of us would be in the same fix.

September 29, 1944

The cornmeal was poison to the post-bacillaries, amoebics, and colitis cases, but we had little else to eat. Inflammation of the intestines, followed by cramps and abdominal distension was a natural result. Our doctors, attendants, and nurses were as sick as the patients they cared for.

September 30, 1944

The women who cleaned vegetables for the camp staged a battle royal every day with internee guards. After their work was over, they sneaked several handfuls of vegetable peelings in their aprons and baskets in order to take them to their shacks to cook.

October 2, 1944

On liquids again! If only I could eat rice and cornmeal!
Depressed, weak, and hungry all the time.

How desperately we scanned the skies for signs of our bombers!

October 3, 1944

Catesy was elated today because I retained the rice mush, and already I seemed to feel stronger and more cheerful.

October 4, 1944

If I had the strength, I'd bawl like a baby with colic. Back on sulfaguanidine and humming-bird portions of watery rice. The sulfa killed the bacillary but it was killing me, too, in slow stages.

Today, nothing could perk me up except a raid by our bombers.

How I had changed! From a mild-mannered pacifist, I became a bloodthirsty belligerent.

October 5, 1944

Via the "basura (garbage) wireless" we heard today that the *Nishi-Nishi* was preparing the Filipinos for the ruthless invasion by the enemy. How corny can the propaganda boys get?

October 7, 1944

The camp folks jerked themselves out of their lethargy when the siren started to wail. People scurried into the building while the Commandant, waving his sword excitedly, tried to hurry us along. With pulses leaping, we waited expectantly, but nothing happened. Disappointed and depressed, we want back to our work.

October 8, 1944

Last night I had a wonderful dream. I was roasting a duck, and every time I opened the oven door, the tantalizing aroma of the roast fowl struck my olfactory, setting off a fountain of saliva in my mouth. But just as the duck was roasted to a beautiful golden brown, I awoke.

October 12, 1944

We continued to lose weight at an alarming rate. Verbal and written protests from both medical and executive committees regarding our starvation diet were ignored by the Japanese. The Commandant repeatedly reminded our leaders that we were on the same rations as the Japanese soldiers. We had only to look at the Japanese soldiers garrisoned in camp to learn that this was a lie. All the soldiers in camp were fat as butterballs. Their filthy cummerbunds completely failed to restrain the layers of greasy and repulsive fat around their bellies.

October 13, 1944

"It looks like Santo Tomas will be the last line of defense!"

Catesy looked a bit grim as he facetiously made the remark to Mr. Mack.

221

All morning, we had watched the Nips unloading huge piles of airstrip rods in front of their office. Trucks and other types of vehicles roared into the camp from which the soldiers removed heavy packing cases, which looked suspiciously like U. S. Army property. We were consumed with curiosity. What was in the cases? Food or guns?

During the night, we were kept awake by a steady traffic of trucks roaring into the camp. As soldiers removed the heavy cases, they chanted, groaned, and broke into snatches of militant-sounding songs.

Fortunately, my legs weren't the edematous stumps that so many walked on, and I managed to do my personal and camp chores. Only severe leg cramps nagged me today, but I was considerably cheered by the heavy traffic of our bombers yesterday. We had not seen them nor had we seen the bombs dropping. But we heard muffled detonations of bombs bursting from a long way off, and it was music to our ears.

October 17, 1944

The area in front of the Big House was completely covered by mountainous piles of packing cases and soldiers.

Each day, we went about our work with lessened strength. Food was our primary interest. Next in importance was the return of our bombers.

The hospital was filled with beri-beri cases. The older people, and those who had eaten poorly for the last three years, were dying.

October 19, 1944

Just as we finished our dismal breakfast of dirty mush, our dear enemy returned!

Kay and Margo were already on my bed, when Catesy and I ran into my room. While Catesy crouched by the window, I joined the girls on my bed, and for the next half hour we were exhilarated to the point of exhaustion, watching the thrilling show.

There was no doubt in our minds that the Nips were being softened in preparation for early landings. As excited and thrilled groups discussed the bombings and possible liberation, food was forgotten.

This was the shot in the arm that we needed!

October 20, 1944

We heard today that Leyte landings were a reality, and we were certain that help was near.

October 22, 1944

In a morning *Nishi-Nishi* thrown over the wall by a brave Filipino, the editorial stated that: "A Grave Mistake Had Been Made by Landing at Leyte Instead of Mindanao."

The cynics and doubters who had read the paper were now convinced that the Leyte landings had come to pass.

October 22, 1944

We saw only seven of our bombers dropping their loads over Nichols Field.

There were reports of new landings in the Philippines nearly every hour, and according to unreliable sources in camp, twenty-seven landings had been made by nightfall.

Some of the wives received cards with a few official lines from their husbands at Billibid, the military camp only a few blocks from us.

"Love is just around the corner," said Kay sadly after she had read the few pitiful lines that her husband had written her.

October 26, 1944

Another smuggled *Nishi-Nishi* reported: "A large American convoy had been sighted northeast of the Philippines. At Leyte, the Japanese had retired to the hills to await an opportune moment to crush the Americans."

The air was charged with excitement and joyful anticipation as we read the above lines. We expected heavy bombings tomorrow because, childishly, we felt certain that our planes would return on Japanese Navy Day.

October 27, 1944

When our bombers failed to show up today, we could have wept from disappointment.

October 28, 1944

The younger men in camp, who had been doing the heavy manual work, were informed by the Commandant that they would have to start another garden. These men were discouraged and sick at heart, for they felt that it was useless and back-breaking work for men on starvation diets. They knew from sad experience that they would never reap the harvest.

Doctors, nurses, teachers, men and women who had essential camp details, continued with their work despite their illness and exhaustion.

October 29, 1944

Hallelujah! Our bombers came three different times today!

Japanese guns barked frantically but ineffectively at our bombers. Seemingly unperturbed, our bombers taxied in and out of the puffs of smoke caused by the heavy aircraft guns. They dipped, dove, and dropped their bombs and they flew away.

What a show! Most of the bombings were concentrated in Manila Bay and Nichols Field area, and again the Wild Eagles were conspicuous by their absence during the heavy fireworks. Only a few of them ventured into the air after the all clear was given.

The optimists were certain that we'd eat our Thanksgiving dinner in our homes.

October 30, 1944

Our adult death rate was climbing, and many of the older ones who had no supplementary food were dead or on the critical list.

There was another death from T.B. today.

October 31, 1944

The heavy rains beat into our lean-to with its three open sides, and Catesy and I worked frantically to protect our cooking equipment and small supply of rice. We not only had to guard against the rain, but we had to guard our supply from thieves.

Hunger had deadened the moral sense of quite a few of our people, and thieving of food continued despite the fact that if caught, the people were thrown in the jail, and their names publicly announced over the loud speaker.

As I watched the carretela carrying today's dead out of the camp, I saw that there was not only a scarcity of food but everything else. One of the coffins was far too short, and the corpse's feet stuck out of the coffin in a grotesque manner.

November 2, 1944

Two more deaths today from beri-beri.

November 3, 1944

The faces of the elderly people in camp had a drawn and fixed look and their legs, no longer resembling legs, were grotesquely edematous.

The men, with their larger frames, appeared weaker and more emaciated, and many of them lacked the cheerful optimism that the women displayed. Some of the younger women, despite their scrawny bodies, kept up appearances and a show of courage that was a boost to the morale of many. Perhaps in a small way, the fact that many of us still used lipstick and wore hibiscus flowers in our hair kindled the faith of those who had given up hope that help would arrive in time.

November 4, 1944

A death and a birth today!

November 5, 1944

This was a thrilling and exhausting day! Five air raids!

During the first raid, we watched over two hundred of our bombers dropping their loads over North Bay.

We watched hundreds of bombs falling in the vicinity of Marikima Valley, North Bay, Grace Park, Nichols and Zaballan Fields, and because of our convenient peephole, we missed very little of the exciting show.

We wondered if this was the final stage of the softening-up process.

Several of our people were caught outside of the buildings gazing heavenwards to get an all-over view of the Big Show. The Nips punished them by forcing them to stand all day in the broiling sun with heads directed toward the sky.

Two deaths today.

Gone were the days when the campus grounds resembled a Country Fair at night with its lights, people in cool summer clothes strolling about, while internee vendors shouted, "peanuts, candy, and ice-cream."

An outsider coming into this place would have known at a glance that this was a concentration camp where men, women, and children were slowly starving.

The most depressing sight of all was the long line of hungry-looking people standing in the food line awaiting their meager scoopful of slop. The rear of the Big House where we stood for our food, as well as the long dining sheds where we ate our scanty meals, was a dismal and dirty spot. The air was polluted with the stench of tainted fish and rotten vegetables, while hungry blowflies flew into our eyes, mouth and food as we ate.

In the last few weeks, Holy Mary, the good Christian who had worked at menial tasks so that she could earn money to share it with the penniless, had taken to preaching to us at odd times. Her parchment-like face was ghastly pale and sad, but her black eyes were lit by the fires of compassion and fanaticism.

Dully, we listened to her exhortations, while words and phrases like: "Come to Jesus, sinful people, be prepared," reached our deadened brains.

Our conscientious sermonizer went on and on, and though her words had become more persuasive, her repetitious words had lost their meaning.

Suddenly there was a rude interruption.

"Hallelujah!" jeeringly shouted Tientsin Mary, as she vulgarly slapped her thigh.

There was a shocked silence among the hundreds of listeners. Holy Mary's face turned red with annoyance and, for a moment, she paused in her sermon to cast a reproving glance toward Tientsin Mary. Quickly regaining her composure, she extended her arms in a circle toward the watching hundreds.

"Come to Jesus!" Her voice had become urgently entreating.

"Hallelujah!" screamed Tientsin Mary with more feeling and enthusiasm than the first time.

One of the internees standing near Tientsin Mary took her arm and talked to her in a whisper.

There were no more interruptions, and the sermon went on with the words, heaven, hell, doomsday, and sin beating about our ears. We listened to this deeply earnest and sincere woman with mixed emotions. Respectfully, attentively, pityingly, indifferently, or with no feeling at all. The religious dissertation ceased only when everyone had disappeared from the food line and dining sheds.

November 7, 1944

At 4 A.M., my aide and I stepped out of the hospital door to watch our bombers dive-bombing into the Bay Area. It was a beautiful moonlit night, and though we could not see the bombs dropping, we heard the loud detonations after the delivery of each bomb.

After breakfast, our bombers returned and this time they poured their deadly load in rapid succession over the Bay Area, Zaballan Field, and Grace Park. It was impossible to estimate the number of bombers that had participated in today's "softening-up" process, but most of us were agreed that over three hundred bombers had taken part.

As the bombings increased, the Japanese became meaner to us. All their pent-up fury seemed to be directed on us as they increased their face-slappings, and cut down on our food. How clearly they demonstrated their inferiority when they started to nag and bully us about bowing to them! They made a fetish of bowing, as though it was the most important thing in their lives to make the "degenerate Americans" bow to them. Any old bow wouldn't do. We stood in the corridors and in the shanty areas in long double lines awaiting the cocky young lieutenant and his henchmen. Sometimes we stood at attention in a long straight line with eyes ahead for more than an hour in the broiling sun, until the great man came by. Some of our people became faint from standing still so long on edematous stumps; some fainted, while the rest of us were consumed by a cold fury and resentment against our jailors. But no matter what happened, we had to master the bowing art, for as the lieutenant said, "We bowed out of gratitude for the protection that we received from them."

The searching and the snooping was intensified. Today, various sections of the camp were surrounded by soldiers so that no one could enter or leave the area, while the dreaded Military Police searched every section. The uneasiness and terror that struck us at this time are difficult to describe, for we all had something to hide.

While Catesy worried about the money we had buried in our lean-to, I worried about my thick diary nestled among the drainpipe, mops, and brooms. Catesy thought I had already destroyed it, which only increased my tension. I had called the Japs many names in my diary when I had felt ill and depressed. Some of the names were unprintable, and worriedly, I wondered what was the punishment for vile name-calling. Firing squad or beheading?

November 8, 1944

Today was another day of tension and anxiety, as the Nips continued with their surprise raids on buildings and shanty areas. They hounded us to give them the rest of our money, and over the P.A. system we were reminded constantly that if we were caught with more than fifty pesos, we would be severely punished.

Internee Shylocks continued to act as contact men to purchase beans, rice, sugar, and cigarettes from Japanese soldiers and Filipino garbage men. Their risk was great, and so were their profits. One of these piratical traders boasted that he had made over sixty thousand pesos in the last few months. In exchange for a few pounds of beans, rice, cigarettes, or sugar, they received diamonds, wrist watches, expensive jewelry, fountain pens, dollars, and Philippine pesos. No one traded with Mickey Mouse any more. Even the Japanese soldier had lost faith in the occupational currency.

The number four typhoon signal was up, and worried shanty owners were tying their shacks to stakes and trees and praying that their homes would withstand the storm. By nightfall, the wind had turned to a shrieking gale, and the driving rain lashed against our windows and balcony doors. I pitied the shanty dwellers in their frail homes during a storm like this.

November 9, 1944

The Military Police from Fort Santiago made another surprise raid on the camp. This time it was the Santa Catalina hospital. Again, they paid particular attention to electrical fixtures and mosquito wiring, and they snooped through all the belongings of patients, doctors, nurses, and attendants. Once more, they drew a blank, and the secret radio with its operator was still safe.

November 10, 1944

Roosevelt won by a landslide and the Americans made another landing in the Philippines! This was the news passed around today, so we knew the renegade radio was working.

How times had changed! I could remember when I used to do twelve- and twenty-four-hour nursing in New York and Pennsylvania and I still felt fairly fresh when I came off duty. Now, after a four-hour stint, I was alarmingly exhausted. But there were many worse off than me. I met Zest, the army nurse, en route to the Big House, and I was shocked when I saw how she had failed in the last few months.

We were a fine pair of prospective brides. If the Yanks didn't

227

return soon, we'd spend the rest of our days in wheel-chairs, instead of walking up the aisle.

November 11, 1944

"Here she comes with her wee-wee can!" announced Catesy. Though he winked at me, he wrinkled his nose distastefully.

It was Mrs. Greenshoes stomping belligerently through the corridors with her Lactogen can. Every day, just as hundreds of us started to eat our lunch in the corridor, the huge double doors of the museum would swing violently forward, and Mrs. Greenshoes would emerge from her boudoir, carrying her Lactogen can filled with urine. No matter how ingeniously she disguised the open can by placing a discarded pechay leaf or a hibiscus flower on top, she could not disguise the stench of the concentrated urine that assaulted our olfactory nerves. Glares, murmurs of protest, and open threats had no effect on her. She and her swinging Lactogen can with its grisly contents were inseparable, and it had to be emptied when the corridor was the most crowded—precisely at lunch time.

How we hated that old woman for her selfishness, thoughtlessness, and lack of consideration for others! Why, that old girl was altogether without feelings!

Later in the afternoon, she stopped me in the corridor and gave me one of her poems to read, and because I didn't want to seem rude, I read the stanzas impatiently and hurriedly. Then I read it the second and third time. There was a simplicity, a rhythmic cadence in the lines of her poetry, and the moving words flowed on like Gray's "Elegy in a Country Churchyard." Each stanza was a song, and each word beautifully expressed, conveying from birth until death man's yearnings, ambitions, heartbreaks, and faith in a Supreme Being. She called her poem "To a Raindrop," and I thought that her lines carried the same truth, beauty and philosophy that I had found in Walt Whitman's works.

I saw this old woman in a new light. She was still a cranky old woman, thoughtless and selfish, but I tried to overlook her bad habits, and some of my animosity and intolerance toward her disappeared. When I thought of myself at eighty-two, I found myself wondering how I would have behaved in a boiler factory, while I slowly starved to death.

We had hoped that Armistice Day would bring back our beloved raiders, but we searched the skies in vain.

We had one, two, and sometimes more deaths every day. From now on, our death rate would increase.

November 12, 1944

One of our neighbors near our lean-to became hysterical tonight after eating his tiny scoopful of watery rice and tainted fish.

228

"I'm starving!" His loud and unrestrained scream woke us momentarily from the despairing lassitude that seemed to push us down these days.

Then in the same hysterical manner, he shouted, "In another month we'll all be dead!"

November 13, 1944

Our bombers raided the Bay area, and what a shellacking they gave the Nips! They came wave after wave and, like marionettes, they executed their work with precision and order. Against the snow-white clouds and the dazzling blue of the sky, our bombers looked like streaks of silver cavorting in the heavens. Enemy aircraft fired furiously, and we were saddened to see one of our bombers struck. A cry of horror went through my room as we saw the doomed bomber burst into flames. It zigzagged dizzily and dropped rapidly, until it disappeared from our view.

By late afternoon, a mammoth blanket of smoke covered the entire city.

Another death today among the T.B.'s.

November 14, 1944

Enemy aircraft awakened me more efficiently than my alarm would have done at 2:45 A.M. I looked out of my window and saw that the sky above the entire Manila Bay area was aglow with a dazzling light. Apparently, our bombers were on the job, for the heavy aircraft guns kept up a continual barking. I wanted to stay by my window and watch the show, but it was time to go on duty.

By seven-twenty-five, I was off duty and just barely made it to my room when the siren went into action. A few seconds later, we heard the smooth hum of more than a hundred of our bombers, and when a few of them flew low over our buildings, we danced with joy.

Our bombers returned on an average of every thirty-five minutes throughout the day, and they concentrated their bombs on the enemy ships in the harbor.

The deafening detonations of our bombs were music to our ears, and no vitamin B or blood plasma could have been as efficacious as the lift we received from watching our bombers in action.

By 7 P.M., most of us were in bed. We were utterly exhausted, happy, and hopeful that liberation was just around the corner.

November 15, 1944

The reign of terror continued. We had another cut in our rice ration, and the searching of rooms and shacks was intensified. We now had two roll calls daily, and there was more yakamashi than ever before over stupid bowing and scraping. Meanwhile, people became hungrier.

The hundreds of pigeons that used to roost on the roof of the Big House, and promenaded nonchalantly on the plaza while hundreds of us milled around, were gone. People used to save scraps of food to feed them, and they had become friendly and tame. But they, too, disappeared into the stew-pots just as the cats and dogs had disappeared.

An internee stopped to chat at our lean-to today, to report on the cat supper he had attended the night before.

"How was it?" I inquired curiously.

He pursued his lips thoughtfully, and in an Oxonian accent, said, "A bit gamey." He added, "I've been to several dog parties, too. It's much more tasty than cat!"

November 16, 1944

The rumor persisted that more landings had been made in Luzon. Surely, it wouldn't be long now.

Another death today.

November 17, 1944

How desperately we wanted to believe the Luzon landings! How closely we watched the actions of the Nips in here, in the hopes that they'd give themselves away.

Two deaths today. One of them was Mr. Greenshoes, and because Mrs. Greenshoes had lost her devoted husband and slave, she was removed to the hospital.

November 19, 1944

We always expected our bombers on Sunday and they didn't disappoint us today. Again, the Manila harbor area received a great deal of punishment, and though the consistent and steady firing of enemy aircraft resounded throughout the city, we didn't see any of our bombers hit.

Today our bombers were at a considerable distance over the water, and we had to strain our eyes to see the bombs dropping. The raids were more or less sporadic all day, but the smooth humming sound of hundreds of planes high in the heavens assured us that our bombers were headed for other areas.

November 20, 1944

Who would have thought a year ago that rice would become so precious?

We had another cut in our rice ration.

Kay's delicate sister sold her last keepsake from her husband, a military prisoner at nearby Bilibid. It was her diamond engagement ring. One diamond ring for several pounds of dirty rice! She and her two small children were desperately hungry, but alas, they never ate the rice, for a heartless fiend stole it from under her bed.

Many of our people experimented in cooking canna bulbs, lily bulbs, hibiscus leaves, pigweed, and many other leaves. Many became ill after eating strange leaves and roots, and the doctors in camp warned us about this dangerous practice. The most versatile of all leaves were those of the hibiscus. It was eaten, smoked, and used for tea.

Another dangerous and disgusting practice brought on by the acute hunger was picking and eating condemned vegetables and other refuse from the camp garbage.

November 21, 1944

We had eleven new cases of bacillary at the kids' hospital, and as I doled out the sulfa to the kids, I took twice the dosage for myself. It was heartbreaking to see with what eagerness these poor kids swallowed the pills. They never had to be coaxed to take their medicine. To these poor hungry kids, the medicine was food, another filler to ease hunger pains.

November 22, 1944

The hungrier we became, the more we talked about the expected arrival of the Red Cross kits.

The Nips were approached today by our patient Mr. Grant and other camp leaders regarding our food situation. As representatives and spokesmen for the camp, these outstanding men had taken insults and abuse from our jailors since the beginning of internment. Today, when they begged for more food for our five hundred or more kids, the Nips told them to kill all the cats and dogs. But, alas, the cats and dogs had long ago disappeared into the stew-pots.

Two deaths today.

November 25, 1944

Distressingly tired and ill again, and though I tried to conceal it from Catesy, I knew that he knew. Knowing that he was worried about my eating only increased my nervousness as I tried to swallow the rice mush.

If I could only stay in bed to get some strength, but nurses and doctors were needed desperately. The nurse who relieved me at 7 A.M. had long since given up her work because of illness. I saw her at the laundry troughs this morning and her face was gray-white in the harsh morning light. It was hard to believe that only three years ago she had been a radiant bride. I wondered if she was just as shocked by my looks.

November 26, 1944

The frequent visits of our bombers pepped us up.

Today we watched many of our raiders diving and dropping their bombs, and when one of our bombers burst into flames, we were sick with anguish. Frantically, we watched for the parachute to open, but we watched in vain. The disabled plane plummeted downward and disappeared from our view.

In a last effort to get more garden workers, the Nips threatened another rice cut.

Another death today.

November 29, 1944

Camp energy had reached a dangerously low ebb. School had to be closed as students and teachers were far too hungry and weak to concentrate on their work.

We were facing a new problem. Fuel shortage. The camp's and private supply of charcoal was nearly exhausted, and already many people were chopping up chairs, desks, benches, and tables for fuel.

Pushcarts heaped with vegetables, fruit, and eggs stood outside the gates of this camp. They were gifts to us from wealthy residents and charitable organizations in the city, but the Nips sent them back with the message that we had enough food.

Six of our neighbors around our lean-to became violently ill today from eating lily bulbs. Fortunately, they had eaten only a small amount by way of experimenting. Otherwise, there would have been eight deaths today instead of two.

The Military Police made another surprise raid on the camp, striking terror in the hearts of us all. What a fool I was to keep my diary! Catesy thought I had already destroyed it, and I didn't want to worry him about it.

December 3, 1944

Close to two hundred men, women, and children were being shipped to Los Banos, and most of the men in the group, chosen because of the hard work at Los Banos, were a sorry-looking bunch. Most of them were over fifty and all of them were weak, emaciated, and with swollen legs.

Uniformed Japanese rummaged through suitcases, tampipis, and bayongs in a most thorough manner. As they pawed over finery, such as evening dresses, dinner clothes, furs, and fine linens, I was struck by the incongruity of such foolish possessions under these conditions. Yet, we all clung to our bits of finery. Pitiful and foolish as it seemed, it was our last link to the life we used to know, but how gladly we would have traded all of it for a square meal!

December 4, 1944

The Japs were jittery and nervous and we felt certain that something was brewing.

When there was no news of landings, and we saw no bombings, we felt hungrier and more depressed.

The blood plasma, B. and C. shots, that came in the last Red Cross shipment a year ago were nearly exhausted. What little was left had to be saved for those who had a chance to survive. Some of it was carefully doled out to the hard-working men and women who had to stay on their feet to care for those sicker and weaker than themselves.

December 6, 1944

Those duck eggs that we stored in slack lime many months ago proved to be a lifesaver. By now, they were ripe, high, and obnoxious in smell, but they were wonderfully light, fluffy and tasteful. Once a week we took four eggs and beat them to an incredible lightness. When I poured the eggs into my iron skillet, it seemed as though I had used twice the number of eggs. While the omelet cooked, our neighbors would shuffle by and quickly avert their gaze in a manner that was pitiful. Just to see those eggs cooking was more than they could bear. Some admitted that they had been unduly optimistic regarding an early liberation and as a result they had not stored away food for a rainy day.

We had looked forward to our feast for days, but all the joy of eating it was gone. As we ate it quickly and almost surreptitiously, we felt guilty because we could not share it with our neighbors.

The quart of coconut oil, now rancid, and which we bought over a year ago, was almost gone. Every other day we carefully measured out a tablespoonful of it to pour on our watery rice. We still had a little rock salt left, but many of our people had been without salt for a long time, and they needed it and craved it more than sugar. Though we salted our food moderately, Catesy and I both craved salt, but this, too, we conserved and doled out to make it last as long as possible. Though we still had an occasional private supplementary feeding, we were weak, hungry, and we suffered from polyneuritis. How weak and hungry were the hundreds who had nothing to add to the line chow?

Two deaths today.

December 9, 1944

Heavy rains and a roaring wind deepened the gloom and depression that shrouded this camp.

Two more deaths today from beri-beri with the usual myocardial complications.

December 10, 1944

A peculiar though understandable mania had seized the camp.

Men, women, and children copied recipes from morning until night. These recipe addicts copied and exchanged recipes with others addicted with the same mania. They dug up old magazines and gazed longingly at colored pictures of temptingly arranged and prepared food. What made the mania so pathetic and futile was that they copied and concentrated on recipes that called for hard-to-obtain ingredients even in a normal world. It stimulated their desire for food, and it used up energy that they could ill afford. It seemed like the cruelest form of torture.

Two more deaths today. T.B. and beri-beri.

December 15, 1944

Our hunger at this time was a living thing, like a torturing pain. It was with us day and night. Most of my little patients were awake by five and their first question upon awakening would have wrung the heart of a sadist.

"Is chow ready?" they would ask eagerly.

"Pretty soon. Go back to sleep a little longer." I coaxed.

Intrepid Wild Eagles buzzed over our heads, and the sight of the orange sun depressed us.

December 12, 1944

We listened to the earth-shaking and rumbling noise of heavy tanks and marching soldiers passing the street in front of Santo Tomas.

Were the Nips leaving the city? Delightful thought. If only it were true!

We had a further cut in our daily rice and corn ration and now we received 210 grams per day. When our internee men in charge of supplies weighed the sacks of corn and rice allotted to the camp for the week, they found a shortage of 240 kilos. This was the short weight trick that our friends practiced on us, and the various Commandants, when confronted by our leaders regarding short weights, had usually gone into a "so sorry" routine. But our present Commandant, the much-hated Lieutenant Tamura, threw a tantrum and accused our men of insulting the Imperial Japanese Army.

December 14, 1944

After nineteen days of absence, our wonderful airforce boys returned to drop their loads over Grace Park and Nichols Field.

Just as soon as we had heard the powerful hum of American motors, instead of the Model-T racket made by the Wild Eagles, we hobbled into the buildings for choice ringside seats. We rushed from window to window in order not to miss any of the air activity, while Japanese soldiers patrolled the buildings and shanty area in hopes of finding an interested spectator to punish.

Two more deaths today. A T.B. and a stillborn.

December 15, 1944

Today the Nips were busier than a dog infested with fleas. From dawn until dusk our bombers visited the city every half hour, and sometimes they returned in fifteen minutes to go over the area

234

they had just shellacked. Enemy aircraft kept up a furious tattoo of firing, but not one of our bombers was struck.

Because of the bombings and strictly enforced ruling that there would be no movement from building to building, we had no food since five last night.

Flares, searchlights, anti-aircraft, bombs bursting, and machine-gun firing kept us awake most of the night. As we peered out of our windows from our darkened rooms, we saw large and awesome fires in various parts of this large city.

December 16, 1944

Our bombers had the freedom of the skies! They bombed and strafed various sections of the city the entire day, and there was less enemy aircraft firing. The Wild Eagles, of course, were no-where in sight!

December 17, 1944

Liberation seemed a long way off when our bombers failed to visit the city, and naturally, our depression and hunger were more acute on those days.

This afternoon I passed the Santa Catalina Hospital, where many of my fellow internees were passing their last days on earth.

From one of the barred windows, a mentally deranged American woman screamed abuses and obscenities at the Japanese guards who were stationed in the hospital grounds. For her sake, I prayed that none of the soldiers understood English. Who could tell what horrifying experiences this poor woman had gone through when she had been outside on sick leave? She was quiet and reasonably rational when the Japs were out of sight, but the moment she saw one of the soldiers, she became a raving maniac. The foul words and insults that this ordinarily gentle woman shouted at the Japanese were shocking to all who heard them.

December 18, 1944

A few days ago when our bombers kept the Nips busy, we were certain that we'd be out for Christmas, but now that there was a lull in the air activity, we weren't quite so sure.

December 20, 1944

Many people childishly set today as the deadline for the kits to arrive. When nothing happened, they gave up hope of ever receiving them.

There was another drastic cut in our rice ration. Our leaders quoted international law to the Nips and exhausted every protest and argument in an effort to prevent this last cut, but to no avail.

Many of us believed that the Japanese planned to kill us by slow starvation. If their plan was to make us suffer, they had succeeded.

A bullet would have been more merciful.

Two deaths today.

December 21, 1944

Those on the critical malnutrition list were mounting.

At this time, we had two distinct types of scarecrows. Men and women who looked like skeletons with folds of baggy skin that had lost all elasticity and life. With drawn faces and eyes fixed on the ground, they walked around on pipe-stem legs.

The people in the second group were usually over fifty, and their faces were large and edematous, their abdomens distended, and they hobbled around on grotesquely swollen legs. These people would soon be in their graves.

Our stock of food had shrunk to a dozen of our stored eggs, six or eight ounces of salt pork, a few pounds of rice, and a few cans of meat.

Another death today.

December 22, 1944

As we moved around our work slowly and lethargically in a half-dream world, we thought only of food.

I kept having the most wonderful dreams about eating oatmeal, and canned milk with gobs of butter and sugar. I felt certain, if I had oatmeal, my tortured bacillary intestines would heal. While many people talked and dreamed of steaks, French fries and bread, I concentrated on oatmeal.

We were suddenly aroused from our half-comatose state this morning by American planes. Never before had they flown as low and close to us, and now we were certain that they had the freedom of the skies.

There were no Wild Eagles to intercept them and no enemy guns to fire at them. They dropped their bombs over Nichols Field and the Bay area, and the rapid detonations of their bombs was beautiful to hear. A short time later, dense smoke covered the bombed areas for many hours.

Tonight this place was in a turmoil. The Japanese bodega had been robbed during the night, and mongo beans, sugar, and rice had been taken. Most of us thought that it had been the work of Japanese guards who had been selling rice and other food to us for watches, pens, diamonds, and good currency.

The Commandant was on a rampage and the entire camp was searched several times. While one area was being searched, we rushed around hiding and burying whatever we thought might be incriminating.

Catesy and I resurrected our Lactogen can, now only partially filled with good money, and buried it in a new spot, and I hid my last pathetic hoard of rice in the trash can by our sink.

A few hours later, the hated Military Police entered my room, and this time I felt that the jig was up. My apprehension mounted as I watched one of the brutish-looking officers with a huge paunch conducting the search. I thought of my diary and the miserable hoard of rice. When one of them examined the sink and kicked the trash can with his boot, I stopped breathing for a second, and when two of them walked out on the balcony where my diary was hidden, I saw myself facing a firing squad, as many had been liquidated for less than that. The dirty names I had called them were there in the diary in black and white. If I ever got out of this mess, I vowed, I would destroy the thick manuscript.

For a moment, their gaze seemed to be fixed on the drainpipe, but instead of moving toward the mops and brooms, they turned around and came back to the room. When we finally bowed out the three Nips, my roommates and I started to breathe normally. But the reign of terror was not over yet. Not for Mr. Grant, and another one of our leading men in camp. Their belongings were searched and both of them were thrown into the camp jail.

December 25, 1944

This Christmas Day would have been bleak indeed if our planes hadn't dropped leaflets over the city and camp bearing this wonderful greeting:

"The Commander-in-Chief, the officers and men of the American Forces of Liberation in the Pacific, wish their gallant Allies, the People of the Philippines, all the Blessings of Christmas, and the realization of their fervent hopes for the New Year!"

The joyous and thrilling excitement that filled everyone's heart as they read those inspiring words was indescribable. Lucky internees who had found these leaflets passed them around so that every person could read them. One proud American had mounted his leaflet in a handsome silver frame and a long line of people stood waiting in the back corridor to get near his prize, while spotters watched either end of the long hall for snooping Japs. Many stood in line twice to reread the beautiful message.

Another death today.

December 26, 1944

One death and two births today.

The nurses and attendants were a bit resentful at the additional food and work required for these mothers and newborns. I cannot blame them, for half-starved as they were with legs disfigured by beri-beri, they had a difficult time caring for the many patients.

The fear-inspiring police from Fort Santiago again searched the camp, and this time when three of them came to my room, none of them went to the balcony.

I was safe again! If I kept my diary this long, perhaps I could hold out a little longer.

For the last few months, Catesy and I had been too dejected to make any plans, but tonight we felt optimistic, and we spoke of wedding plans and a new home.

Another death today.

Tonight we had mashed camotes, sweet potatoes with skin, grit, worms and all, and we enjoyed every bite. We hoped we'd soon have it again.

Another death.

1 9 4 5

January 1, 1945

The corroding influence of boredom, hunger, and hopelessness had left its mark on our people. Those who kept on working despite weakness and swollen feet, reminded themselves that it wouldn't be long now.

Some stayed on their beds and cots to stare at the ceiling all day. They refused to do any personal or camp work. They had lost all hope and faith that our forces would return.

Another death.

January 5, 1945

Three years ago today we entered this prison camp on the day we would have been married! On the days I felt low and ill, the altar still seemed a long way off.

Mr. Grant and three other men were taken outside, and the camp felt that these innocent men had gone to their execution. The three older men's wives were in the States, but the young man's wife was in camp, and her eyes were swollen and red from weeping. A few weeks before the war, she had been a bride, and now she would be a widow.

January 6, 1945

We began our fourth year of internment today!

Our blessed planes bombed and strafed various parts of the city throughout the day, and we were keyed to a joyous exhilaration. All that overhead activity could mean only one thing: liberation and food!

Two more deaths today.

January 7, 1945

Were the Nips leaving the camp?

This question was on everyone's mind as we watched them going about in great excitement and confusion. They packed food and other supplies into trucks. They burned papers and barked last-minute orders to subordinates. From a safe distance, we watched all this activity with rising excitement and fiendish glee. History had repeated itself and now we had the unusual opportunity of witnessing how the other side behaved as the conquering forces drew near.

As our large four-engine bombers strafed and bombed different sections of the city, everyone remarked about the lessening of enemy aircraft activity.

Everyone talked excitedly about the good food our army would bring us. Bread, butter, and beans were the favorite choice. What could be more tasty and wonderful? What could be worse for our shrunken stomachs?

I thought only of well-cooked oatmeal with plenty of canned milk and sugar.

We were horrified to see two of our bombers struck by enemy aircraft, and it was with a sinking feeling that we watched the crew bailing out in their parachutes. Fragments of the demolished planes fluttered in the sky like worthless bits of paper before falling to earth. We all prayed that the crew would be saved.

Tremendous billows of thick smoke surrounded the city. How soon would our forces reach the city? How soon would we eat?

Another death.

January 10, 1945

The city was taking heavy punishment as the Japs were apparently carrying out a scorched-earth policy, just as our army had done prior to the enemy's occupation three years ago.

For the last week, we heard heavy blasts and earth-shaking rumbles, which our camp engineers attributed to dynamiting. The heavy blasting went on day and night. North, east, south, and west—everywhere we looked we saw smoke and flames. If the water and power were included on their scorched earth list, we were doomed.

The air alert was no longer sounded, and our planes bombed and strafed strategic areas, while enemy aircraft was practically nil. When our huge sky monsters buzzed our camp, we screamed like delighted kids. They dropped their bombs over Grace Park and Marikima Valley and we cheered and pounded each other over the backs. Many of us had abandoned caution as we watched the show from our windows. Now that the shoe was on the other foot, we had become a little more independent and cocksure, while the Nips, ever inconsistent, became a little nicer to us, or a little meaner, depending on the Nip and the occasion.

Today we were given cigarettes and permitted to sit outside until 6:30 P.M.

240

January 11, 1945

At noon today we went completely wild when two of our planes came so low over the Big House that we could plainly see the goggled pilots.

January 12, 1945

From the downtown section of the city, only a short distance from our camp, we continued to hear earth-shaking blasts day and night, and the sky was brilliantly illuminated by huge fires.

Two more deaths.

January 13, 1945

We thought that the enemy had already evacuated the city, but we knew better when our bombers were met by considerable enemy aircraft firing today.

There was no water on the second and third floors of the Big House, and the first-floor toilets were jammed with people day and night.

Despite aggravatingly long lines at the toilets and intense hunger, our spirits were high, as we expected our forces to enter the city momentarily.

When I went on duty this morning at three, I heard the firing of machine guns and rifles. I heard screams of terror outside our walls, and everywhere I looked the sky was aglow from mammoth fires.

While our little patients slept, my aide and I drank huge quantities of hot water to appease our hunger, and we talked about our dreams.

January 17, 1945

One death last night and one today. The deceased today was the father of three young children.

January 17, 1945

The tremendously active kids that used to tear around the campus like savages were now little old men and women. Hollow-eyed, skinny, and listless, they sat around and talked about food.

Another death.

January 20, 1945

Our hour of liberation was drawing near. One could sense it by watching the behavior of the Nips.

From my window, I watched young and apple-cheeked soldiers tearing up the lean-tos of several internees in the Father's garden. The young soldiers were all heavy-set and well fed, which belied the often repeated statement of the Commandant that we were on the same rations as the Japanese soldiers.

January 21, 1945

A great number of our bombers were headed toward the Mari-

kana valley. Something really big was about to occur! Of that we
were certain. The most repeated question these days was: How
soon would we eat?

Violent explosions shook the city after dark tonight, and it
seemed that a monstrous torch had lighted the city. It looked like
the Nips were making certain that there would be very little left
of the city when our forces returned.

January 22, 1945

Though we felt that our troubles might soon be over, a cloud of
gloom hovered over the camp when we heard of the latest death
today. Just before passing, the man became violent and shouted,
"I'm starving! I'm going to die!" A few hours later he was gone.

Coffins, like everything else in here, had gone though a transi-
tional stage as the months passed. At first, they had been beautifully hand carved and plush-lined, but now the coffins were rough
boxes hastily made.

January 24, 1945

Three deaths today.

As food became still scarcer, thieving and cheating became more
prevalent. Some of the people sneaked through the food line twice
in order to get an extra scoopful of mush and bilge water, which
passed for gravy.

A buy-and-sell exchange had been set up by a well-heeled and
greedy internee where one could buy a pound of rice for a hundred
dollars. A bar of chocolate sold for twenty-five dollars, and a six-
ounce can of salmon went for twenty-two dollars. Naturally, all
transactions were strictly for cash and in good dollars or Philippine
pesos.

One man, a former car dealer, offered a brand-new car, if and
when, for anyone who would loan him three hundred dollars so
that he could buy three pounds of rice for his hungry family.
Another man offered a fellow inmate $350.00 for a pound can of
powdered milk and the offer was turned down. One young man,
who used to buy for the camp, still had a case of corned beef left.
Though he didn't want to sell it, a family man gave him fifteen
hundred dollars for the case of corned beef.

Two more deaths today.

January 26, 1945

Hunger had become a living thing, like cancer. It ate into our
bodies and minds. We thought of nothing else but food and hate.

No one was interested in gossip as in former days. No one cared
to hear about a new twosome or who was shacked up with whom.

Sex had taken a back seat. A classic example of this disinterest
in the opposite sex was demonstrated today by Don Juan. When

I saw him this morning, I was startled to see the change in this likeable, man-about-town Cassanova. No eye-filling blonde clung to his arm, and he looked like the rest of us, gaunt and hungry.

"Where's your blonde?" I could have bitten my tongue off after the question, for it was common knowledge that she had shacked up with another man who still had some canned goods left.

"Tess," he said gravely, with a trace of his former sly humor, "if Lana Turner stood before me in her birthday suit, I wouldn't give a damn!" Then, grinning impishly, he added, "Unless she had a ham sandwich in her hand."

January 27, 1945

The faces of all our people were grey and vacuous. Without food, freedom, and a purpose in life, we were sunk in apathy. Those who had lost hope and faith in God were like the dead. They gave up and stayed on their beds, while the stronger ones looked after them.

As I looked at my roommates, I saw the changes that the years had brought. All were thin and all of them were hungry.

Daphne, too, had lost her vivacity, and she no longer came around with typewritten transcripts and humorous puns about the Nips, the British, and Eleanor Roosevelt.

Laura, who had written many of our humorous jingles, was ill all the time, and if help didn't come soon, she, too, would be another vital statistic.

Three deaths today.

January 28, 1945

Could it be true that our forces were less than thirty miles from us? I wished desperately that I could register elation, but I felt tired, empty, and dead.

Two deaths today.

January 29, 1945

How I envied the people in our midst who had crawled into a snug four-cornered little wall of security! These were the escapists from reality; the mentally ill who had been too weak to face reality and the hardships that surrounded them. Ever since the enemy entered the city over three years ago, these people had to be cared for. They had to be fed, washed and dressed, and most of the time they stayed in their beds staring at nothing. While the nurses and attendants who cared for them became weaker and their legs more edematous from beri-beri, these people remained comparatively strong by staying in bed and expending little or no energy.

January 30, 1945

Catesy and I opened a can of corned beef and ate one quarter of it for lunch, and the remainder will be stretched out for three more days. Only three four-ounce cans of food stood between us and starvation.

Four deaths today.

January 31, 1945

The head of our medical council, a young missionary doctor, received a sentence of twenty days in jail because he had refused to change malnutrition and starvation to beri-beri on the last eight death certificates.

Three more deaths from starvation.

February 1, 1945

The Nips butchered a carabao today while hundreds of starved people stood in a circle watching, hoping, and praying that they would receive a handout.

One large carabao for only 140 Japanese! No wonder they remained as fat as pigs!

Just as soon as the Nips disappeared with their freshly quartered meat, men, women, and children rushed to the spot and, like voracious dogs, they clawed around the blood, entrails, dust and grit, searching for tail, ears, hooves, or anything that resembled food.

Late that afternoon Catesy and I sat in our lean-to talking about food and playing our macabre guessing game of who would go next, when Tientsin Mary walked in carrying a small package wrapped in a dirty *Nishi-Nishi*. Her beady black eyes gleamed roguishly as she greeted me.

"Hi, honey-girl! I brought you a present!"

Surprised and touched, I accepted the package which I held awkwardly in my hand.

While Catesy and Tientsin Mary watched me, I unwrapped the soiled newspaper and my startled eyes gazed at a sandwich. Two slices of thick white bread! Something we hadn't seen for several years. When my trembling fingers lifted the top slice of bread, I saw a thick slab of boiled carabao meat.

"But where did you get it?" I cried in astonishment. The day of miracles wasn't over!

"Ask me no questions, and I'll tell you no lies!" sing-songed Tientsin Mary.

I colored as I met Catesy's glance, and I saw that his eyes twinkled with amusement. I didn't care where or how that beautiful sandwich came into her possession. I was going to eat it. With fingers that shook, I divided the sandwich into three equal parts, and I handed a third to Mary.

"Not for me, honey-girl! There's more where this came from!" she said gaily, as she started to leave, swinging her hips wickedly.

We watched her disappear around the corner of the building. As Catesy started to heat hot water to go with the sandwich, I noticed that he furtively brushed away a tear. My eyes were flooded with tears, and I let them fall unashamed.

February 2, 1945

The Japanese butchered another carabao today, and the same grim and pathetic tableau of starving people looking on was re-enacted. The well-fed Japs, with their bare and repulsive bellies hanging over grimy cummerbunds were a sharp contrast to the skeletons that watched them.

The destruction of the city went on. Heavy blasting day and night, and there was an overhanging curtain of smoke over the entire city.

Our bombers continued with their bombing and strafing, and it filled us with joyful expectancy. It kept us going. Anything could happen now, for we felt that our forces were close.

Three deaths today.

February 3, 1945

Just as the sun set, and the sky dazzled our eyes with the colors of a Master's brush, something wonderful happened.

Six of our bombers flew over the Big House! This time they came so close that we thought they'd scrape their paint on the high tower of our building. While screaming adults and children waved and cheered, the goggled and grinning pilots dipped their wings, and one of them threw an object into the east patio. It was a pair of goggles, to which was attached a note with this ringing message: "Roll out the barrel, Christmas will be either today or tomorrow!"

A few minutes later, every person in camp knew the contents of that note by heart. Though every version of the note was different, each repetition made the message more inspiring and promising.

Several hours later, as we sat in the corridors talking excitedly about the pilots, the note, and early liberation, we suddenly heard the rumble of heavy tanks outside the camp. It was followed by wild cheering and shouting coming from thousands of throats.

We listened attentively with wildly beating hearts. Then our startled eyes saw many flares shooting heavenwards in the front of the camp.

Between the heavy rumble of the approaching tanks, we heard rifle shots, machine gunfire and tumultuous shouting. The tanks lumbered closer with their earth-shaking noise, and we saw that the flares were directly above the front gate.

We watched, waited, prayed, and listened with trembling excite-

245

ment. We dared not believe! Not just yet! We had been fooled so many times!

The sky above us was lit like a giant Christmas tree by the many flares shooting toward the sky.

"Honey, they're here!" shouted Catesy into my ear as he hugged me tightly. "Let's go to the front of the building and see what's going on!" He grabbed my arm excitedly and dragged me through the long corridor to the front. Since the Nips had pulled the switch, we were in darkness, and we stumbled over other people who were also rushing to the front.

Screaming men, women, and children, in danger of falling out of windows and balconies, were leaning out recklessly, as they waved and cheered. They behaved like people who had lost all sense and restraint.

I still didn't believe that our forces had arrived. We simply had to get near those windows to see for ourselves. Just as Catesy and I squeezed our way to one of the windows, we heard the loud crash of a tank tearing through the front gates of our prison.

As in a dream, we watched the armored monster, the lead tank, with powerful searchlights, coming up the familiar road toward the Big House. We saw soldiers, tall and bronzed, in peculiar-looking uniforms, walking between and on the sides of the tanks. All of them walked cautiously with guns in readiness. Like hypnotized subjects, we watched the tanks and men come closer. We saw the long and wicked-looking gun in front of the tanks, and we saw uniformed men with sub-machine guns standing in the tanks and poised for action. Some of us were still dubious that they were Americans. Not until we saw the American flag draped over the lead tank did we really believe that, at last, the realization of a beautiful dream had materialized. When we saw the lovely Stars and Stripes, our throats constricted and our eyes were blinded by tears.

When the lead tank reached the plaza, we saw two beautiful American words printed on the tank: "Georgia Peach." It was then that we went berserk with joy and excitement! We clapped, cried, shouted, screamed, and cheered. A few fainted, while still others were completely bewildered. They were unable to comprehend what their eyes were witnessing.

"Where are the Japs?" shouted one of the tall officers from the Georgia Peach.

"In the Education building!" screamed hundreds of people, as they waved and pointed to the large building to the left of us.

"Get Lieutenant Tamura!" shouted many voices bloodthirstily.

Like the last day of school, we poured out of the buildings

shrieking like delighted kids. We wanted to get near the tanks and those wonderful men! We wanted to shake their hands! We wanted to touch them!

Before the men in the tanks knew what was going on, they were pulled out of them and lifted on the shoulders of our scrawny fellow internees. It was impossible to hold back the worshiping and joyous internees, and it never occurred to any of us that our men still had to clean up on a hundred and forty Japanese garrisoned in the camp.

We shook hands with our soldiers, we hugged and kissed them; and when the soldiers of the First Cavalry passed out candy bars and chewing-gum, the children squealed with delight. When the men and women near the tanks and soldiers were given cigarettes and canned rations, they wept unrestrainedly.

While soldiers mingled with delighted internees, the artillery-men went about the grim business of coaxing sixty or more trembling Japanese who had barricaded themselves in the Education building.

The tanks roared into position on the side of the Ed Building, and their 75 millimeter cannons crashed through the building with a terrific *c-r-u-m-p!*

But, unfortunately, the Nips also had over two hundred internee hostages, including a few women and children, barricaded in the building with them. When the commander of the First Cavalry was informed of this, they ceased blasting the building, and for many hours after that they continued to negotiate with the Nips in an effort to release the trapped internees.

That night we went boisterously and joyously mad. We threw caution to the wind, and those who still had a can or two left opened them and shared them with the soldiers. Blackout regulations were forgotten, and hundreds of fires were started with chairs, tables, and benches.

As we shared our miserable food with the soldiers, we laughed, talked, and listened to their experiences. How desperately we tried to catch up on the years we had lost!

How wonderful those boys looked to us! Their presence acted as a heady wine and we couldn't seem to get our fill. We wanted them by our side all the time.

We watched the soldiers digging small holes throughout the camp and we were consumed with curiosity.

"What in the world are you doing?" asked Catesy of one of the boys.

"Digging a fox-hole, Mac," replied the soldier.

"What's a fox-hole?"

"Watch me, and I'll show you!"

After he finished digging, the young soldier spread his raincoat—only he called it a poncho—and then he lay down on it.

"Catch on?" He grinned up at us.

This was a new world! So much to learn and so much to forget.

We slept very little that night because of the heavy firing all around us. Snipers were everywhere, and the enemy, fifty to sixty thousand strong, were only a short distance from us across the Pasig. In the entire city of Manila, there were only a few American tanks and eight hundred American soldiers, and they were all in Santo Tomas with us.

The Americans had done it again! They had bluffed the enemy with only a few tanks and eight hundred men, and, fortunately, we internees were too elated and naive to realize the danger we were in.

February 4, 1945

Every time an army truck tore into the camp we rushed to doors and windows to see if they had brought us food. Our camp ration of rice was increased and we had lima beans for lunch, but, unfortunately, hundreds became ill.

Elements of the 37th Infantry Division arrived today, and our camp was buzzing with handsome officers and soldiers. There were tanks, trucks, jeeps, bazookas, machine guns and other artillery all over the front grounds. The girls in camp were besieged by dates and they were starting to primp and pay more attention to their appearances.

We received letters from home today. There seemed to be no end to the wonderful surprises in store for us, but many of us still behaved as though the beautiful dream would vanish.

Via the grapevine, we learned that the Nips had planned to massacre us just as they had massacred thousands in the ruined city. Our underground had learned of the plot through a Christian Japanese and, for this reason, the First Cavalry had made its spectacular dash through enemy lines to rescue Santo Tomas.

Lieutenant Tamura, the undersized enemy who had been the living personification of all that was hateful in our lives, was dead. He had been killed at the front gate by our tankmen.

His body was in the rear corridor of the Big House for all to see. A long line of men, women, and children passed by to take a last look at the enemy. To us, he was more than one dead Japanese officer. He personified the entire Japanese Empire, defeated and cowed. He was General Tanaka! He was the War Cabinet! He was General Homma, the Butcher of Bataan! With him lying dead, we had become human beings once more!

What did I see in the stony expressions of my fellow internees as they slowly passed his body? Bitterness? Triumph? Satisfaction?

Following the example of some of their elders, I saw four- and five-year-old American kids spitting on the dead man. This, too, the war had done to young children.

February 5, 1945

The internee hostages in the Education building were free! They had spent thirty-six hours of nightmare with sixty-seven fanatical and trembling Nips armed to the teeth, and they never knew when the enemy would put an end to them.

After many hours of negotiations, the Nips were given safe conduct to their lines, and they were permitted to leave with their side arms.

We had good army chow today! Wonderful army slum-gum, canned fruit, and coffee with all the sugar and milk we wanted! No food had ever tasted this good! No food had ever made people more ill! A few hours later, hundreds of us were seized with cramps and diarrhea, and many of us were too ill and weak to reach the toilets.

We were caught in a cross fire! Shells whizzed over our heads from both directions and snipers continued to harass our camp.

The Nips across the river had their big guns turned on us, and our own artillery was set up outside the camp to fire at them.

As the shells tore through the air above us, we ducked each time—as though that would have saved us. The whistling shells above us reminded me of the tearing sound of hundreds of yards of taffeta being ripped by a giant and ruthless hand.

There was no electricity and very little water. Fortunately, the army had dug many latrines.

In spite of diarrhea and illness, we could not leave the good food alone. Despite the shells tearing through the air above us from both directions, many of us remained unconcerned. We thought only of eating, and the presence of our soldiers made us feel immune to danger.

Refugees of many nationalities and races sought shelter in the camp. They were in a pitiful state, and their stories were all the same. The retreating and enraged enemy had gone on an orgy of massacre, rape, burning, and destruction. They killed whites and Filipinos alike, and they committed unspeakable atrocities. Husbands and sons were machine-gunned before the eyes of stricken relatives. People were locked into burning homes while the enemy stood outside with machine guns and hand grenades to prevent any escape.

We knew that the fanatical enemy across the river would never surrender, and we also knew that they were making a last stand in the Walled City, the Post Office, Legislature Buildings, the Manila Hotel, and several other large public buildings.

Our big guns outside our walls continued to pour the heavy stuff at the enemy while they in turn returned the fire. As the shells continued to rip through the air above us in both directions, we began to get worried, especially when most of the war correspondents and photographers from all parts of the world moved out of the camp. They had come in with our liberating forces, and most of them admitted that they hadn't seen as much shelling and destruction in Europe and South Africa as they witnessed now.

Late in the afternoon an enemy shell struck the water tower of our building and the terrific crash threw us into a panic. Catesy had been leaning out of a third-story window looking down into the patio where I had been talking to one of our newspaper men. When the shell struck the building, the newspaper man and I ducked, but first I grabbed a dishpan to place over my head.

Now that the enemy had our range, anything could happen! There was no place to run and hide, and we knew there would be no warning before a shell struck. We saw that the commanders of the First Cavalry and 37th Infantry were gravely worried. Santo Tomas was a sitting duck to those big enemy guns across the river, and we were at the mercy of fifty to sixty thousand fanatical Japs.

We spent a sleepless night, as the noise of the swishing shells over our heads made us uneasy.

This day had been a nightmare! There had been many direct hits on the Big House and many of our people had been killed and wounded. We were stunned and almost in a state of shock as we went about our work cleaning up the rubble and caring for the wounded and dying. What a pity! we kept thinking as we went about our duties. After surviving starvation, and then having to go like this!

A large room on the first floor of our building had been opened to care for the wounded, and I gave up my work with the children to help in the new emergency.

Stunned and weeping relatives walked through the narrow aisles to identify their dead and wounded, while doctors and nurses tried to do their work.

I saw many of my fellow-members badly wounded. Many were dying.

Moving from bed to bed in a daze, I did what I had to, and I was indifferent to the shells that whistled over the building. I moved to a cot occupied by a severely wounded man. His head was badly mutilated, but I immediately recognized Mr. Mack. His breathing was stertorous, his pulse thready, and I knew that he had only a few minutes to live. But where was Mrs. Mack? She must see him before he died. Bitterness overwhelmed me. It was not fair, not right that he should go like this! He above all, with his optimism and faith.

"Where's Mrs. Mack?" I asked Dr. Fisher who stood beside me.

"In Catalina Hospital with beri-beri. Will you tell her?"

"Please don't ask me to do that!" The frightened plea in my voice made him pat my shoulder kindly.

"All right. I'll do it!"

A missionary was also among those that were killed today. A severed limb and an arm was all that was left of her, and her inseparable companion was grief-stricken and alone.

Billibid, the military prison a few blocks from us, was liberated, and there were many happy reunions between husbands and wives. It was a day of sadness for those wives who learned that their husbands would never return. No one could realize what torture and anguish these bereaved widows went through as they watched happy reunions between husbands and wives who had been separated all this time.

Kay's husband returned to her today. He was crippled and partially blind from malnutrition, but her joy was something beautiful to see as she led him around the campus.

Kay's sister's husband was dead and it was believed that Margo's husband had died too. There were many other wives whose hopes of being reunited with a loved one were gone forever today.

Leslie's son, an officer, came in with the liberating forces, and her roommates were thrilled to see her happiness. Since her husband's death during the early months of internment, we had watched her trying to conquer her grief.

Sophie's husband also returned. He had hid in the hills after the Nips had taken over the gold mine where he worked, and eventually he had joined a guerrilla outfit.

Jinny, the nurse who had asked me to go with her to Bataan shortly before the occupation, was now a widow. Her husband had died in Cabanatuan.

Some of the extremely ill military prisoners from Billibid were brought to our new camp hospital in the Education building.

Today, when I went through the narrow aisles between long rows of cots, I heard someone calling me by name.

I looked at the pasty-faced, emaciated man with the staring

black eyes and I had no idea who he was. With his completely bald head, he could have been seventy or forty years old.

"Don't you remember me? Sergeant Johnson from Ward Six."

Tears blinded me when I saw the human wreck before me. I had remembered him as a well-built, handsome, and apple-cheeked young man of twenty-five. When I clasped his hands, his eyes brimmed with tears, and for a long time we were too overcome to speak. So much had happened since we left Sternberg Hospital in the black month of December 1941.

I would recover if a Jap shell didn't finish me off, but I doubted if he would survive from the torture and starvation he had endured. As civilians, we had suffered and lost many of our people from starvation, but the many thousands who died in military camps from disease, starvation, and neglect will never be disclosed.

General MacArthur visited the camp today, and he was greeted by yells and cheers. Everyone rushed forward to shake his hands or to touch the great man.

Heavy shelling continued all night. Our shells whizzed over our heads in great numbers and, thank God, there were more going across the river into the Nip's hideout than coming our way.

February 8, 1945

A hundred army nurses arrived today from Leyte and they took over the entire nursing of the camp. How strong, healthy, and beautiful they appeared to us! When I admired their saffron yellow make-up, they laughed and told me it was atabrine, the new drug for malaria, that had caused their skins to turn yellow. I learned something new every day.

When I saw a young woman in army uniform with an unfamiliar insignia on her shoulders, I asked her about it.

"I'm a Wac," she explained kindly.

"What in the world is a Wac?" I asked in wonderment.

Since most of the Santo Tomas nurses were ill and weak, we were glad to relinquish our work to the healthy and fresh nurses. Most of us were completely worn out from dodging shells, caring for the sick and wounded, and witnessing joy and anguished grief.

As the shells tore over our heads, we ran from one section of the building to another. No spot would be safe, and we expected any moment to be our last.

February 9, 1945

Catesy was beginning to show improvement on the nourishing food, but I was still a mess. Mess was the only word to describe me at this time. After each meal I would be seized by cramps and diarrhea. No matter how hard I tried to chew my food slowly and tried to remain calm, nothing seemed to help. I wished desperately that I could have sat down to one meal without starting to bawl. I was beginning to dread mealtime, and I knew that Catesy felt the same. I, who had hated weepy women, was in tears at every meal. How I despised my weakness!

Our death rate was still mounting. Those who died after a shelling, and those who died from starvation. The good and plentiful army chow came too late for them. In many instances, the good food hastened their death.

February 10, 1945

Enemy shells again struck our building, and we had more wounded and dead.

Still no sleep, no baths, and no rest! The shells screaming through the air over our heads had unnerved us, and we wondered if we'd ever see our homes again.

The sick and wounded were moved out of the camp to Quezon Institute, but the rest of us were left behind for the good reason that there was nowhere to go.

People slept in the corridors and outside on the east side of the Big House. They felt that with many thicknesses of walls they would be safer.

Despite the heavy artillery activity and the terrific concussion of the bursting shells, our worn-out bodies finally gave in to sleep.

February 12, 1945

The world had been assured that "Manila was secured." Yet the men who had come from New Guinea, the Marianas, and Leyte told us that the battle for Manila was the bloodiest they had fought.

"Manila was secured!" scoffed a First Cavalry private bitterly. He had sat with us in our lean-to last night. "Why, I'm the only man left in my platoon!"

Most of the officers and soldiers who returned to camp said very little, but all were exhausted and grim-looking.

February 13, 1945

The cornered enemy put up a stiff resistance, though our heavy artillery kept at them from dawn to dusk. The ruthless and enraged enemy continued to kill civilians across the river in the Walled City, Ermita, and Malate sections, and those who miraculously escaped across the narrow Pasig River could never forget the horrors they had witnessed.

February 14, 1945

General Kruger visited the camp today, and he was enthusiastically received by everyone.

The shells continued to sail over our heads. We had to shout to each other to be heard above the terrific noise of the detonating shells.

We wanted to get away! We had had enough of killing and warfare!

February 15, 1945

In my humble opinion, the greatest opportunists, cheats, and two-faced people were those who carried two passports. When the Japs were in the driver's seat, these people flashed their passports from a neutral country and thus they were never interned. Some of them became bloated and rich during the Japanese regime.

When the Americans returned, they tucked their neutral passports into moth balls, and they flashed their American passports so that they could seek the protection of Uncle Sam.

If I am a flag waver, so be it! I am proud of it! I am what I am because I was daily reminded of the blessings and privileges I enjoyed in my land of adoption as a child and a young woman. For had not my parents chosen to emigrate to the United States, I and my whole family would have been swept away like dust under the ruthless boot of the Nazi horde.

We sympathized with the Chinese and Filipino refugees, who continued to seek safety in camp, but the plight of some of the whites, the Nazis, the collaborators, the neutrals, the third-party nationals, left many of us cold and unsympathetic. These refugees, as many of us believed, had lived outside in the comfort and privacy of their own homes while we had lived like pigs in congested surroundings. We had been slapped, pushed around, starved, and some of our men had been executed. Many of these Nazis, collaborators, and neutrals had lost their homes and possessions in the last few days. They had seen their relatives shot before their eyes, and still many of our people remained cold when they heard their stories.

As one internee, a widow, had said, "I lost my home and possessions over three years ago, and I saw my husband die, not with the swift and merciful death caused by a bullet, but by slow starvation!"

God, how calloused and prejudiced some of us had become!

February 16, 1945

Our heavy guns were lined hub-to-hub on this side of the Pasig River, and our artillerists were blasting the enemy in the Walled City.

How could the enemy survive such heavy pounding? The terrific blasting went on day and night and we continued to shout in order to be heard.

Among the refugees that swarmed the camp, we recognized Nazis and Japanese collaborators, and their names were turned over to the USAFFE intelligence operating in camp.

Sniping continued, and today a number of our soldiers died from a poisoned drink given to them outside.

Filipino laborers who came into camp daily were thoroughly searched and investigated.

We were informed by our army leaders that just as quickly as the enemy was vanquished and Manila Bay had been swept clean of mines, our ships would arrive to take us to our homelands. Oh, happy days! Repatriation was in the air, and people rushed around trying to decide which of their moth-eaten clothes should be taken with them.

February 18, 1945

Though Los Banos was only about seventy kilometers from Manila, there was absolutely no communication from that camp. It almost seemed as if that camp, with several thousand men, women, and children, had vanished from the face of the earth. The relatives of these people were gravely worried, as it had been rumored that the Nips planned to massacre the Los Banos internees before they took to the hills.

We consumed vast quantities of coffee mixed with all the sugar and canned milk that we wanted. We wouldn't believe that it would last, so just as quickly as we had drunk the coffee we would rush back to the mobile coffee kitchen with our empty Lactogen cans for more.

Catesy watched the long line of people waiting for refills, and he marveled how people could consume that much coffee. When he spoke to the good-natured sergeant in charge of the coffee regarding his generosity, the sergeant said, "Give the poor bastards all they can drink at all hours of the day, and pretty soon when they realize it's theirs for the asking, they won't be slopping it up all the time!"

It was the same way with our food. We took more food than we could eat and we were always hoarding it.

I visited some of my former little patients and it was good to see how their peaked little faces were beginning to fill out. A few of them, like myself, still had trouble with their food. Their eyes would become as big as saucers when the good food was placed before them, but after a few bites they lost their enthusiasm, and they played with their food.

How we looked forward to the evenings when the boys of the First Cavalry and the 37th Infantry returned from combat duty! Everyone had adopted several of the boys and they ate their meals with their adopted families whenever they could get away.

Tonight the army gave us more than an hour of movie news in the rear of the Big House. We thrilled with pride and gratitude

when the commentator on the screen kept alluding to our heroes
of the First Cavalry, the 44th Tank batallion, and the boys of the
37th Infantry.

We wondered if there could have been another movie audience
in the world who had more realistic battle scenes on and off the
screen. With the fierce battle scenes on the screen, we had the
added sound effect of our shells whizzing over our heads, and the
heavy pounding of artillery only six or eight blocks from us. When
the commentator ended the news reel by saying, "We won't be
satisfied until Manila is taken!" we heered madly. The goose
pimples that crept over my skin felt like heady wine coursing
through my veins and capillaries.

Some of our people gained as much as twenty pounds in less
than three weeks on the wonderful army chow. One little nine-
year-old gir' from my room had gained most of her weight in her
abdomen and she appeared almost disfigured.

The camp children had ceased to be the little old men and
women. They were normal kids again, and they began to annoy
us with their running, screaming, and general rowdiness. The
soldiers were spoiling them horribly. When they weren't stuffing
their mouths with candy, chewing gum, and chocolates, they were
riding the jeeps and trucks in the camp with the soldiers.

February 20, 1945

Catesy and I had our first glimpse of the outside world since
over two years ago. We rode in a jeep with two friendly GIs. This
time, we didn't have to wear the hateful red arm band to show that
we were enemy aliens. The last time I had been out, I had seen
many Japanese soldiers and civilians, and the business section of
the city was still standing. Today it was completely leveled, and
there were no Japs.

We stood at the Plaza Goiti and we looked to the north, east,
south and west, as far as the eye could see. There was nothing
but crumbling walls, and in some blocks there was absolutely
nothing—everything had been leveled off by dynamiting and shelling. We passed the devastated areas and came to crowded streets
filled with hungry and ragged Filipinos who were lined up for
blocks to receive their food rations.

Jeeps, trucks, and other vehicles roared through the torn-up
streets while GIs stood talking to the friendly tienda keepers, who
had nothing to sell. The poor soldiers who had been looking forward to reaching the big city of Manila, after fighting in jungles
for over a year, found a city devastated and still under war
conditions. Many of them had a year and a half of back pay and
no place to spend it. They had nowhere to go! No recreation, no

movies, no beer parlors, and nothing to buy! When I mentioned this to Catesy sitting beside me, he prophesied: "All that will be remedied in a short time, and I'll bet there will be a ginmill on every corner!"

After we left the crowded streets of Ascarraga and Rizal, we rode through sections of residential Santa Mesa. Here everything seemed peaceful and normal, and it was a startling change after the ruins of downtown and the Ermita section.

When we returned to the camp, we were shocked to learn that a ten-year-old boy had accidentally shot a soldier with a gun that he had carelessly given the child.

Three enemy shells struck the camp tonight and we had more wounded and dead.

February 21, 1945

Catesy left for army headquarters in Tarlac, which was about 125 kilometers from Manila. There was a possibility that after talking to some of the officers at headquarters, he would have a better idea whether it was feasible to remain in Manila and re-establish his firm. Many old residents of the city were confronted by the same problem. Stay in Manila, or go back home? Those who had worked for large Stateside firms had back salaries coming to them, but there were many who had worked for themselves, or for local firms, who would be without funds. For this reason, the people in the last group were anxious to get started in Manila. After having lived here for many years, their homeland would seem strange to them. Without funds, it would seem still stranger.

February 23, 1945

The trussed-up and mutilated bodies of Mr. Grant and the other three men who had been taken out of camp by the Nips such a short time ago, were found and identified. The beautiful blonde widow of one of the executed men remained inconsolable.

Catesy returned from Tarlac. He was dirty, tired, and every bone in his body ached from the rough jeep ride over shell-torn roads. He reported that he had never seen as many high-ranking officers in one camp in his life. Only officers above the rank of a lieutenant colonel rated a pillow, he told me with a grin. Most of the officers he talked to told him that there would be no semblance of normalcy or resumption of business of any kind for several years.

"Then you're going back home!" His decision had made me happy.

"Nope! On the contrary, I'm staying. I know how wrong the army can be!"

"Then I'm staying, too!" The happy grin on Catesy's face was well worth my disappointment.

Three hundred and fifty repatriates left the camp by truck in the midst of confusion and a great deal of handshaking and good wishes. More repatriates would follow shortly.

The 17th-century, six-foot-thick stone walls of the Walled City were down at last, and so were all the buildings in that ancient city. It took many days of continual blasting by our artillery to accomplish this. The Nips who hadn't been annihilated escaped to the Port area, and now that section received the full attention of our artillery. Soon these trapped Nips in the Port area would join their Banzai brothers.

In the midst of death, shelling, and destruction, there were weddings galore! The very air we breathed was charged with romance and orange blossoms. Many engaged internee couples were married now, and there were many weddings between internee girls and men of our liberating forces. After attending several of these weddings in camp, Catesy suggested that we get married too.

"Now is our big chance!" he remarked practically. "It won't cost us a cent. No invitations, flowers, wedding cake, or reception expenses. Just think! Why, even the wedding pictures are free!" (The bridal pairs were photographed by the Army Signal Corps, and the pictures were telephotoed to the States.)

"Not for me!" I declared emphatically. "I waited over three years, I guess we can postpone our wedding another few months."

"But why, honey?"

"I want to be a June bride! And besides," I added a bit ruefully, "I'd make a fine-looking bride with my skin and bones."

It was true. While so many were gaining weight, I still looked like a plucked and bedraggled chicken that had been caught in a heavy hail storm. I could tolerate only small portions of food, such as oatmeal, canned milk, and sugar.

Those internees who planned on remaining in Manila scoured the city every day in the hopes of finding a house or a room. With two-thirds of this large city leveled to the ground, this was no easy problem. The Malate and Ermita sections had been completely leveled. I wandered through rubble-torn streets that I could not recognize, as there were no landmarks, no trees, no buildings, houses, or signs to guide me. Yet I had lived in this section for four years before moving to my apartment in the early spring of 1941. I went to the eight-story apartment house where I had last lived and I saw that it had been completely gutted from shelling, mining, and bombing. The vacant houses in Santa Mesa, San Juan, and Pasay had already been reserved for Army and Navy officers, which was just as well, I had to admit, for none of us had cars, and the markets and the business areas which we hoped would soon be established, were miles away.

February 25, 1945

The heavy shelling had ceased, for the time being, and the silence was strange to our ears! The Japs, what there was left of them, were holed up in the Port Area. Soon they, too, would be flushed out as our planes dropped bombs on them hourly.

It was rumored that our Los Banos people had been liberated, and friends and relatives in camp prayed that it was true. Los Banos was in a rough spot with thousands of live Nips all about them.

February 26, 1945

The Los Banos rumor was true! Every person in that camp had been rescued, and the local paper—no longer the *Nishi-Nishi*—carried this headline:

2000 CIVILIANS SET FREE BY DARING RAID AT LOS BANOS. GUERRILLAS AID PARATROOPERS IN BOLD ATTACK.

Their rescue was daring and fantastic, and it was true that the enraged Nips had planned to massacre the helpless Americans and other nationals. It was for this reason that the rescue of the Americans had been so bold and dramatic. It was more thrilling and exciting than any Wild West movie.

When nine American transport planes passed very low over Los Banos, the startled internees saw a myriad of parachutes like giant umbrellas silhouetted against the sky. As the paratroopers descended on the camp, they mowed down the Japs at the front and main gate while Filipino and American guerrillas hiding in the bushes on the mountain side came to life at the precise moment. Screaming like wild cannibals, and with guns blasting away, the guerrillas gave the airborne men the support that they needed. In a matter of minutes they cleaned up the Japanese guards who were at the fences around the camp. The Japanese were taken completely by surprise. While 139 of the paratroopers and the screaming guerrillas were busy with the Nips, a large force of amphibious tanks roared into the camp with earth-shaking rumbles. With the combined efforts of the three separate units, 250 Nips were killed in the camp in a few minutes, while dumbstruck men, women, and children milled around during all this heavy firing. It was another miracle that only four internees were nicked by bullets, and their injuries were minor.

As the American and Filipino guerrillas set fire to the barracks formerly occupied by our people, other soldiers and officers herded the internees into the amphibious tanks. These monstrous tanks loaded with men, women, and children thundered down the road

259

through swamp and lake, and the tanks' big guns roared at the snipers who shot at them from every side. Not one of our people was nicked!

The army had done a beautiful job planning this rescue. For daring, drama, and perfect timing, it had no equal and the kids and adults who were rescued in the alligators said that they would never have an adventure to equal it.

February 27, 1945

The Los Banos people were reunited with their friends and relatives in camp, and as we listened to their thrilling account of the daring rescue, we were again reminded of the clocklike coordination between the different units of our Army.

There were still small pockets of the enemy in the Port Area and in the Marikima valley, and our bombers and artillery kept after them from morning until night.

We fussed about petty housekeeping detail, yet when a shell crashed into our camp, we went about our work, only faintly disturbed. Now, we were fatalistic about those shells. If our number was up—well, that was it!

The collaborators, the Nazis, the Franco people, and the fence-sitters still swarmed into the camp, and it infuriated us old-timers who had served three long years in jail. We felt that only we should enjoy the bounty and hospitality of Uncle Sam. With so many complaints about these people from indignant internees, the USAFFE began checking on them in an effort to weed out the most undesirable. In the meantime, these people ate the good food the army gave us and enjoyed the same privileges that loyal Americans and other Allied nationals received.

We sat up until eleven tonight, an unearthly hour for us, to guzzle huge quantities of coffee as we talked with boys of the First Cavalry and the 37th Infantry. We talked about women, their clothes, shows, 'gator-hunting and fishing in Florida, and food. The Nips, as usual, got a fair share of panning.

March 10, 1945

"Mommy, Mommy! Look! He's a Jap!" shouted the excited four-year-old American boy when he saw a tall and handsome Japanese in the uniform of an American officer.

How well I understood the child's excitement and astonishment, after having seen the enemy in sloppy and dirty Japanese uniforms for so long!

The handsome officer knelt down by the little boy and put his arm around him and said earnestly, "Yes, sonny, I was born a Japanese. But I am an American just like you are!"

The child's eyes remained round with bewilderment and his

mother was silent. If the child could not comprehend, neither could we adults—not for a long, long time to come. We had so much to forget. We had to stop hating, and we had to overcome many prejudices. It was my first encounter with a nisei, and it was not until later that I learned about these brave and loyal Japanese-Americans.

March 13, 1945

A friend of mine coaxed me to go to a cocktail party with her to the home of two colonels. Since Catesy wasn't included, naturally, I didn't want to go, but he urged me to go as he thought the change would be good for me.

What a treat to ride in a passenger car again, to drink good Stateside liquor, and to sit in a comfortably furnished home! I just wanted to sit in the overstuffed sofa and cluck about the delights and wonders of normal living, but the two colonels had other ideas. They had a one-track mind. The old "snow job" about not having seen a white woman for 33 months became pretty tiresome. Every woman from 16 to 60 in Santo Tomas had been handed the same line by our liberating forces, and by now it was pretty stale and overworked.

Their constant allusion to a cozy twosome became most monotonous, and my escort made brilliant plans for a sea-food dinner sometime in the near future, when his new apartment was completed. At the thought of lapu-lapu, giant prawns, and shrimps, I drooled, for I dearly loved sea food, but the anticipatory gleam in the old boy's eyes decided me. No, thank you! I would stick to my army oatmeal at camp. There, at least, the chow was free with no strings attached.

March 14, 1945

When I frothed at the mouth about the neutrals, the Vichys, the Francos, the Nazis and other nationals, I did not mean to generalize, as some of these people of various nationalities helped us whenever they could. A passport was only an official document and it did not make a man or woman good or bad.

Some people who were never interned lost their lives on the outside. I knew of one woman who suffered shame, degradation, and eventually became raving mad. The last time I heard of her, in 1948, she was still in a mental institution. She had lived outside because of her neutral papers. Another woman, also a neutral, and therefore never interned, suffered mutilation and other horrors before she died.

When I learned that my old friend, Mr. Nagy, was a patient at San Lázaro, we went to visit him. Weighing only eighty pounds and suffering from T.B. and a recent bowel obstruction, he was in a pitiful state. The city hospital, where he was, had been stripped of those things necessary for a patient's comfort. Only a sheet protected his skin and bones from the wire springs of the bed. From our friends who were being repatriated, we were able to collect two mattresses, sheets, pillows, cigarettes, milk, fruit, and candy.

How happy we were to be able to help him! Now, he was the enemy national, but of course, in his critical state, he would never be interned. His home had been looted, then burned, and for the last year he had starved just as we had.

Many of our people who, at first, had decided to remain in Manila, now changed their minds when they saw all the devastation around them. In many cases, their homes were gone and they had nothing to stay for.

Soon all our people would be repatriated. Only a few diehards like Catesy and me planned to stay, though we had no home, no furniture, no clothes, and no means of transportation.

Every day we walked for miles in search of a house. We knocked on doors, and friendly and sympathetic Filipinos listened to our story, but no one had an empty house, not even a room. We returned to Santo Tomas tired and footsore, and completely discouraged.

Perhaps we should go back to the States, as things looked pretty hopeless. Then one day, Jim, an American mining engineer, asked us if we would care to share a house with him. Would we? We jumped at the chance.

The house was only a few blocks from our camp and it was built on the old Spanish style with large garage downstairs and tiny living quarters in the back of the garage. The upstairs rooms were large, with a sala and dining room combined, two bedrooms, a tiny kitchen, and a bath and a half. There was ornately carved Spanish furniture in the sala and dining room. As the fine Filipino family who lived downstairs showed us around, we admired the dark Philippine mahogany paneling on the walls, but when we saw two huge rats scampering around as though they owned the place, we were a bit worried. The dead, Japanese and natives alike, were still unburied, and the rats had practically taken over the city.

Though we had lived in comfortably furnished homes and apartments before the war, now we were happy to share a house with bloated rats in the most disreputable section of the city. But to us that house looked like a palace compared to the boiler factory we had occupied for the last thirty-nine months.

The day we moved from Santo Tomas was a happy one! Through the colonel in charge of our camp, we were given an army truck to move us out. No truck ever carried such an assortment of junk! Not only our junk, but junk left to us by close friends who had been repatriated. We could not bear to part with any of it! We had tin cans, bottles, five old beds, school chairs, charcoal stoves, bayongs, tampipis, suitcases, paper boxes, chipped and assorted crockery, dime silverware, and an accumulation of canned milk given us by the army.

We placed the five beds in the boys' dormitory and there wasn't another stick of furniture in the long and narrow room.

My room across the hall had one huge Spanish bed with bejuca matting, and there was a grand Spanish apparador complete with a full-length mirror. There was no other furniture in the room but, since there was plenty of wall space, the boys built wide shelves from discarded lumber we had brought from the camp. Those wide shelves we hoped to fill with canned food, as we all agreed that no wall decoration, no matter how rare, would have the same eye-appeal to us as rows of gleaming canned goods.

We felt certain that Catalino and Adoracion were dead. If they weren't dead, they were ashamed to contact us. It was too bad, as I would have forgiven them for pinching and selling my stuff. War had done strange things to many people.

Soon Jim's former housegirl joined our happy household, and though she spoke no English or Spanish we got along beautifully.

Friends and relatives in the States wrote their men in the armed forces about us, and when these men had leave to visit the city, they called on us. Cousins, nephews, friends of friends, and distant relatives of both Catesy and me called on us. Some came to dinner and stayed for weeks. Those who were stationed in the city came back day after day, and several of the officers moved into the boys' dormitory and lived there for months. The five beds were always occupied, and if there had been space we would have added more.

Wacs, USO girls, army nurses, and Red Cross girls—all of them came to call. Jeeps, trucks, and weapon carriers were always outside our door.

Protestant chaplains, Catholic chaplains, newspapermen, photographers, and an opera singer were guests in our house. It was a gay, happy, amusing and confusing household. We were never alone, and we loved every minute of it now that we were free and eating.

Though we had no electricity, no phone, no car, and very little water, we were sitting on top of the world!

Several of the officers who lived with us went to the commissary and Catesy would hand them a fifty-peso bill and tell them to get everything that they could. Our eyes would lean out like a frog's when they returned with a jeepload of groceries, while Filipinos in the streets would offer us money to sell them some of the food. We shared our good fortune with the kind neighbors downstairs. We exchanged fresh meat and canned food for fresh fruit and vegetables.

The shelves in my bedroom were stacked high with canned goods, and every time I went into the room I would feast my eyes on them, like a rare painting. Every time we had a new visitor, he or she was taken to my room to admire our gleaming rows of cans.

Soon, we had to hire two more girls to help with the cooking and washing.

A group of Air Corps officers, highly skilled in the art of scrounging, discovered us one day, and they became permanent members of our family. After that, we never worried about groceries, and the terrific prices. They flew their jeepload of rice, bacon, and other canned goods in their C 46 from Leyte. There was so much black marketing, looting, shooting, and killing that it never occurred to us that it was wrong to accept all the food donations scrounged from the army. With food prices still out of our reach, it would have taken a Rockefeller to feed all the officers who stayed with us.

There were always eight or ten at our large table at night, and after I had dressed up the powdered eggs, dehydrated potatoes, and Spam with plenty of garlic, onions, and herbs, the boys thought they were eating Stateside food. For salad, I would use the lowly cincamas, thinly sliced, and mixed with more garlic and onions.

Tiendas with shoddy souvenirs, gin mills, pom-pom houses, and pro-stations sprang up in all parts of the city as more than a million and a half of our armed forces eventually sought the bright lights while on leave.

There were pro-stations on practically every street corner. There was one a half block from our house. A noisy gin mill, frequented by sailors and soldiers, did a flourishing business across the street from us and, fortunately, the eleven o'clock curfew closed it promptly at that hour. Next to this gin mill was a popular pom-pom house also frequented by soldiers and sailors.

The Barbary Coast had been namby-pamby compared to postwar Manila. As the city began to get on its feet, more ramshackle gin mills and tiendas were set up on Rizal, Escolata, and various parts of the city. Sailors and GIs by the thousands roamed the dirty streets seeking diversion and souvenirs.

From experience, I learned never to stand or walk past our wide picture windows in the sala, for just as soon as I did, a soldier or a sailor from the gin mill would dash across the street and try to get into the house.

One afternoon I was awakened from siesta by considerable commotion and loud talking coming from downstairs. Sleepily, I donned a housecoat and walked down the stairs to the garage-like room that led to the outside of the house. My astonished eyes saw three young sailors. None of them could have been twenty-one. They were wrestling with my youngest housegirl who was backed against the wall, pleading. "Sir, I am not a pom-pom girl!" she kept repeating earnestly, between sobs.

Outraged, I broke into this disgusting scene, and in my iciest tone, I stormed, "Don't you know a decent, respectable, American home when you see it?"

To say that the young sailors were startled to hear a feminine American voice, was putting it mildly. They took one look at me and backed out of the doorway. Two of them were speechless, but the third one kept repeating, "Jesus Christ! Jesus Christ!" He backed out of the door so quickly that he knocked his two companions into the slimy gutter.

It made me furious and sad to see such behavior. This, too, was a part of war.

One afternoon, several officers were sitting around in our sala sipping junglejuice and talking about this and that. One of the officers was Bill, the husband of my life-long friend, Marge, from Pittsburgh. Suddenly, our conversation was interrupted by the appearance of a very dirty and disheveled-looking soldier. His shirt tails were flapping and his bare chest was exposed in the repulsive fashion of a Japanese soldier.

The officers looked startled, and I jumped up and confronted the soldier angrily. "What is it?" I inquired haughtily. I was shocked and disgusted to see an American soldier looking like a Nip.

He took one long look at me and blushed. Then in a long, Southern drawl, he said, "Ma'am, I think there has been a mistake!" In an embarrassed and apologetic manner he produced an official-looking paper, which I gave to Bill. After reading the paper, Bill started to roar with laughter and he handed it to the other officers. When Bill told me what it was all about, I was outraged. The soldier was a member of the military vice squad and it was his job to investigate pom-pom houses. Apparently, the madame of the popular pom-pom house across the street, thinking that I was infringing on her business, had reported me.

How those officers laughed! The more they laughed, the more furious I became. Then I became furious at myself for being furious. What else could I expect living under these conditions in such a neighborhood?

"Tomorrow, I'm going to the Chief of the Military Police of this city and get a sign to post on my door!" I announced haughtily.

"What will be on the sign?" inquired Bill, wiping the tears of laughter from his eyes.

"Believe it or not! This is not a pom-pom house!"

The men howled, and when the humor of the situation struck me, I joined them.

Naturally, since the occupation, all imported goods from the States and Europe had ceased to come into the country. There was a shortage of everything! This shortage, of course, was most acute in the pharmaceutical lines.

When the Army medical depot asked Catesy to help set up drug distribution points throughout the city, he was glad to help. His large wholesale-and-retail drug firm received the first major shipment of drugs from the States. Catesy also helped to place about 150 of his firm's former employees in medical depots, and they helped with the distribution until the emergency was over. Catesy worked from sunup to sundown, as he was in charge. The older executives had either died or they had been repatriated because of illness. It was a heartbreaking and backbreaking job. Heartbreaking, because, while he sold the precious drugs to retail outlets at legitimate prices, the ill and desperate public paid black market prices for aspirin, penicillin, and other drugs, and there was no way that Catesy or the army could check it.

While Catesy worked with the army medical depot, he tried to reestablish his firm's business in a building that was in partial ruins. While wrecking crews tore down four-storied walls, and bomb-disposal crews removed mines and booby traps from the building, Catesy tried to keep his wits about him as he ordered long lists of supplies from the States.

With the Philippines used as the jumping-off place for the big push in Japan, men, equipment, and acres upon acres of army supplies were scattered throughout the city and country. These mountains of supplies were poorly guarded and exposed to the elements and robbers. Every night one of these huge supply depots was looted by organized gangs of robbers—and in many cases the robbers were our GIs. Finally, when the loot amounted to truck-loads, the armed guards were instructed to shoot to kill and ask questions afterwards.

Black markets flourished! Lawlessness was in the air we breathed!

Under the Nip's domination, people had lived by their wits to survive. Some had cheated, stolen, and killed for over three years, and now the criminally bent, lured by fantastic gains, did not change their behavior pattern.

Filipino robber gangs, in many instances led by white and Negro GIs, broke into homes, and with machine-guns terrorized the households as they stripped them of valuables.

Because of the poor and disreputable neighborhood we lived in, we were comparatively safe from such terrorizing gangsters. Then, too, we had a captain of the MP's as a permanent guest. Whenever a shooting, a killing, or other rowdiness occurred, our captain would crouch by the window-sill with a pistol cocked and ready for any emergency.

An efficient organization of car, jeep, and truck thieves operated on a grand scale in the city, and just as quickly as the vehicle was stolen, an army of workers dismantled and changed the vehicle, making identification difficult and almost impossible.

Bootleg liquor, some of it deadly, was sold at fantastic prices, and some of the men and women of our armed forces lost their eyesight and their lives. On Rizal Avenue, a huge cloth banner was stretched across from one side of the street to the other, bearing this legend: "Four Died Today from Wood Alcohol!"

Farther on, there was a sign in a restaurant with this information: "We Serve in a Sanitary Way." I looked inside, and the place was unbelievably dirty.

On a telegraph pole, there were these words of warning: "Do not buy ice cream from the vendors. It is filled with human feces."

Because civilian white women were rare, GIs and sailors followed me for blocks and their line of patter was always the same. Do you suppose she speaks English? Is she Spanish? No, she's too light. I'll bet she's one of them white Roosians. Knowing how lonely and lost they were, I would have loved to stop and chat with them, but I would have had difficulty in preventing them from following me home. Our home already bulged at the seams. Every bed was occupied and there were no more leaves to add to our dining table.

One night Catesy came home grinning and acting in a secretive manner. After considerable worming, I found the cause. He had cabled to a Los Angeles firm for the biggest home refrigerator that they had in stock.

"But do you think anything will come of it? You know the war is still on!"

The thoughts of having a refrigerator again made me dizzy with delight. Ice for our drinks, making ice cream, and a place to store our perishable food! That would be living! Few people in this large city had a refrigerator, as the Nips had made a thorough job of stripping homes and business houses of furnishings, refrigerators, stoves and other appliances, which they shipped to their homeland.

One day, about six weeks later, I heard loud talking and a great deal of commotion outside our house. Forgetting my precaution about getting close to the window because of the GIs and sailors across the street, I leaned out to see what was up.

A truck had parked outside our door and in it were ten Filipinos and the largest and most beautiful refrigerator I had ever seen. As the men started to unload the refrigerator from the truck, all the yakamashi and music at the gin mill stopped, and entertainers and patrons rushed outside to see what was going on. It looked like even the pom-pom house next to the gin mill had called a recess, for the sullen and buxom-looking madam with her four frowsy girls were leaning out the wide Spanish window and making excited conversation over our refrigerator.

Somehow, ten workmen got the refrigerator off the truck, and then came the hardest task of all to carry it up the steep staircase.

Meanwhile, Tito (uncle), Lola (Grandma), her daughter, son-in-law, and Vidal, her eight-year-old grandson from downstairs, had joined the interested spectators.

While the men puffed, pulled, tugged, sweated, shouted, and got in each other's way, Lola alternately wrung her hands in agitation, and dramatically slapped her cheeks with the palms of her hands as she kept repeating, "Jesus Maria! Jesus Maria!" Dear old Lola worried that the house would collapse from the heavy two-door, 22-cubic-foot refrigerator.

Just as quickly as the refrigerator was installed, three Filipino carpenters reinforced the house below the refrigerator with 6 by 4 beams.

The snow-white gleam and the glistening chrome of that mammoth refrigerator against the Philippine mahogany walls in the dining area was the most beautiful décor I ever saw. The hum of its motors almost, but not quite, drowned out the noise of the gin mill.

Through my good army friends, I obtained ice cream mix in gallon cans, and then began an orgy of ice cream making and eating. That night I ate twelve soup bowls of ice cream and had no ill effects. Vidal, my eight-year-old neighbor, came close to topping my record.

The San Lázaro City Hospital was only a few blocks from our home, and every day I went to visit my old friend, Mr. Nagy. Each day I took him some dish I had prepared, and I kept him supplied with cigarettes, milk, candy and fruit. We spent many happy hours talking about books, music, and his old life in Budapest and Shanghai. With his keen political sense, he predicted that our next adversary would be the Russians, with the Japanese fighting by our side. He never ceased to wonder at the power and might of the U. S. Army. He admired everything that was American, from our huge aircraft carriers to the tiny package of Life Savers that were so cleverly wrapped and sealed. More than once, he expressed his regret that he had never been to the States. Now it was too late.

He often spoke of his approaching death; not with fear or doubt, but with a longing desire for rest and to see what was on the other side. As each day he grew a little weaker, he longed for rest.

Death came for him peacefully and quietly one morning at four. Several men of the military police stationed at the hospital came for me, as he wanted to see me once more before he died. As I walked to his bedside and reached for his hand, he opened his eyes and looked at me. Like the faint flutter of a dying moth, his fingers pressed my hand, then he closed his eyes forever.

I wrote to his sister, a baroness in Budapest, but I never heard from her. With Hungary overrun by Nazis and then by the Russians, it was doubtful that she was alive.

Don Juan, the chaser of blondes, had given up his pursuit forever, and for a good reason. A clever blonde had caught him permanently, and he seemed to enjoy the role of a married man.

The last time I heard about Tientsin Mary, she was still in the Orient.

Harvey Jones, who did more than any person in our camp to lift our morale, gave so much of himself that for a long time it was feared that he would never recover. He spent several years trying to regain his health, and now he is back as an entertainer in the night spots of Manila, and he is happily married to an English girl who was also in camp.

Laura, my poetic roommate who was ill for many years after liberation, has now recovered, and she and her husband enjoy life in Palo Alto, California.

Just before Belle and Toinette left on the first repatriation ship to the States after liberation, we embraced, wept, laughed, and wondered why we had stopped speaking to each other for over a year, though our beds nearly touched throughout internment.
Belle now lives in San Francisco, and her daughter, Toinette, married a handsome medical officer in the U. S. Army.

Mrs. Greenshoes, that hardy octogenarian, survived Santo Tomas. She went to live in Texas, and she probably would still be alive, enjoying her reading, poetry writing, and Buddhist discussions if she hadn't died in a hotel fire.

The ending of Margo's story followed the lines of the fictional Enoch Arden. Many months after the war was over, the War Department sent her an official notice of her husband's death. On the eve of her marriage to the man she met during the occupation, her husband returned alive, but critically ill, from long months in a prison camp in Japan. The marriage, of course, never took place, and the last time I heard, Margo was nursing her husband back to health.

Zest, the army nurse, was hospitalized for a long time with T.B. and the army retired her. She and Henry are now married and living in the Philippines.

The pretty chief nurse of Corregidor lost her fiancé in a prison camp, but she is now happily married to a general.

Leslie, our faithful and efficient room monitor, lives in California with her aged mother. Near her are her married sons, with their wives and children.

Kay nursed her husband back to health, and her widowed sister with the two little children remarried a few years after the war was over.

Mrs. Mack recovered, and she now lives near her married sons in the States.

Grandma, now an American citizen, lives in the States near her grandchildren and great grandchildren.

Since Catesy and I fully recovered from our various illnesses, we do not regret our three years of internment.

While many couples drifted apart in the unusual environment, we were drawn closer. Our long years of imprisonment with its privations had made us appreciate the little things in life—such as a loaf of clean bread, a cellophane-wrapped box of Wheaties, and a glass of fresh milk.

We learned that hate, greed, and prejudice were not confined to the enemy alone. Among other lessons, we learned that yesterday's enemy could be today's ally, and vice versa.

We also saw, at first hand, the bitter lesson of unpreparedness, and we witnessed the tragic results in lost lives and colossal destruction.

But, above all, it made us appreciate our freedom, our blessed freedom that we all take for granted. Borrowing a phrase from Col. Memory H. Cain (ret.), who survived the Bataan Death March and other infamous treatment in military prison camps, we learned that: "Freedom is Not Free! We have to work at it daily. We have to cherish and protect it in order to enjoy its privileges."

June 24, 1945

This was our wedding day! We finally made it! Three years and six months later!

This time, there were no interfering Japs and no prison gates!

In a few hours we would be standing before an army chaplain, in a ruined and roofless church that had only one tottering wall standing.

All the fluttering and bothersome details connected with a wedding had been completed; all but the few odds and ends, such as picking up the cake and taking care of the table. But these details had been left in the hands of our capable and eager army and navy pals, Bud, Gene, Russ, Bill, Charles, and our friendly neighbors from downstairs. From the moment that a wedding had been mentioned a month ago, these friends had been busy and up to their eyebrows with plans. They were almost as excited as the bride.

As I dressed, I peeked out of my bedroom and saw Lola, Vidal, his mother, and her sister-in-law fluttering around the table.

The fragile white butterfly orchids in the center of the table were beautiful enough for a Vanderbilt wedding, and the GI silverware and oddly assorted plates with its many patterns and colors, strangely enough, did not detract from the beauty of the table. The dishes had served time in Santo Tomas, and most of them had been willed to me by friends who had been repatriated.

Our refreshments, liquid and otherwise, both unattainable at this time unless one wished to go into debt for life, were being handled by a group of highly skilled army and navy scroungers.

Bread, at this time, was selling for two and three pesos a loaf. To spend a dollar to a dollar and a half for one loaf was a crime, and to buy twenty or more loaves for our reception would have constituted sheer stupidity. Especially after I had seen U. S. Army trucks piled high with the precious staff of life driving into the courtyard of Billibid Prison where the Nazis and other enemy nationals were now interned. Surely, if the Nazis and other collaborationists had free bread, I ought to have it for my wedding without paying a king's ransom, I reasoned, woman-like. I explained my difficulty to my army and air force pals, and they told me not to worry about it; and so bread was flown from Leyte by our friendly air corps boys, while a group of efficient medical men furnished us the alcohol. The night before, the prospective bride had filled dozens of bottles with watered alcohol, to which she had added juniper essence and glycerin. The finished product had the same desired effect as the genuine liquid from Holland.

In my bedroom, I was surrounded by two giggling housegirls and my new Wac friend, Sylvia, from Brooklyn, who was to be my maid of honor.

Jullya, one of my girls, told me that my dress looked like the one Deanna Durbin had worn in her last picture, and I was pleased by the compliment.

My wedding dress was a housecoat! In 1940, when I had returned from a shopping spree to Hong Kong and Shanghai, I had shown Catesy my loot. When he had seen the housecoat, he had said, "That would make a wonderful wedding dress!"

How I had laughed! How like a man, not to know the difference between a housecoat and a dress! A wedding dress! The very idea! Yet five years later, I was married in it. It was a beautiful housecoat with yards and yards of fragile ivy-colored Peiping gauze shot with a delicate bamboo pattern over peach taffeta. The stiff and heavy taffeta shimmered and swished in a fashion that was pleasing to the ear. Catalino had sent it to me in Santo Tomas and, at the time, I had thought it was the most ridiculous of all my useless possessions in camp. I had covered the housecoat with the native go-go bark and this had successfully kept the cockroaches and silverfish from destroying it under my bed.

My gold slippers had been borrowed from a Filipina friend and they were tarnished and war-weary, but who cared? No one would see them, as the sweeping folds of the housecoat hid the shoes.

The crown of my bridal hat was intricately woven with white gardenias, white orchids, and it was the work of a male milliner. A microscopic bit of veil barely covered my eyes.

As I looked at myself in the old apparador mirror, I was not displeased by what I saw. All the oatmeal, milk, sugar, and ice cream I had consumed in the last few months had paid off. My face was full, there was color in my cheeks, and my bones were now generously padded.

As Hilaria handed me my bridal bouquet of white orchids, gardenias, and the fragrant sampaguita, she told me that I looked like Deanna Durbin. Though I pooh-poohed the idea, I was childishly pleased.

Catesy looked extremely handsome in his one and only white sharkskin suit. It was one of the three items salvaged from the war. The other two were a pair of golf shoes and his golf bag complete with all the clubs. They had been saved for him by a faithful houseboy.

We drove to the church in a staff car, furnished by our lieutenant friend, who was an aide to the admiral.

The best man was Jim, our mining engineer friend, and I was given away by Bill. How I longed for Marge to be at the wedding!

There was an embarrassed pause for a brief moment before the ceremony started when the chaplain mistook the admiral's aide for the bridegroom. No wonder! With all the sombre combat uniforms in the church, the navy lieutenant glittered and shone in his white uniform, gold braid, ribbons, and medals, and he almost stole the spotlight from the bride.

Our wedding reception was a howling success! No other word would describe it! Everyone smiled and laughed, and since there was still plenty of jungle juice left, the wedding feast went on far into the night.

Perfectly strange GIs, mistaking our house for another gin mill, strolled in and out to join the merrymaking. They were given drinks and made welcome, but when they encountered the high brass and realized it was a private wedding party, they discreetly left.

Only a few of my fellow ex-internees were present, as most of them had returned to the States. One of the guests was a silver-haired and respected American judge from Manila who had served time with us in prison. He had quoted international law to the Japs on more than one occasion when he pleaded for the life of a fellow prisoner or for more food. Though he had fought for us in a fearless manner, the Nips had never molested him, perhaps because of his age and white hair.

My youngest guest was a four-year-old American girl. She was an orphan. Her mother had been a friend of mine before the war, and during the occupation, while hiding in the hills with her husband, she had been boloed to death by a demented housegirl. The child's father had died of pneumonia and privations, and the little girl, who was less than a year old at that time, had been cared for by kindly Filipinos. The only English words she knew were yes and no.

Our wedding pictures were taken by General MacArthur's photographer, and our pictures were telephotoed to our home cities in the States.

Since there was an "Off Limits to U. S. Personnel" on the pom-pom house across the street, some of the photographers dreamed up the idea of having us pose for some of our pictures with the sign as a background. As we laughingly posed for the picture, the ugly and buxom madam watched us suspiciously and sullenly.

It was a strange wedding! Bizarre! It was a beautiful wedding, and no newlyweds could have been more happy.

Instead of a trip to Europe, we went on a honeymoon trip to the States. We spent more than a month crossing the Pacific on the long voyage back.

But it was a strange honeymoon! For, due to the wartime conditions, we sailed on different ships!